The
Accelerated
Learning
FIELDBOOK

The Accelerated Learning

FIELDBOOK

Making the
Instructional Process
FAST,
FLEXIBLE,
and FUN

LOU RUSSELL

Jossey-Bass
Pfeiffer

San Francisco

ISBN: 0-7879-4639-7

Library of Congress Cataloging-in-Publication Data
Russell, Lou, 1957–
    The accelerated learning fieldbook : making the instructional process fast, flexible, and fun / Lou Russell.
        p.   cm.
    Includes bibliographical references and index.
    ISBN 0-7879-4639-7 (pbk. : alk. paper)
    1. Business education. 2. Businesspeople—Training of. 3. Business enterprises—Study and teaching. 4. Industrial management—Study and teaching. I. Title.
HF1106.R87 1999   99-6756
658.3'124—dc21   CIP

Printed in the United States of America

Published by

350 Sansome Street, 5th Floor
San Francisco, California 94104-1342
(415) 433-1740; Fax (415) 433-0499
(800) 274-4434; Fax (800) 569-0443

Visit our website at: www.pfeiffer.com

Acquiring Editor: Matthew Holt
Director of Development: Kathleen Dolan Davies
Developmental Editor: Diane Ullius
Copy Editor: Thomas Finnegan
Editorial Production Manager: Jeff Wyneken
Manufacturing Supervisor: Becky Carreño
Interior Design: Gene Crofts
Cover Design: Bruce Lundquist
Illustrations: Richard Sheppard

Printing 10   9   8   7   6   5   4   3   2

 This book is printed on acid-free, recycled stock that meets or exceeds the minimum GPO and EPA requirements for recycled paper.

CONTENTS

Resources

Index

About the Author

Receiving requires a genuine humility that may be uncomfortable and difficult to achieve, whereas giving poses the risk of arrogance which, unfortunately, is easy to come by.

—Robert K. Greenleaf, *On Becoming a Servant Leader*

Writing my first book has been a learning experience for me, on many levels. Without the help of the people at Jossey-Bass, including Matt Holt and Kathleen Davies, I never would have even started this large a project. Detail work is not my forte, and that aspect has been intimidating. The joy of creativity, however, has balanced the discomfort of details.

My best friends and office partners, Margie Brown, Vija Dixon, Carol Mason, and LuAnn Woodruff, worked hard to keep the business away from me whenever I had to write. They picked up the detail work, knowing it was not something I do well. Jim Highsmith encouraged me as he experienced a parallel set of expectations with the publication of his own book (a new approach to complex projects), called *Adaptive Development.* It was wonderful to have someone understand. Marty Morrow composed and produced a music CD for this book after only a brief lunch meeting and with no help from me. Thanks are not enough.

One of the things I was reminded of by the editors was that the book was about you, the reader. The first draft of the book had an awful lot about me and what I thought, which I didn't notice when I wrote it. I learned that this kind of thing can sound pompous to people who don't know me, and it did to the talented editors. My friends who reviewed the book were more gentle, of course, because they know the passion I have for learning. It permeates every aspect of my life. In fact, my personal mission is:

To ignite, affirm, and sustain learning

This is something that I try to remember every morning in starting the day. This is why I have been sent here. This is why I have been blessed with the talents I have. This is what I have tried to do in this book.

I have always been a learner waiting to learn at every opportunity. Yes, I am one of those people who watch public television and listen to National Public Radio. Knowledge is a powerful driver for me, and my family started it all. My father, Earl Russell, a microwave engineer and entrepreneur, helped me grow my logical/mathematical intelligence and taught me to never stop learning. My mother, Peg Connors Russell, an elementary educator, helped me grow my spatial/visual intelligence and my joy of learning; she passed on the strength of a long line of Irish women. My brother David taught me to enjoy life and laugh. My sister, Jody Russell Dobson, taught me how to look at myself clearly, and she continues to help me do this. My brother Chris amazes me with his linguistic/verbal intelligence; he taught me to love words, beginning with the sad story he wrote at an early age about a fly drowning in a cup of coffee. It is a creative and energizing family, and I am proud to be in it.

Numerous people in the business world have strongly influenced my beliefs about learning, and I won't be able to name them all. I learn something new in every class I facilitate. Michael Ayers, at 3M, continues to teach me how to think thoroughly. Also at 3M, Cathy Muckala has taught me the importance of passion. Kathryn Auckland, previously with the same company, taught me a great deal about planning products and markets. Darryl Johnson and his trainers at Elanco have taught me more about swine than I ever wanted to know—but they have also taught me that accelerated learning works for any topic, in any country, and in any business. Nadine Winnick Martin, at Northeast Utilities, continues to teach me that enthusiasm and energy create learning, regardless of the current realities of the business world. (She is also competing with me for the "Most Kinesthetic Learner of the Year" award.) Helen Minchik is a friend I don't see enough, but she has a wonderfully creative way with learning events. She has drawn a beautiful coloring book for our learners to doodle in while learning about learning theory. Leah Colville, at Conseco, continues to teach me the importance of aligning training to the business. Lea Toppino, also at Conseco, has shown me the importance of focusing on performance when dealing with business learning.

Accelerated learning practitioners entered my life a little more than ten years ago and changed it in an amazingly positive way. Connie Perren, then at the University of Houston at Galveston but now at Shell Oil, facilitated a one-day workshop on accelerated learning for our local technical training group, and it rerouted my focus—and eventually my company. Jane Bail, whom I have not seen in many years, helped us write our first accelerated learning workshop. Ole Anderson, Chris Brewer, Doug McPhee, David Meier, Ann Nedi-Herrmann, Thiagi (S. Thiagarajan), and many others in the IAL (International Alliance of Learning) group have continued to inspire me with their passion for learning. Sue Miller Hurst and Peter Senge brought learning to business's attention. In the learning trenches, Maria Ging, my daughter Kelly's third and fourth grade teacher at Fall Creek Elementary School in Fishers, Indiana, has modeled for me multiple intelligence in action. She and I have shared many tips and techniques, but I still wish I could get a class under control the way she can. I am also thankful, with adults, that I generally don't have to.

Thanks to the Fishers library for providing me with a quiet place to write and a plug to juice up my laptop. Similarly, thanks to the wonderful folks at Einstein's Bagels on 96th street in Fishers, who let me sit in there as long as I wanted, typing away, plugged in or not. Thanks to Todd Bickendorf, who, during one of my most difficult writing periods, modeled accelerated learning techniques while he was selling me a beautiful new Audi.

Finally, there are those important people in the background of my life who really keep the whole thing together. This book is as much because of their hard work as it is because of mine. This is the team that helps me balance the many facets of my life. Thank you, Susie Coffing, the second mother of my children, for teaching them to love learning. As one of my younger daughters said to me, "I'm clever, aren't I?" Yes, you are, and it is thanks in part to Susie. Thank you, Donna Hoffman, for keeping my world in order, but also for modeling for me the importance of hard work and never giving up. Carol Ernst, my professional coach, continues to help me be clear about my mission and vision and do what I must. Her support and listening skills have supported me through this project. Scott Conder, my best friend, always keeps reminding me how special I am.

This book-writing business is pretty tough on the people closest to you. My oldest daughter, Kelly, and my husband, Doug, have both taken to stopping by and saying, "What page are you on now?" The little girls, Kristin and Katherine, know only that I have been working at night, which I almost never do. They are all anxious to be done with it, as am I. I know they are proud of their wife and mom, as I am so proud of them.

In closing, thanks to Rich DeFiore, who reminded me that there are actually *four* intake styles and that one is completely outside of us: from God. I believe that this book is His plan for me. These words may bounce off your ears, because the business world hides from the life of the spirit yet craves it at the same time. I believe that learning is a gift from God, and I thank Him for the mission He has given me.

"Faith is the realization of what is hoped for and evidence of things not seen" (Hebrews 11:1).

Indianapolis, Indiana   LOU RUSSELL
October 1999

CHAPTER 1
**Starting the
Learning Journey**

**Business
Success**

CHAPTER 12
Your Learning
Journey
Continues

PART ONE
How People Learn

CHAPTER 2
A Contract for Learning

CHAPTER 3
Learning to Take More In

CHAPTER 4
Learning Through All
Your Intelligences

CHAPTER 5
Learning with
Your Whole Brain

CHAPTER 6
Remembering What
You Learned

PART TWO
**How Successful
Learning Is Delivered**

CHAPTER 7
You Are the Deliverer

CHAPTER 8
The Environment
Delivers Learning

CHAPTER 9
Music to Deliver
Learning

PART THREE
**How Successful
Learning Events
Are Built**

CHAPTER 10
Developing Learning
Events

CHAPTER 11
Selling the Dream

CHAPTER 1

Starting the Learning Journey

What we are trying to do is get people to ask questions they haven't ever thought to ask.

—Michael Ayers, 3M

Paul Nawa was teaching in Indianapolis when he was assigned to the city's Key Middle School. Key Schools use a variation of accelerated learning (AL) to create an effective learning environment. After a few years, Paul left to become a training manager at a company that supplies parts to a major automobile manufacturer. Facilitating learning in both environments drew his attention to similarities. In a letter to the editor in the *Indianapolis Star* (1998), Nawa observed:

> Production managers have no latitude to second-guess anything. Training time is expensive because costs are tripled. Production managers have no time for educational theories. The managers and the training department worked constantly to find ways to provide efficient and effective training methods. Here's what we know:
>
> - Herding people into a classroom and teaching at them for long periods of time mostly teaches them to play classroom games to avoid boredom.
> - A nonadversarial learning environment must exist, where learners and instructors are focused on subject matter.
> - Direct contact with real material, equipment, processes, and people is the more effective and lasting means of learning.
> - Learners must value what is being learned.
> - Different learners have different strengths and weaknesses (intelligences) and learn best through teaching that capitalizes on those strengths.

- Learners need some latitude and input on what is to be studied and how it is to be studied.
- A mentor is needed after the initial training to fine-tune the learner in order to bring the learner up to his or her maximum skill and growth potential.
- People need to know how to work in groups and resolve conflict, how to communicate effectively, and the steps to solving problems.

These are all ideas that Pat Bolanos, the Key School principal, discussed during the year I spent there. I didn't buy all of them while I was at the school, but one by one, they fell into place in the "Real World."

Accelerated learning has been moving into the school systems in the United States and around the world for many years. You'll probably find inspirational examples of learning success in schools in your own backyard; I discovered many in mine.

You will also find less successful schools. Concerns about inadequate learning, lack of vision, undefined processes, limited funds, and flawed evaluation are not confined to the schools, though. You'll find them in business as well. That comes as no surprise when you consider that the schools are growing the people who run the businesses.

You are about to begin a journey toward improved learning. This chapter helps you understand the scope of the challenges and helps you choose how and where to focus your learning energies. This chapter addresses

- What accelerated learning is
- Why accelerated learning is critical for business today
- How to navigate this book to maximize your learning

WHAT IS ACCELERATED LEARNING?

What is accelerated learning? Even though its practitioners can't agree on a definition, in this chapter, and throughout the book, you will encounter mine. As you experience the learning both in this book and in your application of the ideas, I hope you will continue to grow your own definition. Mine is still growing.

Accelerated basically means that speed is increasing. *Learning* is defined as a change in behavior from new skills, knowledge, or attitude. Combined, accelerated learning means "changing behaviors with increasing speed."

Lots of learning occurs in businesses every day, but it is not always the right kind of learning. This book deals specifically with learning focused on improving the business. Choosing the learning that will move the business toward its strategic objectives, and then facilitating the learning as effectively as possible, creates the best return.

One of the objectives of this book is for you to learn to maximize learning by honoring the differing needs of individuals. Traditional corporate training programs are rooted in the assumption that all learners learn in the same way. The key reason AL helps people learn more quickly and efficiently is that it honors the diversity of individual learning preferences.

Putting all these pieces together, I propose this definition of accelerated learning in business:

> Quickly creating learning that is of benefit to the business, with long-term retention, by honoring the different learning preferences of each individual.

When implemented well, AL challenges the learner and the trainer to address the question "How can we learn better?" Learning is not restricted to the learner; the trainer is learning, too. This partnership is a cornerstone of AL.

Many people mistakenly assume that techniques such as playing music or awarding prizes amount to accelerated learning. The techniques are one aspect, but the philosophy is the critical part. Accelerated learning requires a mind-set toward better learning. The techniques then follow.

Table 1.1 contrasts traditional corporate training with accelerated learning.

Many managers have successfully used AL to increase the learning in their organizations to grow business success. Some of their stories are described in more detail in later chapters. Here are some examples of how managers increased the effectiveness of their businesses:

• At Northeast Utilities in Hartford, Connecticut, an information technology training team led by Nadine Martin applied a creative AL approach to a company-wide Microsoft Windows 95 (and soon after, Windows NT) rollout. Using a highway-system metaphor (with maps, trip planners, and other creative ideas), the team showed learners how to navigate their networks and the resources for help. More important, learners discovered how to continue learning on their own after their brief classroom exploration.

TABLE 1.1.   Traditional Versus Accelerated Learning.

Traditional	Accelerated
Linear	Nonlinear, systemic
Knowing about	Knowing how
Formal, structured	Informal, flexible
Conscious	Unconscious
Memorized facts	Intuitive and applicable knowledge
"Have to" learning	"Want to" learning
Hard work	Fun, effortless
Emotion-free	Emotional
Passive	Active

• The SAS Institute in Toronto, led by Bill Fehlner, has been using AL to teach programming and systems workshops. The facilitators use metaphors, choral readings, and games to make learning easy and fun.

• Under the championing of employees Cathy Muckala and Jan Quinto, 3M has integrated games, movement, and color into sales and software training programs, achieving impressive results.

• Warren Harper at Elanco in Indianapolis, Indiana, created a new-product-orientation sales workshop to teach salespeople in the Far East (who were accustomed to selling chicken products) how to sell new pharmaceutical products developed for swine. Through lecture games, experiential learning, and role playing, the salespeople acquired new product knowledge with impressive retention.

In case you're still not sold, here's a chance to experience the difference:

> You're in a personal computer training class. The trainer has been lecturing for two hours about a new recordkeeping system that your company has purchased. The system is not installed yet, and there are no computers in the room. The trainer calls your name and asks you to recite the steps in entering a new record. You have no idea what the answer is, and in embarrassment you fan through the User's Guide until you find a section on entering new orders. You read that page to the trainer.

This is what trainers do to their learners when they simply lecture at them. Instead of helping learners learn, they inadvertently bore them to death with overheads. The learners, in turn, do whatever it takes to get through the experience, understandably forgetting as much as they can when they leave.

Corporate training is largely ineffective, and it has been for a long time. It's time to stop settling for that, and make a drastic change.

> Now imagine you're working a long weekend because you have some projects you must complete by Monday. You remember that the vice president has insisted that you use the new recordkeeping system as part of your projects. Fearing the computer and having no idea of how to start, you stumble along trying to figure out how to enter the new records. You remember that the User Guide had something in it about doing the records, so you look it up. After a couple of false starts, you get the records into the computer. You're pretty proud of yourself for figuring it out.

Different experiences. The first discouraged learning, and the second created it. Notice that the second experience is emotional, relevant, and active. That's one big difference between AL and traditional corporate instruction. This emotion, relevance, and activity occur when the learner has a desire to learn. In Chapter Two you'll find out about the importance of learning objectives, and in Chapter Ten you will learn how to create them. Part of the responsibility of the trainer in an AL classroom is to keep focused on the learning that the learners want, not on the lecturing that needs to be done.

With AL, there is plenty of learning and satisfaction for everyone, facilitator and learner alike. If you're the kind of trainer who loves to see that "a-ha!" look come across a learner's face when she really understands something for the first time, you are ready for AL.

There are many innovative approaches that you can use to encourage the learner to learn. As a facilitator of learning, you are no longer responsible for pouring material into people's heads. Instead, you provide the material to the learners interactively such that they can easily and enjoyably partake of it. With a focus on learning, innovative and effective techniques emerge. Without a focus on learning, the best techniques in the world will fail. This book is full of techniques, but by themselves they are nothing. Always resist the temptation to allow the techniques to take precedence over the learning.

The issue is not a minor one. AL is not (just):

- Little prizes given out in class
- Music playing during class
- Candy on the tables
- Colored and fragrant markers with colored paper on the tables
- Meditation and guided imagery
- Koosh balls
- Fun pointers and magic tricks
- Manipulation and trickery
- Entertainment without business benefit
- Learning without context

This last item, learning without context, is risky business. Knowledge for knowledge's sake is highly valued. For example, scientists have learned how to create nuclear weapons and to clone animals, but no one has learned how to deal with all the deep implications of this knowledge. Should there be nuclear weapons? Is it okay to use them? Should animals be cloned? Humans? Who chooses who will be cloned? Complex, ethical dilemmas remain unanswered.

Although these are extreme examples, similar learning can and does occur in business classrooms. For example, say employees are forced to attend a Taking Risk workshop, but the executives haven't considered what will happen if all the employees start taking more risks. In a bank or hospital, risk taking might have disastrous side effects. If the training plan ensures that learning is focused on a more specific business need, the business learners know and ask the questions before, during, and after the learning. In Chapter Five, you'll read about how accelerated learning helps to create a complex and realistic context for learning, to ensure that the changing behavior will be appropriate and useful.

WHY ACCELERATED LEARNING IS CRITICAL FOR BUSINESS TODAY

In business today, time is the most precious commodity. People are working more hours and bearing increased responsibilities. The fear of failure in this pressure-filled setting keeps people locked into status quo thinking. As you will learn in Chapter Five, fear triggers a physical response that shuts the brain down so learning cannot occur.

Many brains are shut down in business today as individuals fight for survival. It is a perfect time for accelerated learning.

"What is the major difference," Robert J. Graham and Randall L. Englund ask in *Creating an Environment for Successful Projects* (1997), "between those who survive and those who do not? It is the organizational ability to learn, a desire to survive, and the ability to adapt" (p. 174).

Many executives have been trying to create learning organizations since they read about them in *The Fifth Discipline,* by Peter Senge (1990). They agreed with Senge's belief that businesses that can learn outdo their competition. Senge identifies five disciplines for learning organizations. Table 1.2 explains how accelerated learning encourages and supports the adoption of these disciplines.

More recently, businesses have looked to knowledge management to create competitive advantages. Mistakenly, many technologists have viewed knowledge management as a computer initiative. Businesses that have built giant computer databases of customer information are still waiting for the knowledge to come as employees shy away from using the systems. As Nonaka, Takeuchi, and Takeuchi wrote in *The Knowledge-Creating Company* (1995), knowledge management is first a people issue. On an individual level, knowledge is created, exchanged with another, and then transformed in the people involved in the exchange. Knowledge grows through a conversation between people who are willing to both share and receive.

Accelerated learning is critical to this initiative. If individual learners can become more effective in their ability to learn (create new knowledge) and communicate with others (exchange new knowledge), the business will become more innovative and flexible. Knowledge cannot be created through technology. Once people have increased their knowledge, they may then appropriately use technology to enable more knowledge acquisition.

To summarize, Table 1.3 lists the benefits of accelerated learning.

HOW TO NAVIGATE THIS BOOK TO MAXIMIZE YOUR LEARNING

In keeping with the philosophy of accelerated learning, the book has been structured to increase your learning. In this section of this chapter, you will read about the music CD and about planning your path through this fieldbook.

TABLE 1.2.   **The Learning Organization and AL.**

Learning Organization Disciplines	Description	Accelerated Learning Benefits
Personal Mastery	Growing your personal ability to learn	By honoring the diversity of each learner, application of AL creates an optimum environment for personal mastery
Team Learning	Growing the team's ability to learn	By facilitating understanding of how others learn, the application of AL creates a language and process for powerful team learning
Mental Models	Assumptions and beliefs that influence behavior	By including attitude, feelings, and emotion as key components of learning, the application of AL encourages the unveiling and evaluation of individual, team, and business mental models
Systems Thinking	Analysis of business issues to identify the causes and effects of the systems within them and how to intervene systemically	By encouraging learning in a complex and realistic context, the application of AL encourages learners to think holistically about the learning and the world the learning will be applied in
Shared Vision	"Why" the business is doing what it is doing; used to prioritize all business activity	By aligning all learning to learning objectives tied to the needs of the business, the application of AL encourages learners to focus their learning energies on what's best for the whole

The CD

My friend Marty Morrow has composed and recorded a special music CD for you to listen to as you read this book. The CD contains two pieces: "Falling Leaves," to accompany reading, and "The Stream," to use as background for the practice exercises. In Chapter Nine, you will learn more about the power of music when applied to learn-

TABLE 1.3. Benefits of AL.

Recipient	Benefits
Individual learner	• Ability to learn more, faster
	• Better retention of learning
	• Better transfer of learning to the job
	• Increased self-esteem
	• Increased ability to be innovative
	• Increased desire to learn
Learning facilitator (trainer)	All the benefits to the individual, plus
	• Increased learning in the classroom
	• Enthusiastic learners
	• Ability to really help the business and its staff
	• Reduced conflict in the classroom
	• Reduced "no-shows"
	• A never-ending journey to improve learning
	• Increased fun in the classroom
The business	• More flexible employees
	• More innovative employees
	• Improved problem solving
	• Employees aligned to the business

ing; for now, understand that the design of the music is consistent with the research described in that chapter. The music will work best if you listen to it through headphones. The CD can be played on CD players and on computers with multi-media capabilities. Each piece is approximately fifteen minutes long.

Listen to "Falling Leaves" while

- Reading new material
- Reviewing material or working on the chapter-ending sections of your personal action plan
- Reflecting on what you have just read

Listen to "The Stream" while

- Working on the many "Practice Boxes" throughout the book
- Working on your own learning materials
- Working or discussing with others (remove the headphones)

In Chapter Nine, you will also read about the copyright limitations of using music that was not sold for classroom purposes. This CD is yours to use in your classes. Also, please feel free to use this music in self-paced training that you create, such as Web-based or computer-based materials (as long as you credit Marty Morrow and this book).

Planning Your Path

Structural elements in this fieldbook mimic the structure of an accelerated learning event:

- In Chapter Two, you'll be asked to choose your most important learning objectives.
- Each chapter begins and ends with the learning objectives covered.
- Each chapter begins with an image of where you are in the book, with the number and title of the current chapter marked in bold.
- "Learning Practice" suggestions in each chapter help you learn by doing. It's up to you whether you take the time to try them, but I strongly encourage it. Remember, learning happens through practice and then through reflection.
- Each chapter ends with a section of a larger personal action plan, so you can reflect on what you've learned.
- The Appendix contains detailed suggestions for learning techniques, many of which are mentioned in the chapters.
- The Resources material at the back of this book recommends books, tapes, suppliers, and Websites to help you continue your learning.

If you are time-constrained, focus on the parts of the book that add the most value for you at this point in your development. Then return to look at others when you need them. For this purpose, the book is divided into three parts:

Part	*Chapters*
One: how people learn	Chapters Two through Six
Two: how successful learning is delivered	Chapters Seven through Nine and the Appendix
Three: how successful learning events are built	Chapters Ten and Eleven

Chapter Twelve, the Appendix, and the Resources have been created so that you can learn as you grow. The chapters in each part are described briefly below.

Part One: How People Learn

Understanding how you learn and how your learners learn is critical to creating an effective learning experience. Chapters Two through Six distill the latest research about how people learn. Some of this material may be review for you, but please skim through to make sure you know why the various tips and techniques are effective.

Chapter Two: A Contract for Learning

You'll read about the importance of learning objectives. In addition, you'll learn how to help the participants prioritize the objectives that are most important to them.

Chapter Three: Learning to Take More In

You'll read about the power of three intake styles (visual, auditory, and kinesthetic), and learn how to manage your own intake preferences as well as those of your learners.

Chapter Four: Learning Through All Your Intelligences

You'll read about the revolutionary work of Howard Gardner and his theory of multiple intelligences. This concept is one of the most important and useful for business trainers.

Chapter Five: Learning with Your Whole Brain

You'll read about the whole-brain approach to learning, including the work of Ned Herrmann on brain dominance.

Chapter Six: Remembering What You Learned

This chapter covers the most recent research about memory and long-term retention. Retention is what learning is all about.

Part Two: How Successful Learning Is Delivered

The next grouping of chapters deals with delivering learning. Although the emphasis is on facilitator-led events, the ideas can also be adapted to self-paced learning.

Chapter Seven: You Are the Deliverer

This is a critical chapter for anyone who facilitates learning. It explains how to clearly define your role in the learning process and how this definition drives learning success.

Chapter Eight: The Environment Delivers Learning

Learn how to create an environment for learning that includes you as facilitator, the room, and the learners.

Chapter Nine: Music to Deliver Learning

You'll read about research and techniques that integrate music and learning.

Part Three: How Successful Learning Events Are Built

The final part is important if you are responsible for creating and marketing (or assessing) learning events.

Chapter Ten: Developing Learning Events

If you do course development, spend some quality time in this chapter for a step-by-step process for creating learning events, or modifying existing courses into an AL format.

Chapter Eleven: Selling the Dream

Here's practical advice for selling your customers on the value of your learning events. Just because you build it doesn't mean they'll come.

Chapter Twelve: Your Learning Journey Continues

The final chapter, along with the materials that follow it, is to help you move on from here. You'll be led through exercises that help you assess your delivery techniques and then guide you to create an action plan and a time line to increase your own learning and the learning in others.

Appendix

Here are additional techniques and ideas for maximizing learning.

Resources

More than a traditional bibliography, the Resources section suggests books, articles, Websites, and other resources for continuing your learning.

CONCLUSION: THE JOURNEY BEGINS

From the Pegasus Communications Website comes this prediction: "The successful organization of tomorrow will be something called a learning organization . . . a place where transformational thinking, a shared sense of purpose, and a commitment to the individual combine to create an environment where the extraordinary can occur."

Come with me on a wonderful journey. Starting today, you can accelerate your learning and that of your learners. This experience can be the beginning of a positive change for you. I hope that the learning that is begun while you read this book will nurture and fulfill you, restoring your own joy of learning. Thank you for walking with me.

PART ONE

How People Learn

Business Success

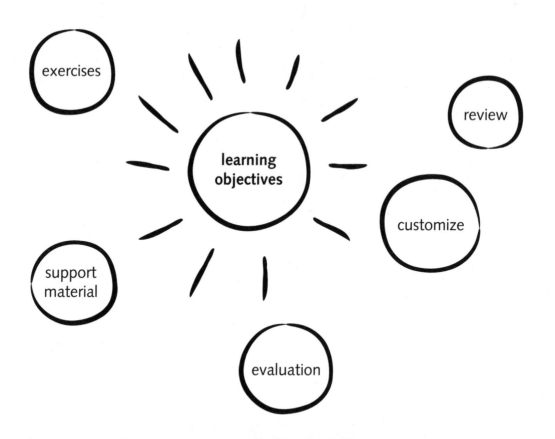

THE LEARNING OBJECTIVES OF CHAPTER 2

After reading this chapter, you will be able to

- Manage effective learning objectives for a learning event

- Create a personal action plan to increase personal learning and the effectiveness of your delivery of learning events

CHAPTER 2

A Contract for Learning

> Let's just all try to create not the cheapest or most expedient programs, but
> ones that are the most intelligent and ecologically sound and in which every-
> one benefits.
>
> —Robert Sylwester, *A Celebration of Neurons*

After you've been successfully teaching for a while, you may start to think that you can teach anything. With all the fun and success of accelerated learning techniques, there is a danger that you may become a fun exercise looking for a workshop to happen, losing your focus on what the learner needs.

I reluctantly admit that this happened to me. I was asked to design a custom workshop on taking risk for—interestingly enough—a Wall Street firm's computer department. The chief information officer (CIO) believed that the information technology staff was too set in its ways and that if people took initiative and tried new ways of doing things, the department and the company would become more efficient and profitable.

I pulled together some exercises on creativity and taking risks, including opportunities to practice "thinking out of the box" and "testing boundaries." What I didn't do was spend enough time with the CIO to find out very specifically what she thought the outcomes of the learning event should be. In other words, I did the course development without defining the learning objectives. Had I done some digging and a lot of listening, I would have discovered that she wanted people to take more risks, but *only risks that would be successful.* Failure, a critical part of risk taking, would not be tolerated. I found this out, instead, from an unhappy CIO after a less-than-successful workshop.

Research in adult education has shown the importance of clearly understanding and managing the learning objectives of a learning event. Without them, the learners do not learn. New AL practitioners often jump into accelerated learning with the thought that its principles completely replace those of traditional adult education. Although accelerated learning challenges many of the delivery methods of traditional education, the belief that learning objectives are critical to learning has not changed. There is no learning, accelerated or otherwise, without a clear understanding of the scope of the need.

 PRACTICE

In your mind, and without looking back at it, picture the star that began Chapter One. Write the number of points on the star here: _____

How sure are you about your answer? Turn back now and see how you did. The chances are good that you didn't do very well and may not have even remembered the star. What prevented you from "learning" the number of points on the star when you first saw it? Write your thoughts here:

_____

_____

Here are some other reasons you may have been less than successful:

- I did not manage your expectation when I showed you the star. I never told you that I would quiz you on the visual later in the book. In other words, you had no learning objectives, and if I had any, I never told you.
- I never clearly defined what I meant by "the number of points on the star" when I quizzed you. I did not clearly say what I was asking for.
- You may have made assumptions and created your own rules. Because I didn't tell you, you may have decided what a star is, what points are, or how important this experience was to you. It could have turned out I had other ideas.

This simple exercise shows some of the same reasons that learning fails in workshops. Such breakdowns in learning are minimized by establishing learning objectives at the very start.

Here are the learning objectives for this book. Later in this chapter, you will prioritize these and perhaps even add some of your own. Later (in Chapter Ten), you will learn how to create quality learning objectives to ensure that learning events meet the needs of the business. In this chapter, you will read about

- Why learning objectives are so critical
- How to prioritize learning objectives
- Concerns about learning objectives

WHY ARE LEARNING OBJECTIVES SO CRITICAL?

In 1991, Elliott Masie performed research that was published in the Masie Institute newsletter (Masie Institute Newsletter, 1995). He was trying to figure out what most correlated to long-term retention in a personal computer classroom. The research revealed two factors, one of which will be covered in this chapter and the other in the chapter on memory (Chapter Six).

The most influential factor was that the learner had something she wanted to learn when she came in the door. Here's an example: suppose you are a learner attending a Microsoft Word workshop. You've signed up because you are having a terrible time with spell check, and you are unhappy about it. When you get to class, you really don't care what the instructor's objectives are. You are determined to learn spell check. You may have to ask at the break, or you may learn it from another learner, but you will learn spell check and you will remember it. Reflect for a moment on an occasion when this happened to you.

I call this learning phenomenon *creative discomfort.* Creative discomfort provokes an individual's need to resolve inconsistencies among experiences, beliefs, or feelings through rethinking. Not knowing spell check is inconsistent with the belief that everyone smart should know spell check. An innate part of our human psyche tries to resolve pain by eliminating it. If learners have an unresolved learning discomfort, they are greatly motivated to eliminate it. This is learning earned, and it is rarely forgotten.

Bringing this research into your classroom means that you must help learners set appropriate objectives for the learning event. A learner may have a great objective, an unreasonable objective, or no objectives. Setting reasonable objectives with participants is a critical driver of learning—so critical that it needs to be the first thing done.

Here are two examples to illustrate the criticality of learning objectives.

First, imagine a corporate workshop where you have been told that the learning objective is (using a calculator) to compute the return on investment of an asset acquisition.

You are given everything you need to learn: a calculator, some sample calculations, some case studies with assets clearly labeled, and a formula to be used for calculating return on investment. You practice and practice, checking your answers against the school solution with success. You feel pretty confident that you have achieved the learning objective.

When the facilitator announces that there will be a final exam, you are a little nervous but grow confident when you hear that you can use your notes. The facilitator passes out the written test. The questions are

- When and why would you compute ROI?
- Who invented the concept ROI?
- Describe another calculation that would provide you with more business knowledge than ROI, and justify its use.

You start to panic because you have no idea what ROI means. After a moment, you suppose it stands for return on investment all right—though you've never been shown that acronym. Even with that discovery, you have not been prepared to answer these unfair questions and you are angry. These questions do not match the original learning objective. The testing does not go well.

Back at work, your boss drops a report on your desk detailing all the expenses of the department for this quarter. She asks you to calculate the return on investment for only the asset expenses, by Monday. As you look at the list, you realize that you have no idea which expenses are assets and which ones are not, and you have no idea how to find out what benefits there will be (on the case studies you were given). You realize that a more useful and complete learning objective for you would have been:

> With a calculator, be able to compute the return on investment (ROI)
> of an asset acquisition by determining asset expenses and their benefits.

The second example is something common in corporate workshops: a learning technique is used that does not map to a learning objective. For example, consider a facilitator who used trivia questions five minutes before the end of a break to entice learners to come back on time. Five minutes before getting back to the course material, she would display some trivia questions; any learners who were back and wanted to play (which was completely voluntary) had the chance to win little gifts. The trivia would be about things outside of class. Let me reemphasize that this was done during free time, not during class.

In a way, it worked wonderfully. Learners would come back from break early, saving class flow. Peer pressure and competition added to the incentive to come back and play. The down side was that the course evaluations had comments like "Wasted our time with trivia," "Get rid of the nonsense trivia," and so on. Many of the learners enjoyed the trivia, but a few in each learning event felt it was not good use of their time. Even though these learners were choosing to use their free time, they perceived that it was being wasted by material that was not tied to a learning objective. The instructor changed the trivia to pertain to the course material and had the best of both worlds: people were back from break early and learning occurred.

 LEARNING POINT

Everything in a learning event must map to a learning objective. You and your learners must clearly know why you and they are doing everything.

This is why learning objectives matter to the corporate learning facilitator. As businesspeople trying to help companies stay competitive, corporate learning facilitators must make sure that every moment of learning is aligned to business goals. In the examples above, specified learning objectives were out of sync with the practice (exercise) of the learning, the final test, or the real-world applications.

 PRACTICE

Read through this list of learning objectives for this book. Select your most important three learning objectives and circle them.

After reading this book, you will be able to

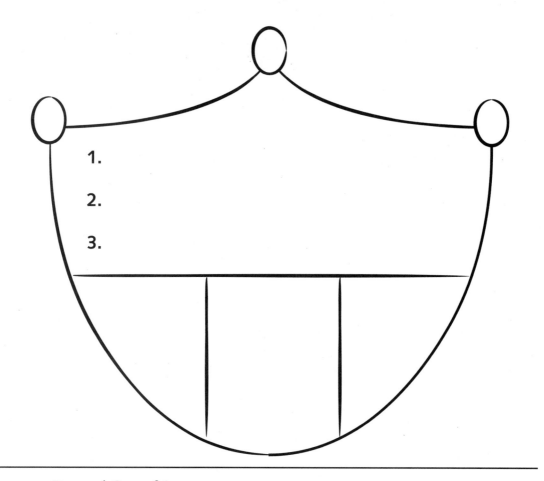

FIGURE 2.1. **Personal Coat of Arms.**

- Identify times in a learning event when you play the roles of facilitator of learning, trainer, and learner
- Adopt specific improvements in how you communicate new learning to learners
- Identify how you learn best
- Identify and rethink those personal beliefs of yours that block learning
- Construct and manage effective learning objectives for a learning event
- Identify your learners' preferences for receiving new learning (intake styles)
- Adjust your intake styles to communicate more effectively with learners

- Assess your preference for processing new learning in terms of Gardner's multiple intelligences
- Use the multiple intelligences to design the logistical flow of a learning event
- Balance the use of both the left and right sides of the brain for learning
- Define the three primary functions of the triune brain in a learning event
- Maximize memory in self and others for long-term retention
- Use music to create focused learning environments
- Develop classroom learning events to meet a specific learning need
- Measure the effectiveness of a learning event
- Create a personal action plan to increase personal learning and the effectiveness of your delivery of learning events

Now transpose them to the Coat of Arms (Figure 2.1). This is my contract with you. Mark this page with a Post-it so you can return to it. Decorate it with color markers or crayons, sign it, and refer to it as you read this book. To reinforce, you will read the pertinent learning objectives at the start and end of each chapter.

HOW TO PRIORITIZE LEARNING OBJECTIVES

It may have been an unusual experience for you to prioritize your learning objectives to read a book. Corporate learners are likewise unaccustomed to being asked to think about what they want to learn. They are used to attending training that is generic—the learning objectives have been picked for them. Their individual learning needs are often secondary to the plan of the course vendor. Still, even with purchased training material, delivery can be adjusted, with minimal effort, according to the priorities of the learners. As in the practice, the prioritized list of learning objectives is a contract between the facilitator and the learners.

The coat-of-arms technique used in the Practice Box is a good example of one way to help a class prioritize learning objectives. When this exercise is done in groups, participants are asked to share their individual learning objectives with the others at their table before taping up their coats of arms somewhere in the classroom. (Ask learners to hang the coat of arms somewhere they will see it often. Remind them not to hang it on a person, because you, as the facilitator, will be a common target!) Not only does this effort provide learning reinforcement for the learner but it also provides the facilitator with the entire class's priorities and decorates the room in a way that gives the learners a feeling of ownership. The downside is that this is a time-consuming exercise that could take up to thirty minutes, so it is best left for multiple-day classes.

Here is a variation for prioritizing if you have limited time. At the start of class, ask your learners to take a colored marker and individually choose their top three learning objectives in their learner guides. The list should be very close to the front of the learner guide and displayed in front of them in the classroom on a flipchart or overhead transparency. Tell them that they have three minutes to choose. Play some quiet music (see Chapter Nine for more information on music choices) while they are silently choosing.

When it seems as if 80 percent of the group is done, summarize the results as a group. As you read through the list, ask the learners to raise their hands if they've picked that objective as one of their top three. Move quickly while you mark the list of objectives with these codes:

- Put a C if a couple of people (or just one) chooses an objective. That keeps you from singling out the person who has a unique answer and keeps them safe (see the next Learning Point).
- Put an L if a lot of people chose it (moderate number of learners).
- Put an M if most people chose it (largest number of learners).

If a learner notices that no one else picked a learning objective that she doesn't understand, she may not raise her hand to choose it; still, she pays careful attention while it is covered. The belief, probably incorrect, is that everyone else knows this, which creates creative discomfort seeking resolution.

Finish by asking for any write-in learning objectives. Notice that this entire process can take less than five to ten minutes. This technique is also useful at the beginning of speeches to ensure that you are providing the emphasis that the participants want.

Many good things come from prioritization. First, the learners have a learning objective. Second, they have been exposed briefly to an overview of the learning materials and have realistic expectations. Finally, they have also been exposed briefly to new learning through objectives that they do not completely understand, and this exposure provokes creative discomfort.

LEARNING POINT

Participants must be safe to learn. It is the facilitator's responsibility to keep the environment safe for all learners. For example, that's why you mark the overhead or flipchart with a letter (C) instead of a number (say, 1) during prioritization. If you write down "1," that individual person may feel embarrassed. Other people may not participate in the vote as it goes on, for fear of being singled out.

Prioritizing objectives can take five minutes (using a list and asking people to choose their top three) to thirty minutes (using a coat-of-arms approach). You must decide which is most appropriate to the length of the learning event and to the people you are with.

LEARNING POINT

The opening of a workshop is always proportional to the length of time the group will be together. The purpose of the opening is to establish initial team dynamics and create a shared vision of learning. You need more or less team trust depending on how long this group of people will be together. In a one-hour session, the opening should be no more than five minutes. In a four-week session, the opening may need to be a full day.

Here are some other creative ideas for sharing and prioritizing learning objectives as part of a workshop:

• If a class has two distinct sections, ask the learners to review and prioritize the first section's learning objectives and then tell them that you will review and prioritize the second set before that section. This keeps people's interest.

• If you have a little more time and want to get people moving, break the class into teams and give each team an envelope containing the learning objectives written on index cards. Explain to them that you are going to give them three minutes to dump out the envelope and prioritize the objectives in order of importance to the team. When three minutes are up, ask each team for its top three and note them on an overhead. This variation is great for workshops in which you are teaching team building, project management, or planning. If that's the case, the learning from the team experience should be debriefed after the learning objectives are prioritized (see Chapter Ten for designing debriefing).

• Ask learners to write a one-sentence description of the content of each unit of the learner guide, or assign each team a unit to review quickly. Accumulate this information on a flipchart page and map it to the learning objectives. This approach is especially useful if the learning objectives are not easily understood and need more supporting information. After this initial review, ask learners to prioritize their top three learning objectives individually, as in the other approaches.

CONCERNS ABOUT LEARNING OBJECTIVES

To finish up this chapter, I'll respond to common concerns from facilitators about letting learners prioritize objectives.

Time

As mentioned earlier, the time to prioritize learning objectives can be as little as five minutes. The payback for this time investment is learning retention. Lack of time is corporate training's favorite excuse for poor teaching and inadequate learning; learning takes more time than does teaching. The choice is between learning and teaching. If your goal is teaching, don't take time to do learning objectives. There is no reason for the time investment.

A nuclear regulatory trainer told me that she felt she was barely getting the material covered—and certainly did not have time to ask learners to prioritize their needs. In addition, she, not the learners, was the expert. The learners were required by law to be there; that was their only need. I encouraged her by saying this would only take five minutes and could save time by creating a prioritization that allowed her to spend less time on some objectives, for example, whatever learning the participants already understand. Ultimately, taking the initial five minutes would make it easier to cover more material, with more retention, in less time.

Required Content

Remember, you haven't asked learners for what they don't want to learn; you have asked them for their top three goals. So, learning objectives that are not chosen are not skipped; they are only minimized. The learning must still be thorough and complete. The prioritization controls the use of time for each objective and also allows adjustment for differences in starting competencies. Asking the learners to choose the learning they feel they need most, while preparing them for testing on required content is the best way for learning to occur.

If no one has chosen an objective that's needed as a prerequisite for other objectives that have been chosen, tell them that. If you skip material, especially pages in the learner's guide, learners might get concerned that they have missed something, even if they didn't care about that objective originally. So, when you get to material that is not on the priority list, remind them by saying, "This was not one of your top priorities, so I will cover it as briefly as possible and move right along to your choices." It's important to remind them and manage their expectations. To minimize time on these objectives, ask learners to read through the guide pages silently and ask questions when they are done. This way no one is short-changed.

For example, in a data modeling class, few learners pick "normalization" as one of their top three objectives. As the facilitator goes over the votes, she says to them: "We need to cover normalization or the unit on design won't make any sense. But I promise you, since I know many of you have struggled with this topic in college, that this will be taught in a unique and fun way that you will enjoy." By sharing this, she has intrigued the learners enough to set a learning objective about normalization.

Learner Competency

Give learners a list of the most learning objectives you could cover to pick from so that the choices are spelled out for them. It is not unusual for learners to come into workshops with little or no existing knowledge of the subject matter. The initial list helps them set some learning objectives and also serves to introduce the content while restricting the choices.

Additional Requests

If the learners ask for something additional that is outside the scope of the learning event, remind them of the list you have provided. This way you have limited the scope of the objectives the learners can choose. I accept write-in objectives but tell the learners in a safe and private way if it isn't an objective within the scope of the class. As Spock says in the film *Star Trek II: The Wrath of Khan,* "The needs of the many outweigh the needs of the few, or one." It's more ethical to talk to a learner at the beginning of a session about a learning objective that won't be met than it is to mutually discover it after having invested a lot of time.

CONCLUSION

In this chapter, you have read about the criticality of learning objectives for retention of learning. People who know what they want to learn will learn it. You have also learned various techniques to prioritize the learning objectives of a diverse group of learners in your workshops. In addition, you have read about many of the concerns you may have as you implement this change in how you deliver learning.

A word of caution before you begin: if you're not willing to change, then don't ask them what their priorities are. This isn't a training trick. If you ask them and then go on your merry way, the learners will be angry with you. You must be prepared and willing to adjust your agenda to meet their needs. The adjustment requires improvisation, and no two workshops will ever be completely alike. Adjustment may be intimidating at first, but you will find it improves the quality of learning for you and your learners.

PERSONAL ACTION PLAN

Please look back through this chapter, and jot down your thoughts below: insights, things you want to do, things you want to remember, games, and quotes. I've added a list of my own to supplement your list. It is better for your learning if you make your own list before you look at mine.

The learning objectives of this chapter were to

- Manage effective learning objectives for a learning event
- Create a personal action plan to increase personal learning and effectiveness of your delivery of learning events

Your thoughts:

_____

_____

_____

_____

_____

_____

_____

_____

_____

_____

_____

Here are my thoughts:

- Learning and retention are maximized if the learners are clear about what they need to learn and why.
- Prioritized learning objectives create a contract between the learner and the learning facilitator.
- Nothing should happen in any learning event, including accelerated learning events, unless it can be mapped to a learning objective.

- Learners must always feel safe in order to learn.
- The time spent prioritizing objectives for a learning event should be proportional to the length of time the participants will spend together.
- It is the role of the learning facilitator to manage the expectations of the learners.
- It is the role of the learner to communicate his or her learning needs when asked by the facilitator.

CHAPTER 1
Starting the
Learning Journey

**Business
Success**

CHAPTER 12
Your Learning
Journey
Continues

PART ONE
How People Learn

CHAPTER 2
A Contract for Learning

▶ CHAPTER 3
Learning to Take More In

CHAPTER 4
Learning Through All
Your Intelligences

CHAPTER 5
Learning with
Your Whole Brain

CHAPTER 6
Remembering What
You Learned

PART TWO
**How Successful
Learning Is Delivered**

CHAPTER 7
You Are the Deliverer

CHAPTER 8
The Environment
Delivers Learning

CHAPTER 9
Music to Deliver
Learning

PART THREE
**How Successful
Learning Events
Are Built**

CHAPTER 10
Developing Learning
Events

CHAPTER 11
Selling the Dream

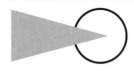

THE LEARNING OBJECTIVES OF CHAPTER 3

After reading this chapter, you will be able to

• Adopt specific improvements in how you communicate new learning to learners

• Identify how you learn best

• Identify and rethink those personal beliefs of yours that block learning

• Identify your learners' preferences for receiving new learning (intake styles)

• Adjust your intake styles to communicate more effectively with learners

• Measure the effectiveness of a learning event

• Create a personal action plan to increase personal learning and the effectiveness of your delivery of learning events

CHAPTER 3

Learning to Take More In

As you grasp the richness and complexity of the operations carried on in every learning brain, you will be in a better position to make the changes needed to teach for meaning.

—Don G. Campbell and Chris Brewer, *Rhythms of Learning*

In Chapter Two, you read about creating learning objectives for reading this book. You learned to set learning objectives before you learn, and before you help anybody else learn. The next three chapters deal with helping you and your learners get new information into the brain. You will learn how to determine the learning profile of the learners in your classes and how to apply techniques to help each diverse learner receive and process more.

You have probably experienced something like this in the corporate classroom. As the trainer, you say, "OK, everyone turn to page 10 for the next exercise." Within the next two minutes, three people will ask you, "What page did you say?"

A couple of learners may notice how many times you have repeated yourself, but not many. Writing the information on a visual (overhead or flipchart) when you say it reduces the likelihood that you will have to repeat. The majority of learners like to get their new information into their brains by looking at it visually.

Accelerated learning practitioners have long had access to some basic information about how individuals prefer to get new information into their brains. Neurolinguistic programming (NLP) researchers have also studied intake styles in great detail.

When there is a communication problem with another person, we interpret it from our own often-limited perspective. This interpretation may get personal, and someone may get hurt or angry, which is not unusual in a learning setting. How someone communicates is judged from our own perspective. We think that everyone else prefers to receive new information in the same way we do. If someone else isn't acting the way we would act in his shoes, then something is wrong with him. This assumption creates conflict in any communication setting where there is simply a difference, not a willful slight or attack.

 PRACTICE

Note the things you do a lot from the lists below. By observing in which columns your choices fall, you get a quick look at your learning preferences (given at the bottom of the chart).

Form mind pictures	Say syllables	Write with finger
Take notes	Use mnemonics	Write lists
Use color codes	Listen to tapes	Pace or walk as you work
Watch TV	Watch TV	Physically "do it"
Watch movies	Listen to music	Breathe slowly
Use charts and graphs	Listen to speakers	Role-play
Use maps	Read aloud	Exercise
Demonstrate	Make up poems	Dance
Use mnemonics	Have discussions	Take notes

Your learning preference is:

Visual	**Auditory**	**Kinesthetic**

It turns out that there are three primary ways people prefer to take in new learning. These preferences influence all aspects of learning.

This brief assessment starts you thinking about your own intake preferences. In this chapter, you will read about

• The visual, auditory, and kinesthetic intake styles
• Other influences on successful intake

- Adjusting for different intake styles in a learning event
- Managing audiences of diverse intake styles

THE VISUAL, AUDITORY, AND KINESTHETIC INTAKE STYLES

Your intake style is not something you should compare with someone else's in terms of whether it is good or bad. One type of intake is not better or smarter than another. Intake preference is not related to intelligence, which will be discussed in detail in Chapter Four. This assessment provides you with feedback about how you prefer to get new learning into your head initially.

It is not unusual for preferences to tie in any rating of the three styles. You may have one strong preference, while the other two are lesser but equal, or you may have two equally strong with one weaker. Some learners have equal visual, auditory, and kinesthetic intake preferences. Although many AL practitioners claim that having three equal intake preferences gives you the most flexibility as a learner, I believe instead that some of these people simply require all three in order to learn. Rather than be able to learn from visual, auditory, or kinesthetic stimuli, they require new learning in the form of all three.

Next you will read about how a person who has a strong preference for visual, auditory, or kinesthetic intake is likely to behave.

Visual

Visual intake is preferred alone or combined with another intake style by about 60 percent of the U.S. public. A person who prefers to take in information visually (highest or tied for highest on the assessment) likes to do so by seeing. He may prefer print, television, video, and some computer-based products. It is possible that a visual learner can't stand television, for example, but he will naturally seek some type of visual input if given a choice. Visual learners may love to read, watch television, and watch movies.

Certain physical gestures are common among people with visual intake. When these people pause to think, their eyes drift upwards. Even if they have attended training in speaking or sales, where they are encouraged to make eye contact, you will see them gaze upward for a split second and then quickly correct.

Visual people are often dressed colorfully and stylishly, as they are conscious of how they look. They will use visually descriptive words when they speak to you: "I see what you mean" or "I can picture that" or "That's a colorful illustration." Their voices tend to be slightly higher in pitch and slightly fast (though this can be trained out of them). Ask a visual person for driving directions, and he will tell you about all the things you will see along the way; in addition to the roads, he may also draw what you will see—for you so that you can see it, too.

Careers that tend to attract people with a preference for visual intake include artist, graphic designer, apparel designer, architect, stylist, and editor.

Visual processing can be done internally or externally. A visual learner may prefer to see things internally in his mind before drawing or discussing with another; this approach looks like daydreaming to someone else. A more external visual learner likes to look at things to process: guides; computers; books; art; and you, if you are talking to him.

Auditory

Moving now from the most common to the least, we find that the auditory intake style represents about 15 percent of the population. People who prefer to take things in auditorily (highest or tied for highest on the assessment) like to do so by hearing. They prefer radio, books on tape, and television (for the sound more than the visual). Many assume that all people with auditory intake will be musical, but that is not the case. Music can bother auditory learners because it jams their intake channel. They often prefer silence when trying to concentrate, and meeting that preference can be a challenge in the classroom (more on dealing with this in the last section of this chapter).

When people who prefer auditory intake speak, they do it slowly, with a measured cadence or rhythm that may be interpreted as slow and monotone by others who are not auditory. There is a definite beat to their voices, which they enjoy hearing.

In terms of careers, people who prefer auditory intake may get involved in music, sound, education, and telephone work.

Certain physical gestures are common among people with an auditory preference. When they pause to think, their eyes look straight ahead. It may give a listener the unsettling feeling of being looked right through, instead of being looked at.

The most telling physical gesture is "the pause." Auditory people will listen intently to what you are saying while looking straight at you. Then, they will pause before answering, for what seems like days to a person of another intake style. The auditory person is repeating your words and the words he is going to say in his head, before he responds to you. In other words, he is practicing in an internal hearing way. The person who has spoken may become very uncomfortable with the silence and may either interrupt or take offense. I find that many learners with auditory intake preference are very introverted in class. This may be because many have been ignored or interrupted so often. They learn to stop trying to talk and settle in to listen instead, which they prefer.

A person who prefers auditory intake will use hearing words when he speaks to you. Ask an auditory person for directions and he will pause, and then tell you slowly and concisely the exact steps. If you are not auditory, you probably don't pay attention for long to the person pausing. If you are someone who prefers visual or kinesthetic input, *you* will probably draw a picture so you can listen to the auditory person. If you interrupt him, he will return to the pause immediately. He will say such things as "I hear what you are saying" or "That sounds good" or "That's music to my ears."

Auditory learners can be either internal or external in focus. The external auditory learner loves to talk and may talk to himself or herself while learning. It's not unusual to find this type of auditory learner as a learning facilitator. Internal auditory learners will talk to themselves inside their heads while learning, but from the outside the only noticeable behavior is the pause.

The ability to listen well, an asset to business learning, has become a lost art at the same time that businesses are lamenting the decline in effectiveness of internal communications. People seemed more auditory fifty years ago during the Age of Radio. Today, such visual stimuli as videos, e-mail, and Web communication further isolate spoken communication and reduce auditory strength. With a little practice and attention, it "sounds" as though businesses could improve their listening abilities just by doing more listening.

Kinesthetic

The kinesthetic intake style represents about 25 percent of the U.S. population. A person who prefers kinesthetic intake (highest or tied for highest on the assessment) likes to learn by doing. Sitting still is difficult, so if a person with a preference for kinesthetic intake watches television at all, he will be doing two other things at the same time. Reading, listening to the radio, and talking on the phone may also be passive enough to be a challenge.

Identifying someone with a preference for kinesthetic intake is the easiest of all three because he is always moving. When he pauses to think, his eyes look down. People who are not kinesthetic, while trying to talk with someone who is, may misinterpret his downward eyes as lack of attentiveness or lack of self-esteem. When he speaks, he speaks and moves very quickly, manipulating his vocal cords just like any other muscle, raising and lowering his voice while changing the rhythm for emotional effect.

Because of the fast speaking pace of this learner, he often interrupts others, especially auditory learners. He will use movement or emotional words when he speaks to you: "Let's get moving!" or "That's fantastic!" In addition, the kinesthetic will talk so fast and gesture so wildly that you may receive much more information than you can absorb. Other common expressions are "I can do that for you" or "I get it" or my personal favorite, "Cool!"

A kinesthetic communicator is a very physical speaker and talks as much with body language and movement as with words. Often a kinesthetic learner will give himself away with body language while he attempts to say words he doesn't mean. He watches the body language of others as much as he hears the words, which is why talking on the phone may be uncomfortable for him.

Kinesthetic people feel emotions as a physical sensation. Fear is a feeling in the stomach; fatigue is felt under the eyes. This is not true for learners who do not prefer kinesthetic intake. Connection to emotion as a physical sensation explains why many kinesthetic processors are uncomfortable as they watch intense movies, exciting basketball games, or emotional television shows—they actually feel as if they were there. Other learners will say to them "It's only a movie!" but to a kinesthetic learner, it is more than that.

Do not assume that kinesthetic learners will be outgoing. Because talking is a form of movement, kinesthetic learners can often be big talkers, or they may be silently moving in other ways. You'll know you're communicating with a kinesthetic learner when some part of him is always moving. For example, he may be tapping his feet or fingers.

Likely career choices for kinesthetic learners are salesperson, firefighter, actor, dance instructor, trainer, and athlete. Some kinesthetic learners are musical performers, as this is very tactile. Listening to music can also be important and can help kinesthetic learners settle down to focus (see Chapter Nine for more information about music and learning).

Ask a kinesthetic learner to give you directions and he will quickly grab a pencil and paper and sketch a map—with all the places to stop and eat (eating is kinesthetic) along the way. When he thinks of going someplace, he recalls the experiences he had, or could have had, on that particular route. Notice that a visual person will also draw a map, but the landmarks will be more sight-oriented than doing-oriented.

Kinesthetic intake can manifest itself internally and externally. External kinesthetic learners prefer tactile, physical touching. They like to learn by actively trying things hands-on and will take massive notes (to simulate "doing") during a learning event. More internal kinesthetic learners prefer feeling out their emotions about learning before accepting it. Both internal and external kinesthetic learners pay as much attention to how the message is delivered through voice and body language as they do to what is said.

OTHER INFLUENCES ON SUCCESSFUL INTAKE

Besides the intake preferences that I've discussed at length, learners also have environmental preferences. Factors that influence learning for various learners include time of day, lighting, temperature, role of authority figure (what others expect), role of self (what they themselves expect), working with others or alone, eating or not while learning, and having choices while learning. In Chapter Eight, you will read about the importance of creating a learning environment to honor these needs.

ADJUSTING FOR DIFFERENT INTAKE STYLES IN A LEARNING EVENT

In this section, you will read about examples of how people with different intake styles behave differently, or behave in the same way but for different reasons. For example, visual learners take notes so they can see them; kinesthetic learners take notes so they can move. Understanding these differences and similarities in behaviors will help you identify intake preferences so that you can adjust to a specific learner. In the last section of this chapter, you will learn how to deal with the multiple intake preferences that are found in a typical learning event. By honoring all three preferences, you meet everyone's needs.

Table 3.1 shows behaviors for various learning settings.

It is important to remember that intake preference can manifest itself in many behaviors determined by not only the highest preference but also the middle and lowest. For example, although taking lots of notes is a characteristic of visual or kinesthetic intake, it would be incorrect to assume, from just this clue, that the learner is not auditory. This

TABLE 3.1.   **Intake Styles and Learning Behaviors.**

Situation	Intake Style		
	Visual	*Auditory*	*Kinesthetic*
Note Taking	Lots of notes; uses them again; may use diagrams and pictures	Few notes; prefers to listen unencumbered and jots notes quickly if absolutely necessary	Tons of notes, some about the meeting; never looks at the notes again
Seating	Sits in the middle to see everything	Sits in the front to hear well	Sits in the back to fidget and move
Remembering passwords or numbers	Sees the numbers in his head and reads them as he enters them	Says the numbers in his head or aloud as he enters them; if on the phone, recognizes the sound of the keys as they are pushed	Remembers the location and movement of the keys; can only recall the number while typing (for example, couldn't say it without moving)
Music	Likes to work to music	Music may jam up his ability to listen if too close or too loud	Music affects his emotions and energy levels
Receiving feedback from others	Wants to see pictures, charts, graphs, and colored reports with lots of pages	Wants you just to tell him what's going on, with minimal fanfare	Wants to get the data fast and then wants to debate the finer emotional points

learner could be equally strong at all three intake modes. In addition, people with the same intake preference may prefer different ways of honoring it. Computer-based training may be best for one visual learner, while reading may be preferred by another. Avoid the temptation to force labels onto your learners; honor the diversity of your learners by recognizing individual uniqueness.

In the classroom, you may be judging others by comparing their behavior with how you would behave in their place. This judgment is based on the mistaken belief that everyone learns exactly the same way.

Actually, there are an infinity of ways people prefer to take in information and learning, as you will continue to find in the following chapters. For example, cultures may reinforce certain intake styles and behaviors. In his book *Brain Based Learning and Teaching* (1995), Eric Jensen writes that women are more likely to be auditory than men. Hispanics tend to be more kinesthetic, while Northern Europeans and Asians tend to prefer visual learning.

Disconnects happen in most, if not, all corporate classrooms. Accelerated learning, whose core premise is to honor each learner, requires that the facilitator learn to modify her own behavior to best meet the needs of the learners.

 ## PRACTICE

Here's a quick quiz to practice identifying intake preferences.

1. You are teaching a class and notice a person sitting right in the front with a very focused expression. You suspect this person is _____.
2. You are in a workshop with a work team you've taught often and—as always—one person is slamming his fist on the table and screaming at everyone. You suspect this person is _____.
3. Entering the office of a customer, you notice that it is very well organized, with beautiful prints of the ocean. You suspect this person is _____.
4. You are in a sales presentation and your client jumps up, turns the lights on, and starts sketching a pie chart on the white board. You suspect this person is _____.
5. You are working with a team member who is very efficient. Things are going very well, when all of a sudden he seems to zone out. He's back in a matter of seconds, and you suspect this person is _____.
6. A friend of yours is an accomplished musician. He is always tapping his fingers to imaginary tunes in his head. You've always assumed he was auditory, but now you suspect he is also _____.

Answers:

1. Auditory
2. Kinesthetic
3. Visual

4. Kinesthetic or visual
5. Auditory (or whatever you are, since you think so highly of the person)
6. Kinesthetic

The next time you think of it, practice identifying intake styles. Try it in a restaurant with the waitpersons, in church with the minister, in school meetings with teachers, or anywhere you remember to do so. Learn to pick up the clues.

Armed with knowledge of your own preferences, you can start to communicate learning more effectively. Aware of your strongest preference, you can begin to recognize your tendency to go there more when you are under stress (as in the next example). Your greatest liability is your lowest preference. The people whose highest preference is your lowest will be the hardest for you to connect with.

Imagine you have a strong preference for kinesthetic with a low preference for auditory intake, and you are facilitating a workshop. As you lecture, you notice that there is a learner who is not taking notes. You don't know it, but this person is high-auditory, low-kinesthetic. Comparing his behavior to what yours would be as a learner, you interpret that the learner is not engaged, is not happy, and is not learning. If the learner were learning, you assume he'd be taking notes just as you do when you are learning in class. This situation increases your stress, because all good facilitators want learning to occur. You go more vigorously into your strongest preference, waving your arms more dramatically, talking more emotionally and quickly, while moving closer to the learner. The learner withdraws, becoming quieter and more stressed. Each of you may eventually interpret that the other is crazy.

What could be done to avoid this disconnect? In a workshop, look for clues to intake styles when you sense a problem with communication. Instead of judging by your own standards, look for such signs as where his eyes are moving, what his body movement tells you, what his choice of words suggests, and if there are any pauses. From the clues given above, you would guess that this is an auditory learner. There really isn't a communication problem. Because note taking is often not useful for an auditory learner, this person may be quite engaged even without taking notes. As a high-kinesthetic, low-auditory facilitator, you would choose to manage your own body language and speech patterns carefully to keep the learner with auditory intake preference stress-free.

Here are some additional ideas on how you can adjust one-on-one when there is a disconnect.

To appeal to a more auditory learner:

- Make eye contact.
- Slow down your speech.
- Keep control of your body language (hold your arms and hands quietly at your side or under the table).
- Resist the urge to draw or write.
- Pause.
- Resist the urge to interrupt.

To appeal to a more visual learner:

- Add visual words to describe what things look like.
- Draw pictures to illustrate your points.
- Bring color brochures or color workbooks.
- Write things down for the learners.
- Consider creating charts.
- Prepare a formal presentation.
- Practice doodling while others speak; learn to draw.

To appeal to a more kinesthetic learner:

- Ask your kinesthetic learner to talk.
- Talk quickly and with your hands.
- Interrupt to move faster.
- Give them something to take with them (toys and laminated cards are great).
- Don't turn the lights out for a presentation.
- Ask about and talk about emotions.

Although in a corporate classroom you often need to adjust your communication one-on-one, you also have to communicate equally well to all intake styles at the same time when lecturing or working with the class as a whole. All learning events are composed of multiple learners with unique combinations of intake styles. In the next section, you will learn to create a communication style for yourself that crosses all preferences.

MANAGING AUDIENCES OF DIVERSE INTAKE STYLES

According to Grinder and Grinder (1991), authors of *The Educational Conveyor Belt,* in a group of thirty learners, twenty-two have enough visual, auditory, and kinesthetic intake aptitude to process, at least for a short while, in any style. The others will be able to learn only in their preferred style. Depending on the discipline or field you are facilitating, the percentage breakdown in your classes will differ from the averages you read about in this chapter. For example, in information technology classes, I have found that the percentage of visual learners is slightly lower while there are more kinesthetic and auditory learners than the average would suggest. Workshops that contain primarily training professionals tend to have a very high percentage of kinesthetic learners. As you have read in a previous section, different types of learners are drawn to different fields.

The occupations of the participants can create problems with intake in a workshop. For example, here's the business problem: salespeople make money when they are out on the road selling. Some would say that they lose money when they are sitting in corporate sales meetings. Therefore, most large salesforces get together only once or twice a year to learn every new product, strategy, and sales technique. With limited time and poorly adjusted communication, frustratingly little learning may occur.

A limit on time seems to encourage sales trainers to lecture as fast as they can for two or three twelve-hour days to cover all the material. All emotional issues are glossed over, with the excuse that they will burn up too much time. Most of these trainers dread these sessions because they know that few of the salespeople remember anything that's said. This is the way it's always been done, and so it stays: the same dry, lengthy lecture.

Can you guess what intake style a salesperson favors? I'd say the answer is that many salespeople are kinesthetic learners, using activity to communicate and generate sales. It is sheer torture for them to sit still for twelve hours while people talk at them, and they are more tired at the end of such a day than if they had run around the building for the same amount of time. Looking for relief, they often rush out to the bars until the early morning hours, losing the last bit of learning energy they have. Although many of the sales and marketing trainers are also kinesthetic learners, they don't mind this kind of day as much, because they get to talk. They see the disconnect as a personal affront—the salespeople just don't respect them enough to listen.

Although this learning problem is common, it is not hard to fix. After settling on a realistic quantity of learning (see the section in Chapter Ten on creating good learning objectives), the solution is simply to build multidimensional ways to cover the material so that all intake styles (especially kinesthetic in this case) are engaged. Using innovative and experiential ways to communicate the new sales knowledge (such as simulations, lecture games, and team problem solving) ensures that there is movement, emotion, hearing, and seeing.

Problems in workshops can often be fixed by better understanding of the preferences of the learners in the particular field. It is rare, though, that any one intake style is completely missing from a workshop of ten or more learners, so even with knowledge of the weighting from the discipline, it is important to honor each style in your communication, as the lecture bingo exercise does.

CONCLUSION

To improve the learning for your participants, adjust your workshops to ensure that you are presenting all new information so that the learners can

- See it (through flipchart visuals, overhead visuals, posters, and color)
- Feel it and experience it (through simulations, note taking, and laughter)
- Hear it (through lecture, review, and time to process)

In the next chapter, you will learn about multiple intelligences and how to honor them; in so doing, you honor all three intake styles.

Practice identifying the characteristics of each intake style, using a person's occupation as one of many clues. In addition, take advantage of and manage your own preferences. The best learning facilitator is the one who recognizes his own preferences and uses them well to help others learn. In every learning event, you will meet people who do not share your intake preferences. How wonderful, then, to be able to adjust slightly and create a mutual learning relationship rather than create a new conflict.

Finally, remember that you hold a magic power with this knowledge. You have the power to understand how communication fails, but with that comes the responsibility to adjust so that communication thrives. As communication thrives, so does learning.

PERSONAL ACTION PLAN

Please look back through this chapter, and jot down your thoughts below: insights, things you want to do, things you want to remember, games, and quotes. I've added a list of my own to supplement your list. It is better for your learning if you make your own list before you look at mine.

The learning objectives of this chapter were to

- Adopt specific improvements in how you communicate new learning to learners
- Identify how you learn best
- Identify and rethink those personal beliefs of yours that block learning
- Identify your learners' preferences for receiving new learning (intake styles)
- Adjust your intake styles to communicate more effectively with learners
- Measure the effectiveness of a learning event
- Create a personal action plan to increase personal learning and the effectiveness of your delivery of learning events

Your thoughts:

_____

_____

_____

_____

_____

_____

_____

_____

_____

_____

_____

_____

_____

Here are my thoughts:

- Intake styles describe how people prefer to take new information in. Style has nothing to do with how smart people are, just how they like to receive input.
- People can take in information in any style, but trying to use an intake style that is not their preference requires more energy and is less efficient.
- Visual intake style is the most common; it is characterized by learning through seeing, visual words, and upward eye movement.
- The kinesthetic intake style is the second most common, characterized by learning through doing, active words, quick physical speech, and downward eye movement.
- Auditory intake style is the rarest; it is characterized by learning through hearing, use of hearing words, slow and even speech, and eye movement favoring straight ahead. It is often characterized by short pauses in the conversation.

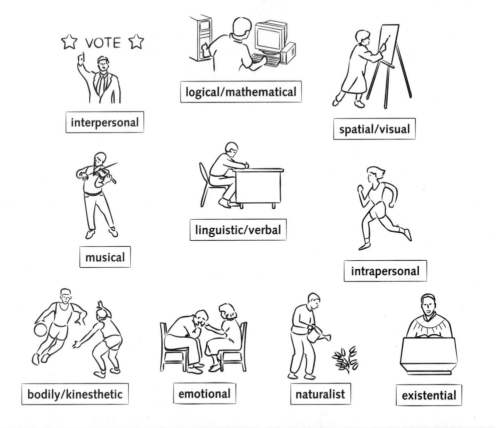

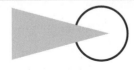

interpersonal

logical/mathematical

spatial/visual

musical

linguistic/verbal

intrapersonal

bodily/kinesthetic

emotional

naturalist

existential

THE LEARNING OBJECTIVES OF CHAPTER 4

After reading this chapter, you will be able to

- Adopt specific improvements in how you communicate new learning to learners

- Identify how you learn best

- Identify and rethink those personal beliefs of yours that block learning

- Assess your preference for processing new learning in terms of Gardner's multiple intelligences

- Use the multiple intelligences to design the logistical flow of a learning event

- Develop classroom learning events to meet a specific learning need

- Measure the effectiveness of a learning event

- Create a personal action plan to increase personal learning and the effectiveness of your delivery of learning events

CHAPTER 4

Learning Through All Your Intelligences

The intelligences are categories that help us to discover difference in forms of mental representation; they are not good characterizations of what people are (or are not) like.

—"An Interview with Howard Gardner," by Ronnie Durie

In Paris in 1900, psychologist Alfred Binet was challenged to create a measure to predict which youngsters would do well in the primary grades of Parisian schools. He created a written test to measure an "intelligence quotient," or IQ. This test was eventually adopted by the United States to test more than one million American recruits during World War I, and after the war it was adopted in U.S. schools and businesses. The pleasing simplicity of the test inspired similar efforts, such as the Scholastic Achievement Test (SAT), which is designed to predict how well a learner would do in college on the basis of math and verbal scores.

People began to believe that intelligence, like height and weight, was fixed at birth. Either you had it or you did not.

This belief did not sit well with practitioners of accelerated learning, who, time and again, saw an individual learner's abilities and knowledge grow, beyond what was accomplished in more traditional teaching methods, through innovative and experiential techniques. This acceleration of learning caused them to suspect that there was much more to intelligence than IQ tests.

In the mid-1980s, Howard Gardner challenged the belief that IQ was fixed with his work at Harvard University, which was explained in his important book *Frames of the Mind* (1985). He hoped to see society move from testing people to growing people, by focusing on the diverse ways people develop skills important to their lives. He redefined intelligence as the ability to solve problems and fashion products that are valued in a culture or community. His research showed intelligence as more complex, more diverse, and less fixed than originally thought. Gardner summarized the results into a preliminary list of seven intelligences, which I'll present shortly. He has recently researched an additional three aptitudes, which you will also read about.

Gardner believes that all of the intelligences have equal importance. No one is more important than any other. He believes that most people are strong in three or four of the initial seven intelligences. This means people have three or four that can be improved.

In the corporate classroom, reward systems can encourage people to limit their development to specific intelligences. They then lose the abilities they once had in other intelligences, or at least the confidence to apply them. Critical to creating a learning organization is finding how to honor and grow diverse intelligences in business. The more intelligences used by an organization, the more learning, and the better the company is able to compete. Peter Senge calls this personal mastery.

Accelerated learning practitioners such as Thomas Armstrong, Dee Dickinson, David Lazear, and Nancy Margulies absorbed Gardner's research and continue to experiment with learning techniques that honor the seven aptitudes he proposed. Gardner himself worked with various elementary schools to refine his theories. Increasing test scores at the these schools, including the Key School in Indianapolis, the Guggenheim Elementary School in Chicago, and St. Augustine's in the Bronx confirmed the value of learning with multiple intelligences.

Multiple intelligence (MI) is sneaking into the corporate world, but it is usually a silent success. Here are some examples you read about first in Chapter One:

• Learning organization practitioners such as Senge and Sue Miller Hurst encourage the development of intelligences as part of personal mastery, one of the five disciplines of the learning organization detailed in Senge's *The Fifth Discipline.*

• Elanco, an animal health product company, has incorporated MI into its new product and sales training. Success has been measured by increased sales through quicker and more accurate retention of new-product information by the salespeople.

• 3M has integrated MI into the workshops delivered through the information technology computer desktop training area. The return to the business is increased worker productivity through the correct use of personal computer desktop software.

• Conseco, an insurance company, has created a project management curriculum honoring MI. A midyear survey indicated that the managers of those learners attending the workshops felt that the learners' project management aptitude had increased significantly compared with the staff who did not. The learners themselves strongly supported the innovative way the workshops were taught and were mindful of increased retention and learning. An increase in business profit—through projects being completed closer to the time, cost, and quality required—has improved the business's ability to compete in the marketplace.

• At Northeast Utilities Service, the training staff used MI to transition employees from an outdated computer platform to a brand new desktop PC in less than a year. Increased worker productivity through quick adoption of new computer skills as well as fewer help-desk support hours through better retention of new technical skills were the return to the business.

These accelerated learning practitioners have seen firsthand the power of multiple intelligence as a part of accelerated learning. The core idea is that people have different aptitudes and ways of processing information internally. As you read in the discussion of intake styles in Chapter Three, you saw that people communicate with others as if the intake preference is exactly the same, which is occasionally true one-on-one but never completely true in a group of learners. The result is sometimes a disconnect. When the variety of internal processing aptitudes and multiple intelligences is considered, in addition to the plurality of intake styles, it is clear that there is even more possibility of a disconnect.

In this chapter, you will read about the relevance of Gardner's multiple intelligences. You will be provided with a summary of the research and with examples of how to apply the knowledge to your classrooms. In Chapter Two, you learned the importance of having a learning objective, which opens you to letting new learning in. In Chapter Three, you learned that individual learners have their own preferences, or intake styles, for getting the new information into their brains. In this chapter on multiple intelligences, you will learn how learners process the new information after they have gotten it inside. You will learn about the intelligences and about MI's impact on learning.

To lead into this material, take a moment to try this practice exercise.

 PRACTICE

Answer this question: How many days are left until January 1, 2100?
   Once you have an answer, think about how you solved the problem:

• Did you close your eyes and picture a calendar in your head?
• Did you talk to someone else or think about talking to someone?
• Did you sketch pictures, charts, or formulas on a piece of paper?

- Did you use a calculator?
- Did you build a mathematical calculation?
- Did you think of the mnemonic "Thirty days hath September, April, June, and November; all the rest have thirty-one, excepting February . . ." or some other similar ditty?
- Did you figure it all out in your head, or did you work it out in writing?

How you approach this problem gives you clues about the intelligences that you are strong in and depend on. As you read on, you may see yourself in some of the definitions.

THE MULTIPLE INTELLIGENCES

In this section, you will learn the initial seven (and later, three more) intelligences. You will then read examples of mapping these intelligences to exercises in learning events. There will be an example of a single exercise that maps to all intelligences, a learning objective that requires multiple exercises to map to all intelligences, and finally an example of mapping the intelligences to improve existing materials—an approach that is common in business. Following these examples, you will learn how mapping to the multiple intelligences takes care of honoring all three intake styles. To begin, you will learn a little more about how Howard Gardner approached his initial research.

Gardner started his research by defining criteria for determining a component of intelligence. He hoped to find that intelligence was not entirely genetic and fixed at birth, that it could be nurtured and grown. The criteria for identifying the components of intelligence were that

- The intelligence would have to be measurable.
- The intelligence would have to be valued by the person's culture.
- The intelligence would be a strength that people defaulted to when they were being creative or solving problems.

Being measurable was a necessary condition for Gardner because that's the world of research. In a sense, there must be some observable change, which proves or disproves the questions being asked. The measurements were not restricted to numeric results or quantifiable calculations, because of the nature of this research. For example, you can measure a person's musical ability by assessing him while he plays pieces of increasing difficulty. It would be misleading (but is often done) to give this person a starting "grade" of 2 out of 10 in music before a music class and then a final grade of an 8 out of 10 after. Why 2 or 8? Numbers are arbitrary when assessing many aptitudes.

Gardner compared children who had various learning challenges with children who were considered normal. By comparing their aptitudes, he defined seven intelligences and their value. When this list was originally published in *Frames of the Mind*, he emphasized that this was a starting list, not a final one.

The Original Seven

These are the original seven intelligences as defined by Gardner:

1. Interpersonal
2. Logical and mathematical
3. Spatial and visual
4. Musical
5. Linguistic and verbal
6. Intrapersonal
7. Bodily and kinesthetic

 LEARNING POINT

To help you easily learn and remember the original seven intelligences, remember this little phrase. It contains the first letter of each of the seven intelligences:

I Last Sued My Landlord in Boston

Notice that linguistic/verbal and logical/mathematical are the only two of the initial seven measured by Binet-like IQ tests (including college admission tests). Are these the only two things taught in management training? Have you ever worked with someone who was brilliant at math and reading but couldn't work with anyone else? The seven intelligences map more completely to the competencies that are recruited and grown within businesses today than do standard IQ tests.

Each of the original seven intelligences is described below. With the definition is an example of a famous person who demonstrates a strength in this aptitude, sample careers, and examples of how a person with that intelligence might react to stress or a need to be creative. You will also find sample teaching techniques that work well for learners strong in this aptitude. Remember, the examples are optional behaviors that might exist for an aptitude; for example, a person could be strongly logical/mathematical but not feel confident in his math abilities. Likewise, the same teaching technique can be helpful for various types of intelligences for varying reasons. For example, having ground rules for teamwork is useful for interpersonal, logical/mathematical, and linguistic/verbal learners because it speaks to their needs for team, structure, and words.

Interpersonal

Interpersonal intelligence is an aptitude for understanding other people and processing through interaction with them. Characteristics include empathy, understanding of human nature, and awareness of the goals and intentions of others. Humor and influence may also be strong. Interpersonal intelligence is how people understand each other; it influences how they communicate. Our relationships with others are managed through this intelligence.

Famous person: Oprah Winfrey
Good careers: Teacher, minister, politician, supervisor, social worker
Under stress: Talks to someone else about his or her problems
Creative: Creates new thoughts by bouncing ideas off others

Some sample teaching techniques:

- Work in teams or pairs (limit two to five).
- Provide ground rules for group work that emphasize collaboration versus competition.
- Change leadership roles often on teams.
- Meet together as groups for a minimum of half a day and then change teams.
- Assign mixed groups, according to gender, culture, background, and experience.
- Perform team role plays (see the Appendix, p. 285, for details).

Logical/Mathematical

Logical/mathematical intelligence is an aptitude for processing analytically. It includes being able to calculate, quantify, consider theorems, and carry out complex mathematical steps. Any market-driven culture that values counting money (like the United States) esteems this ability.

Famous person: Albert Einstein
Good careers: Scientist, accountant, programmer, mathematician, engineer
Under stress: Adds up the pros and cons of the problem mathematically
Creative: Breaks down a problem into concrete, doable steps

Sample teaching techniques:

- Use checklists.
- Detail pros and cons.
- Include numerical summaries and research results.
- Assign logic problems.
- Draw flowcharts with cause and effect.

Spatial/Visual

Spatial/visual intelligence is an aptitude for forming a mental model of the world and being able to play with and change this model in your mind. Strongly visual people can think three dimensionally, picturing how to get to places or easily designing products in their mind. The spatial/visual intelligence is composed of seeing, imagining, and creating.

Famous person: Frank Lloyd Wright
Good careers: Decorator, architect, artist, graphic designer, navigator
Under stress: Escapes through movies or reading
Creative: Creates visually by painting or sketching

Sample teaching techniques:

- Illustrate with charts and diagrams.
- Mind map (see the Appendix, p. 298).
- Use a window pane agenda (see Appendix, p. 305).
- Use a logistics poster (see Chapter Six).

- Guide learners in visualization and imagery.
- Use color to highlight and emphasize.

Spatial/visual learners need the environment to be aesthetically pleasing. Flickering, harsh, or broken bulbs will deter from their learning, as will clutter. They like sitting where they can see everybody—in a circle or at round tables, for example. Lots of color is inviting, including posters, flowers, pencils, markers, and paper. Visual people like overhead projectors and flipcharts. Computer-generated projection may be too fancy, and it may interfere with their learning by distracting them with the glamour of the media.

Peripheral learning (which means putting learning points on posters around the room before and after the material is covered in class) works well for visual/spatial learners. Georgi Lozanov, the Bulgarian creator of suggestopedia, a precursor to accelerated learning, claims that peripheral learning registers new information into the minds of learners even if it is never called to their attention consciously. His studies showed increased retention when peripherals were used. In Chapter Eight, you will learn more about using peripheral learning techniques to create a learning environment.

Musical

Musical intelligence is sensitivity to pitch, melody, rhythm, and tone. This aptitude can be found in both performers and listeners. It is the earliest form of human giftedness to emerge in child prodigies, according to Gardner's research. If you have musical intelligence, you may already have sensed enjoyment in listening to the CD with this book as you read. In Chapter Nine, you will learn more about research on music and its impact on learning.

Famous person: Wolfgang Amadeus Mozart
Good careers: Composer, singer, choir director, sound recording engineer
Under stress: Calms down by listening to music, often through headphones
Creative: Plays a musical instrument to release new thoughts and think

Sample teaching techniques:

- Play music during class (see Chapter Nine).
- Create a rap, poem, or song.
- Perform choral readings (see "performance" in the Appendix).
- Sing new terminology and meanings to common melodies.

Internal music is a typical phenomenon in people with a strong musical intelligence. Do you have a song in your head? You may have assumed that everyone else was exactly like you. As I ask many learners the same question, some say to me, "How can you think with a song in your head?" while others respond to them, "How can you walk around with an empty head?" Once again, the diversity of learning styles is evident.

An article in *Computerworld* talked about the relationship between music and technical people (Melymuka, 1988). There appears to be a correlation between musical aptitude and a strong logical/mathematical aptitude in some. Many programmers and technical experts are also musicians. In fact, two of the relatively technical instructors in my company are professional musicians. This is not to say that all highly musical people are also highly logical, or vice versa; both intelligences manifest themselves in various behaviors, which creates a complex relationship between them, difficult to measure with research.

Recently, physiological brain research on how neural structures develop has caused educators to speculate about the relationship between teaching music to children and developing their logical/mathematical abilities. There is some evidence that early musical experiences lay the groundwork for future logical/mathematical brain development. From 1987 to 1989, the Music Educators National Conference found that learners taking music courses averaged 20–40 points higher on both verbal and math portions of SATs than those who did not take music courses (Campbell, Campbell, and Dickinson, 1992). In the business world, where there is currently a debilitating shortage of technical people, it is an interesting idea to consider whether people with more technical proficiency can be grown through early musical instruction.

That said, Gardner has found through his research with brain-damaged and healthy people that the intelligences appear to be highly independent. He says we must be careful not to confuse interest with aptitude, continuing to say that there may nevertheless turn out to be links.

Linguistic/Verbal

Linguistic/verbal intelligence is the ability to express thoughts clearly through the spoken or written word. People strong in this aptitude think in words and depend on the spoken word to nurture relationships. This aptitude is highly valued in businesses.

Famous person: Maya Angelou
Good careers: Writer, speaker, thespian, teacher, newscaster, therapist
Under stress: Logs thoughts in a journal
Creative: Uses metaphors, analogies, and storytelling to generate new thoughts

Sample teaching techniques:

- Write.
- Read.
- Journal for reflection.
- Give learners word-search and crossword puzzles.
- Compose poems and raps.

Intrapersonal

Intrapersonal intelligence is an aptitude for thinking by way of quiet. Consider it a need to be alone. Through self-knowledge created during reflection time, these people make personal choices. Goal orientation, independence, perseverance, and compassion can also characterize intrapersonal strength. Many corporate settings, with rising time constraints, have lost effectiveness in their people because there is little or no intrapersonal time. There is a tremendous need in business to make it safe enough to learn through reflection.

Famous person: Howard Hughes
Good careers: Monk, forest ranger, distance runner, psychologist, researcher
Under stress: Takes a long walk alone
Creative: Sits alone at a corner table in a coffee shop to think

Sample teaching techniques:

- Ask learners to set objectives and prioritize individually.
- Journal for reflection.
- Use guided imagery for intrapersonal review (see Chapter Nine).
- Debrief with individual reflection before team discussion.
- Balance time alone and team time.

Intrapersonal and interpersonal are not mutually exclusive aptitudes. Unlike the common misinterpretation of the Myers-Briggs assessment tools (someone has surely said to you, "Oh! I'm an E!"), Gardner's research shows that you can be strong in both. Although many corporate trainers are highly interpersonal and love to be with people, they may also have an equally strong need to be alone. You may have noticed, after a full day of facilitating learning, that you need to renew your energy by yourself.

Bodily/Kinesthetic

Bodily/kinesthetic intelligence is an aptitude for physical movement. Bodily/kines-thetic is sometimes broken into two types: tactile and kinesthetic. Tactile learners learn through touch and manipulation of objects. Kinesthetic learners involve their whole bodies; they may process by jumping or dancing.

> Famous person: Larry Bird
> Good careers: Athlete, mom, gym teacher, trial lawyer, waitperson, surgeon
> Under stress: Goes for a long run to sort out issues
> Creative: Thinks while tossing a ball around or clicking a pen

> Sample teaching techniques:

- Role-play.
- Simulate through games.
- Move seating often.
- Use action and emotion-packed stories and metaphors.
- Assign scavenger hunts (good for reviewing long, dull documentation).
- Pass out laminated cards (tactile).

When you have someone fidgeting in one of your learning events, find a way to keep him safe while he does it. He is learning while he moves, but he may be dis-tracting others who do not learn this way. Pipe cleaners to play with, candy to munch on, and note cards and colored markers to write with all provide the kinesthetic learner with a safe, self-contained way to process. Create multiple zones in your room for them to move through: the refreshment zone, the quiet zone, the computer zone, the supplies zone, perhaps even zones for topics. Kinesthetic people love breakout rooms for exercises, and they love to go outside.

One of the challenges that come with the diversity inherent in a multiple-intelli-gence approach to learning is that measuring success is more complicated. For exam-ple, giving a written test to someone who may not be strongly linguistic/verbal or spatial/visual is not a valid measurement. With standard IQ tests, you measured, you got a number, and you were done. With MI, it's more complex. That said, here's a brief list that captures some of the characteristics of each MI.

PRACTICE

In all the columns, circle any statements that you feel apply to you.

1	2	3	4	5	6	7
I have a song in my head	I meditate often	I like to talk about my problems	I liked English in school	I can do math in my head	I think in pictures	I like to play sports
I like to listen to music	I have personal goals	I'm a leader	I like to read	I like rational explanations	I like to draw	I can't sit still
I enjoy singing	I'm independent	I need social events	I'm a good writer	I categorize things	I'm good at finding mistakes	I speak with my body
Off-key notes hurt me	I know my strengths	People come to me for advice	I like to use big words	I like logic games	Color moves me	I feel emotions deeply

Enter the number of choices you selected from each column, and find which intelligence(s) you favor.

• Beware of assessments being pedaled that treat the seven intelligences as a zero-sum game. These are tools that force learners to rank different situations from 1 to 7, purportedly to indicate the strength of each of the seven intelligences. One of the exciting things about Gardner's research is that the intelligences are not mutually exclusive. You can have them all!

• People are not only strong in three or four intelligences; they have a need, even a hunger, to use all three or four of their strengths. For example, a strongly musical person may be drawn to listen to music, a highly visual person may feel the need to draw, and a highly intrapersonal person will crave being alone. Reflecting on your cravings may help you identify your stronger intelligences.

The Three New Intelligences

In August 1997, Gardner published a white paper evaluating five additional candidate intelligences that practitioners and researchers had asked him to consider. He proposed to add three new intelligences to the original seven: emotional, naturalist, and existential.

 LEARNING POINT

Add to the mnemonic "I Last Sued My Landlord in Boston" this tag: "**E**scaping **N**ew **E**ngland!"

Again, the initial letters of the words help you remember the three new intelligences.

Emotional

As popularized by Daniel Goleman in his best-selling book *Emotional Intelligence* (1997), this aptitude is strongest in people who are able to recognize an emotion as they are experiencing it and react to it in a way that is considered positive by the culture. There is discussion about the role that emotional intelligence plays in the rising tide of violence in inner cities and low-income areas. Children in those areas may have never learned to recognize and understand their own anger and may not know how to deal with it nonviolently. Business is not immune to this learning disability. You may have had a learner in one of your business workshops who was unable to deal well with emotions, lashing out at you or other learners because of unresolved or unidentified anger about something outside of class.

Researchers are noticing the increasing stress level in corporate life and watching for side effects. The airlines are seeing an increase in "air rage" incidents (presumably among business flyers); violence in the workplace is up, as average work hours are climbing. Unless employees learn to deal with their emotions constructively in the increasingly difficult world of business, the businesses and the human beings will lose greatly. Sadly, teachers are seeing the side effect of this business stress in the classroom, where stressed-out children of stressed-out parents are also unable to focus well. The additional pressure from concern over struggling children adds to the heavy stress level of your corporate learners. It has become a reinforcing spiral effect.

Famous person: Mohandas Gandhi
Good careers: Organizational developer, guidance counselor, therapist, coach
Under stress: Meditates to identify true feelings
Creative: Checks emotions: how does each idea "feel"?

Sample teaching techniques:

- Use thorough debriefing, including emotions: "How do you feel about that?"
- Use music (see Chapter Nine) to calm or provoke emotions.
- Draw situations, to reveal true thoughts.
- Use guided imagery for intrapersonal review (see Chapter Nine).
- Encourage individual reflection before team discussion.
- Balance time alone and team time.

Notice that many of the techniques that work well for intrapersonal intelligence also work well for emotional intelligence. Emotional intelligence can make use of the ability to process intrapersonally, to go inside to examine feelings and determine the action that makes sense.

Those strong in bodily/kinesthetic aptitude experience emotion as a physical, almost muscular sensation. For example, they can point to the muscle that feels fear, anger, happiness, or stress. Emotion is very important and influential for strongly kinesthetic people. Discussed in more detail in Chapter Six on memory, emotion is a strong link to memory and strongest for people who are bodily/kinesthetic.

Naturalist

Are there some days when the outdoors calls you? This need to be with nature is the naturalist intelligence. A part of this aptitude is strength in categorization. To survive in nature, it is critical to be able to tell the difference between an edible berry and a poison berry, or a harmless snake and a dangerous snake. A 1997 Zephyr Press newsletter suggests that children today may have adapted this naturalist categorization ability to their own "nature"—for example, by their ability to clearly identify members of a gang, or original Beanie Babies, instantly from hundreds of feet away. This natu-ralist aptitude is seen in the business world, for example, through managers' ability to identify the power of another manager according to where her office is located, the car she drives, or what she is wearing. This hierarchical categorization happens at the start of every workshop, with learners jockeying for position in this new team setting. A good learning facilitator neutralizes this activity by assigning seats or mixing up teams as soon as possible.

Famous person: John Denver
Good careers: Park ranger, nature guide, oceanographer, ski patrol
Under stress: Hikes outside
Creative: Sits in a beautiful spot outside to think

Sample teaching techniques:

- Do a few of the exercises outside.
- Take nature breaks, with one lap around the building.
- Bring fresh flowers to class.
- Place live plants around the room.
- Hang nature scenes on the walls.
- Open the blinds and let the outside in.

The naturalist intelligence may partner with some ability to be alone and process intrapersonally. In addition, many people with a naturalist aptitude also have a bodily/kinesthetic strength, for example, hikers or members of ski patrols.

Existential

After considering and rejecting a religious aptitude, which he saw as difficult to measure (what with all the cultural influences on initial criteria), Gardner nominated this aptitude. He defined it as an aptitude for knowing why you are here.

Famous person: Martin Luther King Jr.
Good careers: Evangelist, marketer, motivational speaker, public relations manager
Under stress: Remembers his or her personal mission
Creative: Aligns creativity to personal goals

Sample teaching techniques:

- Create personal mission statements.
- Debrief thoroughly, including emotions: "How do you feel about that?"
- Use guided imagery for intrapersonal review (see Chapter Nine).
- Debrief with individual reflection before team discussion.

- Balance time alone and team time.
- Reinforce shared mission, vision, and values.

The existential intelligence also may make use of some ability to process intrapersonally. People with a passionate existential aptitude can be quite interpersonal as well, for example, evangelists and marketers.

MI'S IMPACT ON LEARNING

When designing learning events (see Chapter Ten), and in the classroom, MI should be used as a litmus test to ensure that the needs of every learner are met as much as possible. It is challenging to offer new information and format every new exercise in ways that honor all ten of the intelligences, but it is very possible. If you honor the multiple intelligences, you also honor visual, auditory, and kinesthetic intake preferences. The difficulty is well rewarded with learning results.

Remember a time when you were offended about something a participant said or did? Rather than give in to your gut-level emotional reaction, it is helpful to think about the multiple intelligences—could it be that you and the learner are just processing in different ways? If you stop and consider the clues, you can often adjust your behavior to maximize the learning for both of you.

Mapping an Exercise to MI

Here's an example of how you can take a simple learning experience and map it to the intelligences. In Chapter Two, you built a coat of arms to help you prioritize learning objectives for reading this book. Assume you are going to use this same coat-of-arms exercise in a workshop with a group of learners. Here are the steps:

1. Pass out colored paper and instruct learners to draw a coat of arms by demonstrating how to do it on a flipchart.
2. Show learners (by showing the pages on the overhead) how to refer to the learning objectives in the learner material.
3. Ask learners to choose their top three learning objectives as well as any additional write-in requests.
4. Ask learners to copy their selected learning objectives onto their coat of arms.
5. Ask learners to personalize their coat of arms with at least their name.

6. Play quiet instrumental music while the learners work.
7. Ask learners to share their objectives with the rest of the participants at their table, and have the table select one that they all agree on.
8. Ask the teams to share their common objective with the class and introduce their members briefly.
9. Ask learners to tape their coat of arms up somewhere in the room where they will see it often.

Here's how this thirty-minute experience maps to the multiple intelligences:

Intelligence	Step in Exercise
Interpersonal	The learners share with their team and the class.
Logical/mathematical	There is a defined process: the learners pick three things, and so on.
Spatial/visual	The coat of arms as well as the personalizing, the flipchart, and overheads are visual.
Musical	Music plays throughout the learners' work time.
Linguistic/verbal	The written and spoken word are used.
Intrapersonal	The learners read, choose, and decorate their objectives alone.
Bodily/kinesthetic	The learners write and then tape their coat of arms up.
Emotional	It is fun to decorate and share your thoughts.
Naturalist	Weak; consider plants and flowers in the room or a room with full windows.
Existential	The learners must choose what they want.

Mapping Across Multiple Exercises

There are times when it is not possible (or not best for learning) to map to all the intelligences. Here's an example of a situation that would not warrant all intelligences. Imagine that you are facilitating a leadership workshop. The learning objectives center on having the learners discover the internal beliefs and past experiences that help or hinder them in their leadership roles.

The first exercise is reflective: the learners sketch the face of a clock. You show them a sample clock face. Starting at the twelve o'clock position, they are to write down life events that have influenced their leadership beliefs. For example, at the twelve o'clock position a learner might write that he was born the oldest child, which led him into an early leadership role. (A detailed description of this exercise is in Chapter Seven.)

Let's look at how this exercise maps to the intelligences:

Intelligence	Step in Exercise
Interpersonal	None; this might be threatening to share.
Logical/mathematical	The progression of time on the clock is highly structured.
Spatial/visual	The clock drawn on the paper is visual.
Musical	Quiet, instrumental music is playing while learners think.
Linguistic/verbal	Learners write down their life events.
Intrapersonal	Learners work alone, reflecting.
Bodily/kinesthetic	Learners are writing, but this is not a strong kinesthetic experience.
Emotional	Thinking about life events brings up strong emotions.
Naturalist	Weak; consider plants and flowers in the room.
Existential	Thinking about life events creates thoughts about personal purpose.

Because of the very personal nature of the thought process, this exercise is and needs to be highly intrapersonal. The more the learning objective has to do with attitude versus skill or knowledge, the more necessary it is to focus on intrapersonal, emotional, and existential intelligences, at least initially. In this exercise, the interpersonal intelligence is not used at all.

To balance, you as facilitator would follow this experience with an exercise that is strongly interpersonal and that also gives the intrapersonal a little rest. For example, learners might be asked to move into teams and tell each other their life stories according to their clocks for a fixed amount of time. Moving into teams shores up the interpersonal and bodily/kinesthetic gaps of the first exercise. Fixing the time gives the learners a safe way to skip over things they'd rather not share. Together, these two exercises honor all the multiple intelligences.

LEARNING POINT

Perceived peer pressure in sharing sessions of this type can force people into sharing things that make them feel unsafe. Skilled facilitators manage this dynamic carefully. Be aware of learners who are looking stressed, and help them with a safe way to not share if they so choose.

This second team-sharing exercise maps out like this:

Intelligence	Step in Exercise
Interpersonal	Highly group-oriented, as learners share with others.
Logical/mathematical	The time limit adds structure.
Spatial/visual	The visual component is in looking at each other and one another's clocks.
Musical	Quiet, instrumental music is playing while the learners share.
Linguistic/verbal	Learners are talking and sharing the spoken word.
Intrapersonal	Little or none (would hinder listening).
Bodily/kinesthetic	Learners physically move to a new team location.
Emotional	Talking about life events brings up strong emotions.
Naturalist	Weak; consider sending the teams outside to talk.
Existential	Talking with others about life events creates thoughts about personal purpose.

Notice the flow of these two activities: the intelligences that were weaker on the first exercise (interpersonal, bodily kinesthetic) were stronger on the second exercise. Likewise, the aptitudes that were weak on the second exercise (intrapersonal, logical/mathematical, spatial/visual) were strong on the first. This balance keeps the energy level of the learners high. If you balance experiences in your classroom, you will notice a marked difference in the amount of material the learners can absorb and a lack of fatigue as they do.

 LEARNING POINT

Use the multiple intelligences to manage the flow of your classroom experiences. Strive to make the learning 80 percent experiential and 20 percent lecture, rather than the 20 percent experiential and 80 percent lecture model in many corporate classrooms. Be especially attentive to varying intrapersonal and interpersonal time to maximize the learning energy.

Notice that in the previous example the logical/mathematical aptitude is not very strong in either exercise. If you had a room full of people with a strong aptitude for logical/mathematical (for example, engineers, programmers, technicians), you might need to add a more exact process for sharing so that people with the logical/mathematical aptitude would be more comfortable. You know you have this need when you overhear learners saying, "I'm not really sure what we're supposed to be doing here; did you get it?" Consider adding structure by asking people to share in clockwise order, or doing something similar.

Mapping Existing Material

A classic business example of failing to honor multiple intelligences is the traditional sales meeting. The once-a-year sales meeting creates a time-pressured situation for learner and facilitator, and many sales trainers try to address the problem by lecturing as fast as they can for hours on end. The learners squirm in frustration and later recall virtually nothing other than the weight of the new-product guides. I described this situation in the last chapter because of its relevance to honoring all intake styles. Let's map it now to MI to continue to analyze the challenges and see how to improve the learning.

As you noticed in Chapter Three, a typical salesperson is a highly kinesthetic processor. The most energy-draining thing you can do to him is to force him to sit still all day and listen. In sales conferences where salespeople don't move (their preferred way to get new learning into their brains), they will retain virtually nothing once they leave. The little they may learn will require a great deal of energy. Investing a little preparation time by designing learning events that honor all the intelligences creates an immediate return on investment for the company. Better new-product knowledge creates a competitive advantage in the marketplace.

Here's an example. A global animal health company needed to quickly switch its international salesforce from selling products exclusively to chicken farmers to selling products to both chicken and hog farmers. There were several business and learning challenges: a geographically dispersed audience, the fact that many learners were working in a nonnative language, differing levels of experience among the salespeople, and the normal business time pressures to get to the market first.

The first step was that the company invested in a large binder containing a textual tutorial on hog basics and sent it out to the learners in advance. The sales training staff suspected most of the salespeople wouldn't read it, so they planned to have a veterinarian lecture for a couple of hours during a two-day annual sales meeting in hopes that the basics would be learned and retained.

Honoring MI, the sales training staff developed a fun "scavenger hunt" as the first exercise of the sales meeting. Teams of salespeople were given sheets with hog trivia questions that they answered together, using either the knowledge of the group or the binders of information. There was a fixed time to answer the questions, and the teams with the most correct answers won prizes. The team aspect of the game made it safe and evened the playing field because some learners had read the binder, some hadn't, some had previous hog experience, and some did not. The competition created a non-threatening way to share the answers, providing a review that reinforced or introduced the learning.

Here's how the scavenger hunt maps to the multiple intelligences:

Intelligence	Step in Exercise
Interpersonal	Highly group-oriented because the learners play as teams.
Logical/mathematical	The list of trivia questions, the rules, and the material are highly structured.
Spatial/visual	Navigating the book and reading the questions are visual.
Musical	Quiet music is playing while learners work.
Linguistic/verbal	Teams record their answers on paper; then, during the review, the teams share verbally.
Intrapersonal	The teams that choose to do so can divide up the question intrapersonally, allowing some people to work alone for part of the time.
Bodily/kinesthetic	The salespeople physically move together to a shared table.
Emotional	Competition is emotionally energizing to most salespeople.
Naturalist	The topic is very naturalist.
Existential	Weak.

The second challenge was the veterinarian's lecture. It was important to the politics and the learning that the salespeople meet and hear from the vet, but there was realistic concern about the effectiveness of salespeople listening to a lengthy, technical lecture. To honor the intelligences, the sales training staff created bingo cards with key terms about hogs on them. As the vet lectured, salespeople marked their bingo cards. The first person to get a bingo stood up and was asked to define the terms to get the prize. The play continued until the lecture was complete.

The positive side effect was that the sales meeting as a whole was fun—fun to attend, and fun to teach. The managers were impressed with the "change" in the facilitator, which was really more a change in how the material was delivered. The facilitator was excited about the success and anxious to continue to add MI to the learning events. In Chapter Five, you will learn more about the link between laughter and long-term retention. Unfortunately, many corporate cultures seem to view fun as frivolous rather than productive.

Keep in mind, also, that the subject matter of the learning objectives carries an orientation toward certain intelligences. If you are teaching material on computer programming, for example, all of the exercises will have a strong logical/mathematical map.

PRACTICE

Let's review the multiple intelligences. But let's do it with a different kind of review.

At the end of this chapter is a whimsical dialogue, beginning right after the personal action plan, at the head "Choral Reading: Effective Skills Practice."

If you are reading this book with others, consider doing the exercise out loud as a choral reading. As a review, after you have done the choral reading you can map this exercise to the multiple intelligences. (Clue: choral readings honor the musical intelligence because they are rhythmic.)

It is a little intimidating for some people to read aloud, but learning is increased because people are so attentive as they read. The participants who do not have a role or do not want to take part can read along with a photocopy of the script that has numerous blanks (you can prepare this by making a full copy of the choral reading, whiting out the italicized words in this master copy, and then photocopying these master pages). The audience members who then use the blank version must listen carefully to fill in the white spaces.

To use this type of review exercise in your workshops, introduce it by showing the learners the filled-in script. This shows them right up front that they won't have to improvise any parts. Very quickly, ask for volunteers (to keep it safe) who want to play a role and read, and pass each volunteer an index card with the name of the part she will be reading. This ensures that you have honored all the intake styles. When the parts are taken, distribute to the remaining participants the scripts with the blanks, and announce that the blanks can be filled in while they listen. Even this part is optional (writing interferes with an auditory learner's ability to listen).

When everyone is ready, turn to the end of the chapter, and begin at "Choral Reading: Effective Skills Practice."

The Multiple Intelligences and Intake Styles

In Chapter Three, you learned to honor all three intake styles—visual, kinesthetic, and auditory—during every learning event. A wonderful side benefit of mapping the learning event flow to the multiple intelligences is that you also cover the intake styles. Notice how the three intake styles are easily "covered" by the intelligences:

Intake Style	*Multiple Intelligence(s)*
Visual	Spatial/visual, naturalist
Auditory	Linguistic/verbal, musical, existential
Kinesthetic	Bodily/kinesthetic, emotional

So, multiple intelligences are everywhere. You have learned to identify all ten intelligences and learned how to map them to your exercises in your learning events. You have seen ideas about integrating the intelligences into your classroom environment; you will learn more about this in Chapter Eight. In Chapter Eleven, you will learn how to use the intelligences to create effective marketing pieces to promote your learning events. Corporate training departments have always struggled with how best to communicate and sell their services. Integrating MI into a corporate training marketing strategy ensures improved communication and sales success.

Before you learn the ramifications of the multiple intelligences to business as a whole, take a minute and reflect on your own strengths, the demands of your life, and what you plan to do about the gaps.

 PRACTICE

Using the chart below, rate the intelligences in terms of their importance in your work and family life. To begin, choose three or four intelligences (or more, if you'd like) that are your strongest in column 2. Then, look at each of the intelligences: are you called on to use these aptitudes never, sometimes, or often in your work (column 3) and family life (column 4)? In the final column, take a moment to create some ideas on how you can grow the aptitudes that you need to improve.

Intelligence	My Strengths	Work Life	Family Life	Action Plan
Interpersonal				
Linguistic/verbal				
Spatial/visual				
Musical				
Logical/mathematical				
Intrepersonal				
Bodily/kinesthetic				
Emotional				
Naturalist				
Existential				

CONCLUSION

I have seen learners get old in their thinking, independently of their actual age. They get lazy about their thinking, set in their ways, or afraid to risk change. They get dependent on fewer and fewer aptitudes until, sadly, they can only process in one or two.

For example, an experienced computer programmer might end up with an arsenal for dealing with work and life that contains only intrapersonal mixed with logical/mathematical processing. Historically, computer programmers have been rewarded for these two aptitudes, but the complexity of business needs (and the nature of computers and software themselves) require more aptitudes than that now. These people are left sadly handicapped and unable to be effective. Essentially, their lost ability to learn in varied ways prevents them from growing the skills and knowledge needed to stay competitive in the job market.

Gardner believes that there may be a genetic limit to everyone's ability to grow within their intelligences; however, the exciting news is that he also believes that this limit is rarely, if ever, reached. The environment surrounding learning is greatly influential to growing the weaker intelligences. High concentrations of exposure to an intelligence—such as the popular Japanese Suzuki Method, developed by Shinichi Suzuki, provides with musical performance—can significantly improve aptitude.

Suzuki spent a great deal of time identifying the factors that matter in developing musical skills in young children and taught these skills to other children, significantly improving the effectiveness of the instruction, and therefore the learning.

Businesses that find a gap in a certain intelligence might look to methods like the Suzuki method and develop learning based on how people who are strong in the intelligence have developed it. For example, how salespeople develop their interpersonal skills might be beneficial to developing a learning strategy for growing the interpersonal aptitude in the computer programmers.

In contrast, if you are never exposed to an intelligence, you will not grow that aptitude, regardless of your strength. This obvious point speaks to the importance of a multitiered approach not just to business learning events but to business as a whole. I have built a three-part model to widen a multiple-intelligence focus from a single business learning event to a holistic business learning approach, based on a similar model developed by Gardner (for a multiple intelligence school) in *Frames of the Mind.* Figure 4.1 shows the three components.

Educational Structures:
The learning environment, the business owners of the learning need, the corporate culture, and the business processes all honor the multiple intelligences in all aspects of communication.

Lesson Types:
The learning content, tools, and techniques map to the multiple intelligences.

Learning Strategies:
The development of learning, the delivery technique of facilitators, and the learning needs of the learners honor the multiple intelligences.

FIGURE 4.1. **A Holistic Approach to Business Learning.**

In business, it is important, but not enough, to integrate MI into the occurrence of a single lesson or learning event (lesson types). You will learn more about delivery techniques in Chapter Eight. More learning will occur if the learning events are designed from the start to include MI and the facilitators are all experienced practitioners of MI (learning strategies). You will learn more about developing learning events in Chapter Ten.

These two components will improve the learning while people are attending the learning event, but they will not improve the likelihood of applying the learning in the environment that they return to. The learners may be unable to apply the new learning because of a corporate culture that does not allow them to process their new learning in the manner they need to. Creating an organization that honors and nurtures MI in all aspects of communication (educational structures) is key to a significant return on investment in business learning. MI holds the key to truly moving toward becoming the sort of learning organization espoused by Senge and others. Senge acknowledges learning at a personal and team level as prerequisites to organizational learning.

 PERSONAL ACTION PLAN

Please look back through this chapter, and jot down your thoughts below: insights, things you want to do, things you want to remember, games, and quotes. I've added a list of my own to supplement your list. It is better for your learning if you make your own list before you look at mine.

The learning objectives of this chapter were to

- Adopt specific improvements in how you communicate new learning to learners
- Identify how you learn best
- Identify and rethink those personal beliefs of yours that block learning
- Assess your preference for processing new learning in terms of Gardner's multiple intelligences
- Use the multiple intelligences to design the logistical flow of a learning event
- Develop classroom learning events to meet a specific learning need
- Measure the effectiveness of a learning event
- Create a personal action plan to increase personal learning and the effectiveness of your delivery of learning events

Your thoughts:

_____

_____

_____

_____

_____

_____

_____

_____

_____

_____

_____

Here are my thoughts:

• Intelligence is not fixed, according to Gardner. It is not limited to logical/mathematical and linguistic/verbal aptitudes. Learning is a multicolored tapestry not yet completely understood and defined. Value the diversity of it, and honor that diversity in your learners. The intelligences, as defined by Gardner, are

Interpersonal
Logical/mathematical
Spatial/visual
Musical
Linguistic/verbal
Intrapersonal
Bodily/kinesthetic
Emotional
Naturalist
Existential

- To ensure that all learners learn in the way that is best for them, the flow of a learning event should be mapped to the intelligences. Any intelligence that is neglected in one experience should be used in the one following. If possible, all intelligences should be honored.
- Learning events that are mapped to MI will also honor all three intake styles.
- MI can be applied to all types of corporate training, including self-paced. It is also useful in any communication setting, such as marketing, advertising, meetings, and brochures.
- MI and its application are building blocks of a learning organization.

CHORAL READING: EFFECTIVE SKILLS PRACTICE

NARRATOR: The setting is a conference room gathering of trainers. Their boss, a middle manager in a Fortune 500 company, has called the meeting. She has arranged the meeting to obtain input from the training team. Her concern: why field managers complain that trainees spend so much time in the training room yet are unable to transfer learned skills into actual practice. Once the issue has been stated, the training staff starts to respond.

GARDNER SEVENS (a learning consultant): I think we really do a great job of presenting new information. Where we may be lacking is in the proportion of time we allow to *practice* the new information, compared to the actual teaching time.

BETSY BOSS: Huh? Oops! I mean can you be more specific?

GARDNER SEVENS: Sure. Global research has proven beyond the shadow of a *doubt* that, in order to substantially improve learning *transfer*, we must *reverse* the amount of time we spend teaching to the amount of time the trainees actually spend *rehearsing* newly learned *information*. According to scientific findings, we should spend *20–30* percent of the time teaching and *70–80* percent of the time allowing learners to activate the material in a *meaningful* way.

BETSY BOSS: OK. I'm intrigued. Tell me more.

GARDNER SEVENS: Many of us in this room have been interested in the research of *Howard* Gardner at *Harvard* University in Cambridge, Massachusetts. His years of intensive personal and *team* research have proven that standard IQ tests fail to measure true intelligence. They only measure linguistic and logical/*mathematical* skills.

BETSY BOSS: So? What's the point? How does this relate to our discussion?

GARDNER SEVENS: Inez, help me out here.

INEZ INTRAPERSONAL: Gardner has clearly determined that, once information has been taken in, whether *auditorily, visually,* or *kinesthetically,* each person has three or four ways in which he or she *processes* the new information. Altogether, *seven* processing styles (or intelligences) have been unequivocally identified.

I confess, I'm at my best when I'm allowed to work alone. It's not that I can't work with others. It's just that sometimes I get overwhelmed by team input and need to be off by myself for a while. That's when my thoughts get real clarity.

Once they've taken concrete shape, I can function better as a member of a team, but not for extended periods of time. Overuse of team activities in any situation causes me to withdraw and not carry through with my best work.

BETSY BOSS: I'm still lost.

LARRY LINGUIST: People like and respect me because I communicate well, both *orally* and on paper. But the same isn't true for Sue. Right, Sue?

SUSAN SPATIAL: Right! And it's not that I value my dominant processing style any less, but I now understand that different people need the opportunity to *process* information in other ways than mine. Not all people learn anything by fooling with a Rubik's Cube! Or designing a twenty-first-century condo! Matt?

MATTHEW MUSICAL: Exactly! I love music and rhythm. But not everyone is engaged by exercises and *activities* that engage that particular preference. For them to learn, they may also *need* rehearsals that involve *logic* and mathematics.

LEO LOGICAL: I learn best by breaking problems down to their smallest *parts.* I find flaws in other people's thinking this way. My middle name is *Deductive*! But, contrary to popular opinion, I don't go to a party . . . even a learning party . . . with my ledgers under my arm! I also love to *interact* with all kinds of people!

IRENE INTERPERSONAL: Wow! Yes! Me too! I know I'm smart all by myself, but somehow, my most wonderful ideas and *solutions* flow best when I'm with other people! When I have to work alone, I feel isolated . . . like I'm working in a *vacuum.* Bev, what about you?

BEVERLY BODILY: Well, you see me always tapping my fingers when I'm thinking. And pacing the floor when I'm working out the details of an idea. Or shifting positions when I have to sit through long classes or meetings. I need to MOVE! I need to be DOING! And when I get fidgety, other people look at me like I'm either disrespectful, not with it, or some kind of FLAKE! And you all laugh at me when I get *emotional*! But *feeling* deeply helps me to learn and grow. That's my preferred processing *style*. Certain kinds of *music* also help me concentrate and clarify my thoughts. And I love the challenge of *analyzing* raw data. I don't mind writing progress reports and usually go to Larry when I can't find exactly the right words. So, I know I process information differently than he does.

BETSY BOSS: Tell me again about percentages, Gardner.

GARDNER SEVENS: In order to maximize the potential of learning *transfer* from the *classroom* to actual *on-the-job* situations, we must do one thing: as quickly as possible, reverse the *ratio* of training time to *practice* time. Ideally, we should spend *20–30* percent of the time training and *70–80* percent of the time allowing learners to practice in ways that honor and *respect* individual processing styles.

NARRATOR: Betsy Boss nods her head wisely. The need for some significant changes must be conveyed and, the change itself, implemented.

Gardner Sevens smiles, confident that the message has gotten through.

Inez Intrapersonal goes off by herself to contemplate her role in this change.

Larry Linguistic sits down at his word processor to draft a letter to other colleagues about the progress that has been made.

Susan Spatial goes off to play with her Rubik's Cube and redesign a diagram for her next training.

Matthew Musical retreats to his cubicle, puts on his Walkman, and plugs in a Bach tape.

Leo Logical mind maps all the possible outcomes of the meeting and charts the most likely scenario.

Irene Interpersonal can't wait to get on the phone and share her thoughts about the meeting with anyone who will listen.

Beverly Bodily paces her nine-by-ten-foot cubicle, chews on her pencil, sits down, stands back up, taps her feet, drums her fingers, looks anxious, and then sits down to summarize the meeting for everyone else!

Business Success

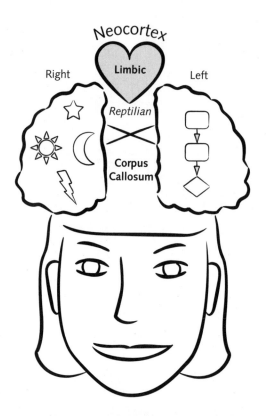

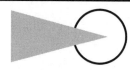

THE LEARNING OBJECTIVES OF CHAPTER 5

After reading this chapter, you will be able to

- Adopt specific improvements in how you communicate new learning to learners

- Identify how you learn best

- Identify and rethink those personal beliefs of yours that block learning

- Balance the use of both the left and right sides of the brain for learning

- Define the three primary functions of the triune brain in a learning event

- Maximize memory in self and others for long-term retention

- Use music to create focused learning environments

- Create a personal action plan to increase personal learning and the effectiveness of your delivery of learning events

CHAPTER 5

Learning with Your Whole Brain

This ability to harness our mental energy through fuller creative functioning
becomes more and more important. The pace of change is accelerating so
rapidly that humans will be unable to handle it with anything short of their
whole brain.

—Ned Herrmann, *The Creative Brain*

I have had the privilege of working with my dear friend Vija Dixon since 1988. Vija
and I have many life experiences in common but came from different occupations.
She was in sales most of her professional life, starting with retail sales and management
and moving into telecommunications sales. I was a computer programmer who moved
into technical training. Then I began growing a small company; I knew a lot (at least
I thought I did at the time) about computers and training, but little about sales. At
that time, she was frustrated by the lack of flexibility in her bureaucratic sales organizations and was looking for a more challenging place to be. It seemed like a perfect
match, and it has been.

Early on, we both attended an accelerated learning workshop where we were
exposed to Ned Herrmann's research on brain dominance. I had assumed that I was
left-brained (which you will soon read means comparatively linear thinking), because I
was in a left-brain field (the computing field); Vija seemed right-brained (which was
more nonlinear) because she was in sales. We were both assessed, and to our surprise we
found out that Vija was high-left and I was high-right! We knew that together we made
a whole brain, but we were surprised to find which side we leaned toward. You will read
more about what brain dominance really means, but as brain researchers know, the best
thing is to use your whole brain—one side is not sufficient. As Herrmann says, we all
have access to our whole brain. Frequently, one mode alone is not sufficient.

In the chapters before this, you learned about how intake styles and multiple intelligences vary depending on the learner. Brain dominance, or the side of the brain that

the learner prefers, also varies from learner to learner. In this chapter, you will learn about brain research that is helpful as you proceed to deliver, create an environment for, and develop AL events. You will read about

- Brain dominance theories
- The impact of brain dominance on learning
- The theory of the triune brain
- The impact of the triune brain on learning

Brain research has changed dramatically in the last ten years as technology such as MRIs and CAT scans allows researchers to actually look inside the brain. This technology challenges many old beliefs about brains and reinforces others. One truth has not changed: the brain is designed for survival. Everything that the brain does has to do with keeping you healthy, happy, and alive. Clearly, if a training class makes you feel unhealthy, sad, or less alive, the brain will attempt with all its power to block it. As the central control center, that is the brain's job.

BRAIN DOMINANCE THEORIES

Many practitioners oversimplify brain dominance. Although preference develops through natural inclination and environment, just like right-handedness or left-handedness, everyone has access to all of the brain. None of us uses exclusively one side.

The Left Brain and the Right Brain

The brain-dominance theories say that the brain has two sides that are each responsible for some kinds of processing. In other words, the sides have specific roles to play in the job of keeping the brain and the body performing well. Each side is equally important, and in fact the brain works best when both sides are playing their roles at the same time. Remarkably, the ancient Egyptians knew of some differences between the left and right brain. More recently, researchers such as Herrmann and Eric Jensen have validated the original work of Nobel Prize laureate Roger Sperry, who documented the functioning differences between the brain hemispheres.

According to your preference, your brain mentally filters what information you process first, what you pay attention to, and how you communicate. The next sections will describe the three primary parts of the brain that are important to the theory of brain dominance: the left brain, the right brain, and the corpus callosum.

The Left Brain

The left brain is like a manager. This mode of thinking likes facts, numbers, black-and-white data, structure, and planning. Some people call it the academic brain. This mode is very organized and likes predictability and repetition. The left brain controls much of the right side of the body. The left mode likes:

- Sequences and steps
- Explanations from detail and facts rather than the big picture
- Words, letters, icons
- Reading the directions before trying them
- Facts, related and not
- Structure and predictability

The Right Brain

The right brain is more like an artist. This mode of thinking likes fantasy, color, emotion, patterns, what-if, and looking at things from a different perspective. Some call it the creative brain, although many people (for example, Einstein) are very creative using primarily their left brain. This part of the brain gets bored easily with repetition. The right brain controls much of the left side of the body. The right mode likes:

- Randomness
- Big picture rather than detail
- Pictures, graphs, charts
- Learning by seeing, hands-on
- Spontaneity, open-endedness, surprises
- Integration

Highly left-mode-dominant individuals will probably have a very organized and clean workspace. A highly-right-mode dominant individual will have piles everywhere. Both will be able to find things in their own spaces, and both will have stress working in the other's environment.

Take a minute and reflect on which mode of the brain a business typically favors.

The left mode of the brain values quantifiable elements, which can be described with numbers. The right mode values measurable but not quantifiable elements, which aren't numeric. For example, the ideal for averaging certification test grades, which is quantifiable, would be left mode. Thinking about the complex factors that influenced that average would be right mode. Certainly, both are critical to success.

In many business curriculums, the learning is oriented to the left mode only, because that is the type of learning that is quantifiable, and so easier to measure. The answers to right-mode questions, such as "Did performance increase?" are more difficult to measure, and often avoided. The problem is that business innovation requires strength in both right and left mode processing. The left mode identifies, sequences, organizes, and analyzes content. The right gives the context, a view of the big picture, and understanding of the impact of that content.

In a learning event, the left mode prefers to learn statistics—for example, using analysis, formulas, and lists of data. The right mode would rather use a hands-on, fun example—such as studying the likelihood of pulling two red M&Ms in a row out of a two-pound bag.

The Corpus Callosum

The corpus callosum is a bundle of nerve fibers that function like a telephone cable between specialized neurons in each hemisphere. Its job is to connect the sides of the brain and allow them to communicate. When learning engages both sides of the brain, the corpus callosum is put to work. For example, using a colored job aid (right mode) with checklists (left mode) triggers the corpus callosum. There is some evidence that music can stimulate both sides of the brain and provide some integration of the two. You will read more about how music influences learning in Chapter Nine.

 PRACTICE

Here's a simple exercise that demonstrates what happens when both sides of the brain are stimulated.

While standing, find a solitary place and read aloud from the first row each of the letters of the alphabet, while simultaneously raising the hand indicated below the letter (L = left hand, R = right, T = two or together). After you have been successful reading the list from beginning to end, read the list again from the end to the beginning, and raise your hand or hands accordingly.

A B C D E F G H I J K L M N O P Q R S T U V W X Y Z
L R R L T T L L T R L R T L R R L L R L T L R R T L

Which direction was easier? Why?

Why was the other direction harder?

When you move your right arm and then your left, you are creating an oppositional challenge that requires both hemispheres of the brain and coordination between them. You are also overtaxing the left mode by asking it to simultaneously interpret two rows of letters, say the letters out loud, and move the right arm.

Forward is easier because you could "read" the alphabet from memory, which reduces the load on the left brain. Going backward brings the need for more concentration, creating a sense of overload and triggering the emotions in the right mode.

This sense of overload happens in business daily, though you are often not conscious of it. This is similar to the children's game where you try to rub your tummy with one hand and pat your head with the other. With practice, mastery can be achieved, but frustration often discourages practice.

Ned Herrmann's Brain Quadrants

Herrmann has delved deeply into Sperry's work and incorporated the triune brain concept (which you will read about later in this chapter) to form a four-quadrant model. In looking for a way to assess brain functioning differences in workers at GE, he developed the Herrmann Brain Dominance Instrument (HBDI), used widely in business settings today.

Herrmann subdivided the sides of the brain into what he called four brain quadrants. His assessment tool measures not only brain dominance but also the intensity of all four quadrants. He has encouraged learning facilitators to honor all four quadrants and vary them while facilitating learning. Figure 5.1 shows Herrmann's model.

A few years ago, Herrmann (who is a gifted sculptor) turned his focus toward the

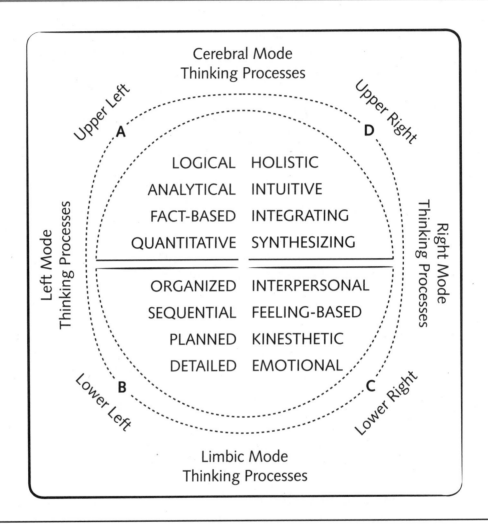

FIGURE 5.1. Ned Herrmann's Whole-Brain Model.

Source: Copyright © 1988 Herrmann International. Used with permission.

creative process. In his book *The Creative Brain* (1995), he details a strategy for moving the brain through all four quadrants to encourage the most creative solution by viewing the problem from different perspectives. Anyone involved in teaching creativity or problem-solving workshops would do well to check out this practical book.

THE IMPACT OF BRAIN DOMINANCE ON LEARNING

Don Campbell, a researcher in the field of music and learning, presented an interesting demonstration during a session at the International Accelerated Learning (IAL, which was then known as SALT) conference in Boston in the early 1990s. He asked for (brave!) volunteers who believed they were tone deaf and proceeded to stand in front of them, sing a note, and ask them to match it. They all failed miserably.

The next thing he did was to stand in front of them again, sing the note (which they still couldn't match), but then move toward their left ears while singing. Attempting once again, each person instantly slid onto the note. Observers could tell by the amazed look on the volunteers' faces that they knew they had.

Campbell explained that matching a musical tone is one of the roles of the right brain. As you read earlier, the right brain controls much of the left side of the body, including about 70 percent of what is heard through the left ear. Campbell was overcoming a hearing dominance by moving to the volunteer's left ear. When he stood in front of the volunteer, the right ear (left brain) was hearing better than the left ear (right brain). As he moved toward the left ear (right brain), musical matching occurred.

Think about which ear you prefer to put the phone to when you talk. Try switching to the other ear and see how well you hear. The ramifications in the corporate classroom are astounding—what if your learners aren't listening with both ears? Researchers now say that the left mode is involved most of the time. Because much of language is processed in the left hemisphere, speak to the right ears of your learners as much as possible.

One of Herrmann's more recent books, *The Whole Brain Business Book* (1996), contains his thoughts on how to predict career success using brain profiles, applying the four brain quadrants to business. In the book, he documents through his research HBDI scores for people who are successful in business roles. For example (and not surprisingly), a programmer and a salesperson have very different maps. Herrmann's organization continues to do extensive research on the quadrant strengths of people in many vocations, as well as the quadrant flow of creative thought.

There are a number of implications for corporate trainers. You may find you need to tailor your marketing of workshops depending on the target audience. A programmer is looking for facts and data, while a public-relations expert is looking for emotional benefit. In addition, you may want to consider the types of exercises you use in a learning event, based on the profiles of the target audience or at least the profiles of the average person in that job. You will find that learning events that are written for a highly technical (left-brain) audience need more facts and checklists, whereas workshops that are aimed at more big-picture (right-brain) audiences need more hands-on experiences.

In summary, what do you do, as a facilitator, with knowledge of brain quadrants?

- Honor the whole brain regardless of the dominant mode of the learning. For example, writing programming code (left) could be done on colored paper with colored markers (right), thereby engaging both sides.
- Be aware of your own preference (take the Herrmann Brain Dominance Instrument), as you will be predisposed to teaching this way in class.
- Honor left and right sides by sharing big picture and details and relating things.
- Ensure that your learning events have both structure and flexibility; for example, the reviews are always at the end of the day, the lunch is always at the same time, it's always safe, but the exercise content is always unique and surprising.
- Show, tell, and let participants experience every new thought or topic.
- Honor the multiple intelligences, which you read about in Chapter Four, and both sides of the brain will also be honored.
- Practice deep breathing with the class to balance oxygen flow and feed the whole brain.
- Use cross-lateral energizers to wake up the hemispheres when energy is dropping. Cross-lateral energizers are physical movements that get the blood flowing to the right and left brains, such as rhythmically touching the opposite shoulder while alternating between right and left.
- Use music to integrate the brain (see Chapter Nine). Music can help your learners get settled and focused enough to learn.

THE THEORY OF THE TRIUNE BRAIN

Originally named by Dr. Paul MacLean, former director of the Laboratory of Brain and Behavior at the National Institute of Mental Health, the triune brain has proven slightly controversial since about 1990. MRIs and CAT scans now make it possible to peek inside the brain, and observation has challenged the belief that the brain has these three physically distinct parts that you will read about below. The functionality discussed below, however, remains unchallenged, although physically these functions might exist in other places. You will find the concept of the triune brain useful in understanding learner behavior and memory in a learning event.

MacLean's research defined the three (*triune* means three in one) parts:

1. The reptilian (R-complex: includes the brain stem and cerebellum)
2. The limbic (midbrain: includes amygdala, hippocampus, hypothalamus, pineal gland, thalamus, nuclear accumbens)
3. The neocortex (neomammalian: cerebrum and neocortex)

Eric Jensen has a wonderful analogy for the triune brain. He asks us to think of an office building. On the lowest level (the reptilian) we find the maintenance workers who are responsible for heat, electricity, air, alarms, and security. At the middle level (the limbic), we find the employees who provide the day-to-day work of the business: the emotion, energy, motivation, and life blood of the business. On the top level (the neocortex), the executive management is working on trends, forecasts, and long-term planning (Jensen, 1995). Building on this metaphor, let's look at the important roles of each of the three parts: the reptilian brain, the limbic, and the neocortex.

The Reptilian Brain

The reptilian brain, sometimes called the brain stem, is known for "fight or flight." It is believed by many to be the most primitive part of the brain and is there to help its owner survive. It controls breathing, heart rate, and all the things the body does automatically when threatened. It gets adrenaline pumping and the heartbeat accelerated to help the body deal with threats. In fact, blood flow is directed away from other parts of the body—including the brain—to power the heart and the extremities, preparing them for quick response. The reptilian brain is triggered by instinct and is very fast-acting. The reptilian brain is responsible for learning

- How to conform socially, for example, with hair, clothes, and attitude
- What your territory is, and how to protect it
- Proper mating rituals for your community
- How to survive in hierarchies (including corporate bureaucracies)
- Proper social rituals, for example, how to greet a customer

The reptilian brain can create problems in the corporate world, if it interprets new learning as threatening. Think of the reptilian area as a gate. When it is closed, nothing is going to get into the brain, so no learning will occur. Most people can clearly remember a teacher in school who triggered a reptilian response. Here is a personal example.

When I was in sixth grade, I had a young English teacher who taught through intimidation and fear. He would demand that his classes memorize and recite things and would loudly humiliate us in front of our adolescent peers if we did not. For the most part, I managed to memorize, but I still had nightmares about his class. To this day, more than thirty years later, I can still recite most of the prepositions. Fearmongers would say, "See! Look how long-term and effective that learning was!" True, the learning was long-term, but it was not effective. I remember the words, but I have no idea what a preposition is, what it is used for, or why I need to know about it. In fact, I'm pretty sure I would avoid anything to do with prepositions or English grammar, given a choice. In a sense, negative learning has occurred.

When the reptilian brain is engaged in learning, our preservation mechanisms allow us to quickly learn the bare minimum needed to avoid punishment. We have no time to understand context or move to higher levels of learning. Threatened with embarrassment, I retained the prepositions themselves, but I never stored the knowledge of how to use them.

Pictures of brains under threat show that they operate differently from nonthreatened brains. The blood flow is increased and rushed to the reptilian area, minimizing the resources available to the limbic and neocortex areas. In a sense, all power is switched to survival. This creates instantaneous and not necessarily well-thought-out reactions. An unsafe learner will behave this way, which is obviously not the best behavior for learning.

PRACTICE

Think of a situation in which you learned through fear or intimidation. It is very easy to remember the emotion of fear that you experienced. Analyze the learning that occurred and the learning that did not. I have used my personal example to get you started.

My situation: sixth-grade grammar class, memorizing prepositions
Learning that occurred: I can—still—recite the prepositions
Learning that did not occur: I do not know how, when, or why to use prepositions

Your situation:

_____

Learning that occurred:

_____

_____

Learning that did not occur:

_____

_____

Consider survival in the corporate world. Although our reptilian brains do not have to worry so much about death and physical trauma, there are endless possibilities of psychological pain. In many corporate cultures, it is never acceptable to fail. Facilitators of accelerated learning must create a learning environment in the classroom that is a safe haven for learning to occur.

If learning is not safe, the reptilian gate stays shut tightly—perhaps forever. The memories up to the closing of the gate are very strong; your brain is ready to deal with the threat that triggered the reptilian response if it ever shows up again. Unfortunately, the long-term effect on contextual and future learning is damage that is difficult to undo. Corporate employees unknowingly carry reptilian learning blocks with them into their jobs; these are often called "learning ghosts."

For example, a learner who is very reluctant to attend or participate in an introductory PC class may actually be reacting to a bad experience with, say, a math teacher in fourth grade. Part of the joy of facilitating accelerated learning is that focusing on learner diversity helps learners have small successes, which can allow them to reopen gates shut by previous experiences. Make time to show learners that they have learned through review. People who think they are novices may have learning ghosts that prevent them from seeing what they have learned.

The reptilian brain is constantly on the lookout, trying to anticipate threats early so there is more time to react. One of the things it does very well is interpret symbols: warning indicators, stop signs, red lights, and icons. Each symbol is linked to a strong emotion. The reptilian brain judges the symbol as either safe or dangerous. As a facilitator, you can use the alertness of the reptilian brain to your advantage. Using symbols to help learners remember things is highly effective because the reptilian brain is alert to them. Notice the effectiveness of the symbols associated with different parts of this book.

The Limbic Brain

The limbic brain is the first to experience a negative threat. It translates the experience into an emotion, and if the emotion is a threatening one it sends control to the reptilian brain. As you read in the last section, the reptilian gate shuts as much as possible to deal with the specific "danger." All other input is ignored so that the focus stays on the threat.

The limbic, or mammalian, brain is where humans experience emotions and where the brain controls the body's physical state. Some of the activities run from this control center are immunity, thirst, sexuality, hormones, sleep, and hunger. All of these tasks are very tightly connected to emotion. The limbic brain ties into the emotional links to long-term memory that you will read about in Chapter Six, on memory.

The limbic brain helps people learn and experience:

- Safekeeping modes
- How to bond socially with business peers, friends, and family
- Sexual feelings
- Emotions, painful, and pleasant
- What is truth (as the person perceives it)
- Historical, context-rich memories
- Long-term memory

Because a workgroup is just a variation of a family in terms of relationships and emotions, all these feelings affect business and its learning events. Even sexual feelings, although kept silent, can have an impact on a learning event. After attempting to facilitate a workshop with a recently divorced couple and the "other man" as participants, I have personally seen the strong impact of sexual desire and sexual hurt in a classroom. The anger and mistrust quickly infiltrated the entire group of learners, and virtually no learning occurred.

As you have read, negative emotions can trigger the reptilian brain to close the gate, so that's not the way to create long-term retention through emotional links. Research on humor has shown that laughter has as strong an effect as fear does on long-term learning retention, and it's a lot more enjoyable. Unfortunately, many learners who have been taught through intimidation are actually afraid to have fun learning. They have learning ghosts that remember being punished when there was fun. Learning facilitators must model an upbeat mood, slowly adding humor as the learners give themselves permission to have fun. It is not a good idea to open a corporate workshop with a comedy routine, even if it is tied to the learning objectives. This is too much humor, too fast, and it may cause guilt in the learners, triggering a reptilian response.

Positive emotions trigger chemicals called endorphins in the brain. Endorphins create a feeling of pleasure and in turn trigger the neurotransmitters that create new connections between brain cells. Learning is really just adding new connections to existing brain cells and connections. In Chapter Six, on memory, you will read that the more pleasurable and complex the stimulus, the stronger the connection. The facilitator can use this knowledge to enrich the learning environment with color, art, music, candy, fragrant markers, and props that encourage a positive mood (see Chapter Eight). To refer back to the previous section, these props also stimulate the right-brain mode by adding more color to the classroom.

In Chapter Four, you read that emotional intelligence is one of the new multiple intelligences. Because emotion is so critical to long-term retention, corporate learning facilitators need to think more about how to help corporate people learn to manage emotions. Emotions have long been avoided in business, to the detriment of communication and performance.

The Neocortex

The neocortex, or thinking brain, is the key to learning. It helps people see, hear, think, talk, and thrive. It is where information is taken in and processed, and where much of memory is stored. It is where people exercise judgment and plan for the future. With the strong link to the limbic brain, the neocortex can turn concepts such as compassion, justice, and caring into concrete actions.

The neocortex helps you

- Think, reflect, and be mindful
- Solve problems and calculate
- Write, draw, and speak
- Plan strategically and work on scenarios for the future
- Visualize and imagine
- Read, translate, and compose
- Draw, sing, and perform

Most of the time, the neocortex is learning without the person's being conscious of it. Emile Donchin, at the Champaign-Urbana campus of the University of Illinois, found in his research that learners pick up the majority of their learning from visual cues, sounds, experiences, aromas, and other environmental cues. You may think learners are learning just from you in a corporate classroom, but they are also learning from the environment and each other.

Memories are not stored just in the neocortex. There is some evidence that memories are stored all through your body. If you've practiced any sport, you have been told about and probably experienced muscle memory. Many Olympic pentathlon athletes practice as much in their minds as they do physically, to give the muscles the memory. Rehearsing in the head ensures that perfect movement is encoded, rather than mistakes, which would occur during physical practice. Like many, I'm still working to get some muscle memory for my golf game.

THE IMPACT OF THE TRIUNE BRAIN ON LEARNING

The concept of the triune brain is useful to increase learning in the corporate classroom. Learning facilitators can apply these techniques to honor the research associated with the triune brain:

- Keep it safe. This is the number one rule of learning: avoid triggering the reptilian brain.
- Present new material in diverse (MI) modes, numerous times, and in different ways to keep the interest of the whole brain.
- Make time to show learners that they have learned, through review. People who think they are novices may have learning ghosts that prevent them from seeing what they have learned.

- Help learners embed the learning by allowing them to create context through their own symbols, metaphors, models, and icons. The reptilian brain is looking for these things all the time.
- Consciously embed context around content. Our brains cannot easily remember facts alone.
- Be conscious of the cues in the learning environment—your attire, the visuals, the posters on the wall, and the learner material—because much of learning is not conscious.
- Avoid negative phrases, for example, "This part is really hard." They speak volumes to the limbic brain, which passes the word quickly to the reptilian.
- Speak to all three parts of the triune brain through words, music, stories, myth, and movement.
- Be sensitive to the learning ghosts learners may have that are blocking them from learning new things.

CONCLUSION

In many corporate classrooms, lack of stimulus creates boredom and anxiety. The brain prefers diverse and interesting input, but most corporate workshops present information in a stripped-down, linear manner. The brain learns poorly if presentation is done in an orderly, sequential fashion, as only part of the brain is used that way.

When learning is complex, interesting, and context-rich, through the whole brain, it becomes nearly effortless. For example, I had the opportunity to teach in Madrid. I had never studied Spanish, and I knew very little about the Spanish culture. Luckily for me, the Spanish people as a whole are warm and helpful when dealing with novice Americans.

As I taught (in English), ate, watched television, shopped, and became immersed in the Spanish community, I absorbed a tremendous amount of knowledge, though not always consciously. In fact, I wasn't aware of many of the things that I learned until much later. This knowledge was not just limited to language; it also included cultural mores, food traditions, family relationships, and history.

Not only did I learn new things but I also tapped into pertinent existing knowledge I didn't even know I had and had never used. One day, it was very warm in the conference room. I was trying to communicate this problem to the hotel staff in English, with little luck. From the depths of my memory, a Sesame Street song popped into my conscious mind:

> *Hace calor, hace calor,*
> could fry an egg on the cement
> it's so *caliente*!

I muttered "*hace calor*" to the man helping me. He immediately smiled, ran off, and turned up the air conditioning.

Where was that knowledge for all those years? What triggered it to come back? The context-rich, whole-brain style of Sesame Street (color, music, movement, and emotion) had stored the memory securely so that when I needed it I could recall it. You will read more about memory in Chapter Six.

As you read about Herrmann's work, you learned that people show a preference for processing something new with one mode or the other. For example, people who prefer to think first with their left mode would approach problems step-by-step and analytically. People who prefer to think first with their right mode would approach problems more holistically, starting with the big picture.

If people develop strong preferences for one mode of processing, they are not making the most of their potential. The left mode alone is less than adequate in dealing effectively with people issues. The right mode would not be best suited to balancing checkbooks. Unfortunately, some companies and fields so strongly emphasize one mode over the other that they inadvertently coerce people to focus primarily on one mode of processing. This overemphasis can create a learning disability, which hinders the ability of a business to grow the skills it needs in the future.

For many years, computer development people worked with word-based computer languages that require primarily left-mode thinking. Today's shift to more visual developments, like those introduced and popularized by the Apple Computer Macintosh interface, and then that create Windows applications, is quite a transition. Adding right-mode processing to the work of people who are used to left mode can cause mental fatigue and even frustration.

Unlike the scarecrow in the *Wizard of Oz*, we are all blessed with amazing brains. The capacity of our brains is nearly endless—a sometimes frustrating prospect for the corporate person: "If I have so much brain, why can't I learn faster? Why can't I retain more? Why can't I use the capacity?"

The answers to these questions are slowly emerging as learning and brain researchers begin to understand more and more about how our brains work. The future in brain research is truly a yellow brick road leading to a learning land the likes of which we cannot even imagine.

 ## PERSONAL ACTION PLAN

Please look back through this chapter, and jot down your thoughts below: insights, things you want to do, things you want to remember, games, and quotes. I've added a list of my own to supplement your list. It is better for your learning if you make your own list before you look at mine.

The learning objectives of this chapter were to

- Adopt specific improvements in how you communicate new learning to learners
- Identify how you learn best
- Identify and rethink those personal beliefs of yours that block learning
- Balance the use of both the left and right sides of the brain for learning
- Define the three primary functions of the triune brain in a learning event
- Maximize memory in self and others for long-term retention
- Use music to create focused learning environments
- Create a personal action plan to increase personal learning and the effectiveness of your delivery of learning events

Your thoughts:

_____

_____

_____

_____

_____

_____

_____

_____

_____

_____

Here are my thoughts:

- Brain dominance is research about the processing differences of the right and left brains, identified initially (after the Egyptians) by Roger Sperry.
- The left mode of the brain likes facts, numbers, black-and-white data, structure, and planning.
- The right mode of the brain likes fantasy, color, emotion, patterns, and what-if.
- The job of the corpus callosum is to connect the sides of the brain.
- Some listening problems may actually be related more to brain dominance (creating ear dominance) than they are to hearing.
- Ned Herrmann has deepened what we know about brain dominance by combining the triune brain concept with Sperry's research to define brain quadrants. He has done extensive research on the quadrant strengths of people in different vocations, as well as the quadrant flow of creative thought.
- Learning event flow must maximize the use of the whole brain in learners.
- The triune brain consists of the reptilian brain (fight or flight), the limbic brain (emotions), and the neocortex (knowledge). Learning must be safe, pertinent, and diverse to get through to the neocortex.
- Brains like to multiprocess.

Business Success

CHAPTER 1
Starting the
Learning Journey

CHAPTER 12
Your Learning
Journey
Continues

PART ONE
How People Learn

CHAPTER 2
A Contract for Learning

CHAPTER 3
Learning to Take More In

CHAPTER 4
Learning Through All
Your Intelligences

CHAPTER 5
Learning with
Your Whole Brain

▶ CHAPTER 6
**Remembering What
You Learned**

PART TWO
**How Successful
Learning Is Delivered**

CHAPTER 7
You Are the Deliverer

CHAPTER 8
The Environment
Delivers Learning

CHAPTER 9
Music to Deliver
Learning

PART THREE
**How Successful
Learning Events
Are Built**

CHAPTER 10
Developing Learning
Events

CHAPTER 11
Selling the Dream

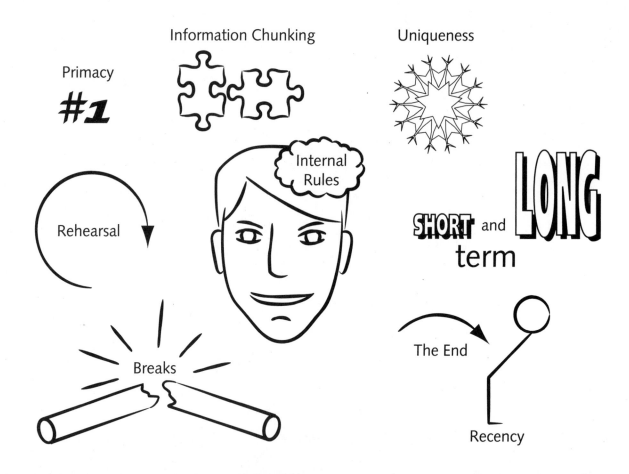

Primacy

#1

Information Chunking

Uniqueness

Internal Rules

Rehearsal

SHORT and LONG term

Breaks

The End

Recency

**THE LEARNING
OBJECTIVES OF
CHAPTER 6**

After reading this chapter, you will be able to

- Adopt specific improvements in how you communicate new learning to learners

- Identify how you learn best

- Identify and rethink those personal beliefs of yours that block learning

- Maximize memory in self and others for long-term retention

- Develop classroom learning events to meet a specific learning need

- Create a personal action plan to increase personal learning and the effectiveness of your delivery of learning events

Remembering What You Learned

It is the profound influence of parenting, schooling, friendships, work and life experiences in general that shape our mental preferences that in turn lead us to do what we do the way we do it. We consider this a message of hope because if we can change what is happening to us we can also change ourselves.

—Ned Herrmann Group

I grew up in Groton, a small town in north central Massachusetts. The main street of Groton looks like a calendar of New England. The beautiful antique white homes create a very different look from the growing young community of Fishers, Indiana, where I now live. My parents still live in Groton, and my mother likes to tell me stories about all the goings-on in town. She writes to me, sends me newspaper clippings, and tells me stories on the phone about people I honestly cannot remember at all. How can I have forgotten almost twenty years' worth of people?

I had a strange experience a few years back when I returned to Groton for a visit. While jogging through the center of town, I suddenly realized that I knew all the names of the families that lived (or had lived) in these houses. I could not name one person while I was in Indiana. The names that I had learned as a young adult were still in my brain, more easily recalled in Groton than in Fishers. Recollection is highly dependent on the context of the memory at the time it was recorded. When I heard the same sounds, smelled similar scents, even experienced some of the same feelings through the memories of experience, I was able to connect to memory that was unreachable from my Indiana context.

Memory is important in accelerated learning because it drives how well learners retain new or changed learning. To accelerate learning, a person must remember and recall with less effort. In this chapter, you will learn how to accelerate learning to improve retention through the use of a diverse, rich context.

In Chapter Two, you learned the importance of having a learning objective, which opens you to letting new learning in and focuses your attention. In Chapter Three, you learned how individual learners have their own preferences, or intake styles, for getting the new information into their brains. Chapter Four revealed the importance of honoring the multiple intelligences for better learning, and then in Chapter Five you learned how brain dominance and the triune brain influence learning.

In this chapter, you will learn how to store and recall this learning by maximizing retention. The chapter addresses two major areas: the process of memory, and understanding your memory.

Figure 6.1 is a picture of the four aspects of memory. To begin, let's look at the process of memory in more detail.

THE PROCESS OF MEMORY

Memory is not a single event or process, but multiple steps in a process. An easy way to remember these four steps is with a simple mnemonic:

Remember **f**or **S**uccessful **R**etention

which maps to

Receive, **F**ilter, **S**tore, **R**ecall

You will read about each in the following sections, but here are some brief definitions to get you started.

Receive	Exposure to learning from outside of yourself
Filter	The unconscious or conscious choice of whether or not you will allow the learning in
Store	The process of putting the new learning in memory and creating paths to access it
Recall	Remembering learning by accessing the paths to it in the brain

Here is each one in detail.

Receive

People can't remember what they don't hear. Hearing requires attention. Part of the strategy in AL is to grab people's attention.

An interesting way to look at it is that a learner who pays attention to something

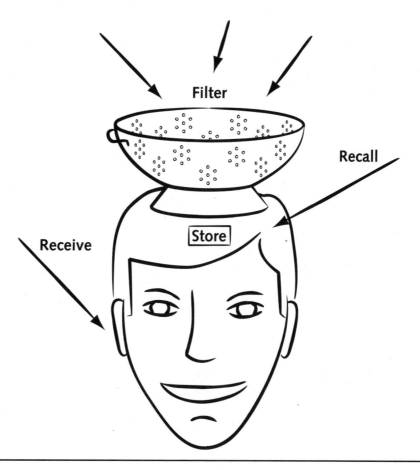

FIGURE 6.1. The Four Aspects of Memory.

is not paying attention to something else. People can't pay attention to everything coming at them—there is too much. Still, for survival reasons, in paying attention to one thing a person is still monitoring the surroundings for changes at the same time. The human body is built for survival, and constant monitoring of the environment is part of that. As I type in these words, I am partly aware of the music changing, or people coming and going. Because attention is compromised when there are too many things going on at the same time, the variety of experiences in an accelerated learning event must be balanced to avoid overstimulation. In traditional training, in contrast, the issue often is understimulation.

LEARNING POINT

A computer-based training developer who had worked as one of the original developers on Sesame Street once told me, "First you must entertain; then you can teach." You can certainly see that strategy in action on that program. Entertainment sounds trite to the corporate training world, but it is a proven tactic in marketing communication. Business training programs must step up to the entertainment factor in their learning events to ensure that they get the learners' attention. Entertainment is not frivolous—it is a necessary step for communicating in today's chaotic business world.

People pay attention in different ways. In Chapter Three, you learned that the intake of the information is dependent on the intake style of the learner and may be any combination of visual, auditory, or kinesthetic. The process of building memory and retention begins by improving learners' reception. Facilitators should capture attention by using color, sound, and visuals, and then use visual, auditory, and kinesthetic variations of the message to get it safely into the learners' brains.

If learning is not received, it cannot be retained. Without the first step, there is no memory. Accelerated learning practitioners know that attention is critical for retention, and they work to achieve it.

Filter

You are bombarded with messages every day. Through television, newspaper, e-mail, and meetings, the noise never seems to end, and you may sometimes have the sensation that your brain is full. Research shows that people don't come anywhere near filling their brains, but it is still an important function of the brain to protect itself from overload. This function is the process of filtering.

The hippocampus, which is part of the limbic brain and straddles both the left and right brains, is the little part that decides what gets in and what doesn't. It bases this decision on two factors: emotional significance and relationship to things already known. In either case, it is easier for the brain to figure out how to file a new memory that has a strong emotional link or a link to an existing memory.

When new input is received, your brain makes a choice. It looks at this new information and says, "What does this look like that I already know?" Just like a good filing clerk, your brain knows that it is a lot easier to file something in an existing file than to create a new one. Your brain seeks to enhance existing knowledge and gets a little confused processing something completely new and unconnected. As comedian Stephen Wright wryly says, "You can't have everything. Where would you put it?"

Your brain is also interpreting these data as it decides what to do with them. For example, right now you are deciding whether to store these ideas that you are reading. Mental filters created from other memories help determine which data are valuable and which are junk. You may have noticed that a small child of one to four years of age isn't very good at filtering and absorbs everything. Around the age of six, the brain learns to filter information to protect itself from overload. The learners in your adult classrooms have become very proficient at filtering new information before it ever gets to the memory. The more overload in the business context, the more likely the learner is to filter out new knowledge compared with a learner who is in a less overwhelming context.

Getting rid of the filter completely sounds great, but it isn't. Neurologists have encountered people with superhuman memories who can recite long lists of facts but cannot think clearly about day-to-day life. Without the filter, these people can't control the noise. "You want to keep the junk of everyday life out of the way so you can focus on what matters," says Columbia University neuroscientist Eric Kandel (Cowley, Underwood, Springen, and Gegax, 1998, pp. 50–51). The ineffective filtering overwhelms the brain. Filtering reminds us that forgetting is as important to our well-being as remembering is.

Store

Once the brain has decided to let the new data in, it has to decide where to put them. If you use a computer analogy here, the data are going from short-term-working to long-term memory, similar to saving a file created in temporary computer memory (RAM). Our brains are actually more complicated than even the most intelligent computer, but the analogy is useful. Storing a new memory makes it available for later use, just as on a computer. Although receiving and filtering may be conscious or unconscious activities, storing is usually unconscious.

Memory and Existing Knowledge

In storage, the brain likes to link new memories to existing knowledge. Here's an exercise to help you experience the difference between learning something entirely new and learning something that you can hook to existing knowledge.

 PRACTICE

Memorize the following list:

                     & $ @ percent * ! = @ & - ? ! *

Now memorize this list:

                     A1B2C3D4E5F6G7H8I9

Which one was harder? Why? What role did existing memories play? Why is it more difficult to store brand new information? How can you use this knowledge to help your learners learn something new?

Your learners remember things that you didn't teach them, or at least didn't mean to teach them. There is a wonderful video available through PBS called "A Hidden Universe." In this video, the commentators ask Harvard graduates and professors about why there are seasons, and why the moon has phases. Most get it wrong. The documentary then turns to a classroom where a teacher is teaching these basic concepts to a group of middle school learners. Although the teacher seems to be explaining the concept clearly and reviews it often, the new knowledge is transformed into a strange mix of new and existing knowledge in the learners. As the knowledge is tested, it is amazing how tightly the middle school students hold on to their old misconceptions—especially (surprise!) the more knowledgeable learners.

LEARNING POINT

It is harder to unlearn than to learn. Help your learners by addressing their existing knowledge before hooking new learning to it. For example, a manager may have been using an older word processing program where the help key was the F15 key. To remember that the new help key is F1, the manager will need a hook back to the existing and incorrect memory. Asking the manager to look for the F15 key (supposing there isn't one) and then explaining that the 5 has been cut off, leaving just *F1,* may help her relearn. By just talking about the F1 key without relating back to the existing knowledge, the facilitator may end up with learners who cannot remember the Help key, and will probably give up trying to use Help, thus hindering their ongoing learning.

You can use the brain's natural tendency to store new knowledge with things that are already remembered by using mnemonic devices to help your learners. An easily remembered mnemonic helps establish existing knowledge to which to hook the new learning. Here are some examples:

• In Chapter Four, you learned about the multiple intelligences. You learned the initial seven using the sentence mnemonic "I Last Sued My Landlord In Boston" (interpersonal, linguistic/verbal, spatial/visual, musical, logical/mathematical, intrapersonal, and bodily/kinesthetic). Then you added the new three intelligences, using "Escaping New England" (emotional, naturalist, existential).

• Use rhymes or rhythmic phrases to help learners remember. In a workshop on data modeling, for example, learners need a way to remember that when they are not sure what to do, they should leave the rule they are defining as optional (signified by an *O*). They can learn the motto "When you don't know, make it O."

• Another way to use a mnemonic is to make up a word or phrase with each of the letters representing the first letter in each word, in a sequence of steps. For example, a reengineering methodology could be taught by reciting the phrase "Make a PACT with your customers." The word *PACT* contains the first letters of the four phases of reengineering: plan, analyze, create, transition.

• Many AL practitioners have had great success using visual keyword mnemonics to teach foreign languages quickly. In this technique, words are used that sound a little like the foreign word to help the learners remember the meaning. An example is that in Spanish, *pato* means duck. Have the learners visualize a duck with a "pot" on its head.

The use of mnemonics is powerful because it proves to learners, through quick success, that they have a great deal of ability to remember and learn. It is a fun and entertaining way to learn.

People tend to fill in the gaps in what they remember with other things they have encountered that seem to fit. For example, you may have trouble remembering the name of a new learner who reminds you a lot of another person with a different name. Relearning is difficult.

Learning ghosts, as we've seen, are existing learning that blocks new learning. They occur when the brain wants to hook new learning to the memory of an unhappy previous learning experience. When this happens, the reptilian brain is called and the brain gate is shut (see Chapter Five). The new learning is blocked because of historical memories that the corporate trainer may not be aware of. Some common learning ghosts with professional adults include math ghosts, computer ghosts, drawing ghosts, and speaking ghosts.

The key to dealing with learning ghosts is to see them coming. Observe your learners carefully, and be prepared to change directions if you see the behavior of a learner who is starting to get reptilian. For example, a learner who is fearful about speaking will not want to participate in a role-play exercise. Instead, the learner can coach someone else to play the part (see guardian angel role play technique in the Appendix, p. 287).

 LEARNING POINT

Different groups will be able to handle different things. Some learners come in ready to try, while others come in afraid. Honor the learning ghosts of the group and take them at the pace they need. It is often the cautious starters that are most open to innovative learning after trust has been established.

Memory and Emotions

Existing knowledge is easy for the brain to link memories to, and strong emotions provide a strong link as well. A useful analogy for remembering with emotions is a filing system. When you file something, you need to have some way to index it so you can retrieve it. Filing professionals have intricate ways of cross-referencing information so it can be retrieved many different ways.

Your brain works that way as well. The more indices the brain can build to a memory, the more ways the memory can be retrieved. Indices are built from the context of the memory around it as it occurred. For example, if you are reading a book on leadership principles, trying to memorize techniques in a quiet library, you are storing the memory with a black-and-white visual and linguistic image only. In contrast, if you have the opportunity to have lunch with Peter Drucker, you will learn leadership quickly and with more depth. The conversation, the setting of the restaurant, the emotion of awe from being in the presence of such a famous and learned man—all these factors build indices to the memories acquired. In other words, the memory is vivid.

Similarly, a project manager in a workshop who has to deliver a project plan in one week has less difficulty learning how to do it than a learner who has no need to know it at this time. Learning how to create project plans for the manager is driven by an intense emotional need to succeed and compete. These emotional links to the memory will be strong and sturdy. Interestingly enough, the project manager in the same workshop will not have the same success learning the other objectives in the project management class—he will be most interested in and will retain the most about project plans. This speaks to the need in corporate training to modularize the learning to ensure that it is timely and focused.

Although in some ways the brain may seem similar to a computer, essentially it is very different. The neocortex houses ten billion nerve cells that communicate by relaying both chemical and electrical signals. Now that the technology to see what's happening in the brain has improved, scientists have made progress defining what storing memories physiologically is all about. "What we think of as memories are ultimately patterns of connections among nerve cells," says Dr. Barry Gordon, head of the memory-disorders clinic at the Johns Hopkins School of Medicine (Cowley, Underwood, Springen, and Gegax, 1998). Every time you pay attention to something, a unique combination of these neurons is activated. The connections between them may be strengthened and tightly connected, creating memory. Anything that activates part of the network activates the memory. For example, the smell of prime rib or the sound of a particular song may trigger the memory of the lunch with Drucker. As with muscles, if this network is not activated the memory will become weaker—like my network with the names of the families in Groton. The more we activate it, the stronger it will be. The more we remember, the more we *can* remember. The storage of the memory strongly influences the person's ability to recall, which you will read about next.

Recall

When you try to remember something, the brain attempts to look up the location of the memory with the clues from the context and the request. These clues are used as the initial indices to find the memory that has been stored somewhere in your almost infinite brain. The more clues, the more easily the memory is recalled. The more indices the memory was originally written with, the better the chance you can recall it with what you know at the time. Here are some of the critical influences on memory:

- Primacy
- Recency
- Breaks
- Uniqueness
- Emotion
- Visual
- Information chunking
- Internal rules
- Rehearsal
- Learner diversity
- Age and memory
- Memory and other people
- Short-term and long-term memory
- Sleep and memory

The Practice Box shows a brief exercise that will let you experience some aspects of the memory process for yourself.

PRACTICE

Following is a list of items. Set a timer for two minutes and memorize as many as possible. When the timer goes off, write as many as you can remember on another piece of paper (no peeking!). Stop writing after two minutes, and read on to learn why you do or don't remember.

apple, chair, newspaper, pen, cement, love, tree, dog, sign, bagel, desk, faith, queen, blue, book, pen, square, vine, orts, cup, down, coffee, peace, boot, smile

Primacy

Most people remember the word *apple* easily from this list. People remember the first things that happen; this is one of the strongest memory influences. When you are transferring learning in your business workshops, there are many ways you can use primacy to increase retention:

• Start the workshop with the learning objectives. Immediately hit the fresh brain cells with the important material. Do not start the workshop with "This is where the bathrooms are"; your learners will figure that out eventually. Instead, put up a logistics poster right near the coffee, identifying the hours for class, lunch, breaks, and any other pertinent information like bathroom location.

• Start the workshop with a fun exercise only if it is tied to a learning objective. The trouble is that these exercises can take up valuable time with trivial results. For example, some trainers ask each of the learners at the beginning of class to take turns introducing themselves and share something like a word association to help everyone remember their first names. This easily takes forty-five minutes in a class of fifteen students. It also fills the fresh, open brain cells with things that the participants are not there to learn. Consider delaying the introductions until the debriefing of the first team activity. This keeps the introductions short, to the point, and in context. Introduce yourself in little bits as you go, instead of taking the learners' valuable brain cells at the beginning with how wonderful you are. Knowing about the facilitator's life is rarely their learning objective.

• Any type of break provides another shot at primacy. Use the time after lunch for active, creative review to reinforce what was learned in the morning. After lunch the learners may be physiologically slow because they are digesting their meal, but they have fresh, open brain cells that need something substantial.

Recency

People also remember the last experience or the last learning point. Recency is not as strong an influence as primacy, but it is useful. In the Practice Box, you may not have ended your two minutes right on the word *smile,* so take a second to think of the last word you were working on. Recency in combination with primacy is a powerful memory enhancement. If you cover the new material at the beginning of a learning experience and then use recency to review that learning at the end, retention will be maximized.

Here are some of the ways you can make the most of recency through review (detailed in the Appendix):

- Koosh ball review
- Jeopardy review
- Review rap or other musical performance

 LEARNING POINT

Review exercises are critical to memory and retention, and they have the added benefit of letting the facilitator and the learner assess the learning up to that point. The facilitator can see the places that weren't covered sufficiently and then readjust. The learners can become conscious of how much learning has occurred.

Breaks

Research has shown that long-term retention increases with many short breaks throughout a day rather than a few long breaks. The more breaks you have, the more primacy and recency, so the more retention.

Learners don't retain well during long learning sessions. The traditional approach of talking faster and longer when time is running out actually reduces long-term retention. Long sessions put too much between primacy and recency. The breaks don't have to be traditional dismissals; they just have to be a change in action. For example, never lecture for more than twenty minutes without some type of learner interaction or exercise. "Biological" breaks should be allowed for five to ten minutes every hour. Contrast this to the traditional thirty-minute break, one in the morning and one in the afternoon. Shorter breaks keep business learners focused on the workshop and prevent them from getting distracted by going back to their desks or checking their messages, while encouraging retention through primacy and recency.

Uniqueness

The word *orts* in the Practice Box is usually retained because it is strange even if its meaning is unknown (orts are table scraps). It catches your attention, and so it engages your memory through an emotional link.

By featuring characters such as friendly monsters and Big Bird, Sesame Street has successfully used unusual characters to capture attention and teach. Research has shown that strange or unusual things can strengthen memory. Negative advertising is consistent with this theory. Sometimes the advertisements that are the most irritating create the best long-term brand recognition.

How can you use this research in your classroom? Here are some ideas:

• Create an environment that is slightly unusual. When the learners walk in, let them see right away that this experience will be unique. Move the tables and chairs around; sprinkle confetti on tabletops or floors, place flowers in the front of the room; add colored paper, markers, and candy to the tables; create an inviting refreshment area; and put unique covers on the learner's guide. See Chapter Eight for more ideas about creating a learning environment.

• Use suspense. Introduce a topic with three parts, and cover only two initially. This strange, unfulfilled goal keeps the learners engaged.

• Use a jingle or mnemonic to remember a set of steps. In a project management workshop, you could use the phrase "Dare to Properly Manage Resources" to help learners remember the first letter of each of the four phases of project management: Define, Plan, Manage, Review.

• As a class, create gestures to reinforce a list to remember. For example, to remember in order the four basic questions to initially ask a customer during a data-gathering interview, the facilitator could ask the class to invent a (clean) physical gesture to remember each question. Each time a new question with a new gesture is learned, all the earlier ones are rehearsed together for review. Here's a sample:

Question	*Gesture*
What do you do in your job?	What "do you do" suggests "doo-doo": look at bottom of foot and hold nose.
Why? What is the business reason?	Hold arms overhead to make a Y (like YMCA).
What information do you need to do your job?	Hands open like a book in front of you.
Where do you get and send information?	Cross arms on chest and point fingers away from body.

• Give out prizes when learners do something you want to reward (see the Appendix, p. 301).

Emotion

Any word that triggers an emotional response in a learner, either negative or positive, makes a beeline to the brain with a strong link to the new learning. Look at the words that you were able to recall from the Practice Box; do any of them create an emotional reaction? *Smile* and *peace* may have triggered strong feelings, or maybe you have a *dog* you care deeply about. Kinesthetic processors are most strongly influenced by emotional connections.

The emotions at the start of a learning event are relatively strong—anticipation, suspense, novelty, and challenge, to name a few. This limbic link to the neocortex explains why the effect of primacy is so vital in a learning event. The emotions at the end of a learning event may be less positive (boredom, fatigue), or they may be similar to those at the beginning, as you anticipate the chance to apply the new learning. If the emotions are positive, they encourage retention through recency. Using an accelerated learning approach by honoring the variety found among learners increases the likelihood that their emotions will be strongly positive at the beginning, at the end, and all the way through the learning event.

In class, you can use emotions to link to new learning by

- Using clip art, cartoons, or pictures to emphasize key learning points. Even if it's just internal, the laughter will create a long-term link. (If using published cartoons, of course, be aware of copyright standards.)
- Provide lots of opportunities for people to connect. The joyous emotions of a new friendship are a great way to create strong links to learning.

Kinesthetic learners feel emotions strongly and can use them to create solid links to memory. Here's a technique for memorizing a list of items created for kinesthetic learners. Notice the strong emotions generated by the movement of the images. (The slightly negative emotions generated by some of the images are not negative enough to close the reptilian gate.)

- Imagine the room in your house you love the most.
- Starting to your left as you walk into it, imagine the items (on the list in the last Practice Box) scattered around the room.

Here's an example:

A smashed *apple* is suspended between the door frame and the easy *chair*. A *newspaper* has been stuck to the wall by jabbing it with a *pen*. *Cement* has been painted on the glass doors I *love*. A *tree* was dragged in by the *dog* and left in front of the television. A *sign* left on the hearthstone says "Day Old *Bagel* Available." The *desk* is upside down by a bookcase with a bumper sticker that says "Have *Faith* in the *Queen*." A *blue book* is being used as a carpet *square*. A *vine* wraps around the piano, where there are *orts* in a pile on the bench. A *cup* of milk has spilled and run *down* next to the *coffee* stain on the carpet. *Peace* fills my heart as I see the baby *boot* on the couch, and it reminds me of her *smile*.

The downside of this technique is that, until you get good at it, it can often be time consuming to think up these images.

Visual

When you recall the words on the list, do you see pictures of the items (like a picture of a *cup*), do you see the words (the word *cup*), do you say the word to yourself inside, or do you mouth the word? How you remember is hooked to your preference for getting new learning in and your strongest multiple intelligences. Because the majority of people prefer visual intake, many people remember by seeing either the word or the picture of the word in their mind. Most of the memory techniques being taught are good for visual learners, but not so great for others. If you have a predominantly visual intake style, you may find it easier to remember visual words: *apple, chair, newspaper, pen, cement, tree, dog, sign, bagel, desk, queen, blue, book, pen, square, vine, cup, coffee, boot, smile.*

People with a visual preference often remember things that weren't there. They enhance the pictures in their head with things that seem to fit when they group items together. For example, they might mistakenly remember *leaf* with *tree* or *crown* with *queen.*

If you have a strong visual preference, you probably find it a struggle to see in your mind and so remember *love, faith, own, peace.*

Applying the visual memory concept to the learning event, you can

• Use peripheral learning to help visual learners. Hang flipcharts around the room with material that will be covered or that has been covered, including learner-created charts. As minds start to wander, their owners will browse the walls and continue learning. These peripherals should have lots of color and pictures, though they don't have to be expertly drawn. Hand-drawn pages are much more interesting to learners than the computer-generated kind. There is also something special in creating peripherals by hand specifically for a class.

• Use visuals on your overheads, slides, and learner material. Put a picture or graphic on every page so there is a link to the learning. In reviews, you will be able to watch the learner rebuild the memory from the picture on the page. This visual link is very helpful to retention.

• Use color as much as you can. Be mindful that red and green are trouble for colorblind learners, and some marker colors can't be read from very far away. Use construction paper around the room with smaller items such as quotes, and place colored markers in colorful plastic cups on all the tables. For more information about color and emotions, read the section on color in Chapter Eight.

Information Chunking

Chunking is useful when remembering long lists of items. In a given situation, people will retain seven items of information, plus or minus two. Chunking separate items into groups could make a list of fifteen items into three chunks of five, which will improve retention. AT&T made U.S. phone numbers follow the pattern ###-###-####. Instead of remembering ten items, you remember three groups.

You use chunking every day. Recite your social security number without pausing.

In the Practice Box exercise, you may have chunked visually by constructing a picture in your brain of things that go together. Removing the emotional aspects of the earlier kinesthetic example, a visual example might look like this:

> An *apple* is sitting on a *desk,* next to a *newspaper, book,* and *pen.* There
> is a *blue cup* with *coffee* in it. A *sign* on the wall says "*Smile.*" There is
> a *tree* outside with a *vine* growing on it. . . .

As mentioned in the previous section, a learner with a strongly kinesthetic intake style will not be very successful at building these kinds of pictures. To review, here's a partial example of a picture that people preferring kinesthetic intake could easily use to remember the same list:

> An *apple* falls from the *tree* and spills the *blue cup* with the hot *coffee*
> all over the *bagel* and *newspaper* sitting next to it on my own *chair.* The
> *dog* I *love,* lying on the *cement* eating my best *pen,* was in trouble for
> eating my *boot* yesterday. There is no *peace* here. . . .

Another technique that helps learners organize new learning is the window pane agenda (see the Appendix, p. 305). Using this technique at the start of class helps learners organize the flow of the class into manageable pieces—never more than nine if possible.

Internal Rules

You may have wondered whether the words had to be memorized in order as you tried to learn the list. Some people give themselves the rule that the words do have to be in order, some assume they do not, and some don't seem to think about it at all.

The learners in your workshops are creating their own internal rules that may limit their ability to store and recall. It is very important to state the obvious during learning events, to try to make sure that the rules (from the learners and from you) are completely clear and relevant.

Rehearsal

No doubt you've seen learners in your classes silently mouthing to themselves (sometimes not-so-silently). You may have mouthed the list yourself as you tried to remember it. This rehearsal is critical to learning; repetition is important to retention. People can rehearse either to keep something in short-term memory long enough to use it (reciting a phone number over and over until you are through with the call) or to move something to long-term memory (a learning facilitator practicing a presentation). This more permanent type of rehearsal usually involves hooking on to other things already in long-term memory, as mentioned earlier in the section on storage.

Learner Diversity

As all of these tips and theories show, memory is strongest when it is stored with multiple links created by diverse context. This is yet another reason why it is so important to use the multiple intelligences as a guide. If you facilitate learning by making use of all ten intelligences, you will create a multitude of strong links to the memory. From another perspective, the learners will be able to recall the memory from many triggers.

Here's an example. Let's suppose you want to convince a learner in a project management workshop that for projects to be successful time must be spent planning effectively and teams must be ready and able to change the plan at a moment's notice. Notice that this type of learning requires learners to hold two conflicting beliefs at the same time, a paradox. Planning and abandoning the plan are both critical. The learning objectives will be to

- List three project failures that can be avoided through thorough preproject planning.
- List three project failures that can be avoided through project plan flexibility.

You decide to use a simulation to facilitate the learning of these objectives. Notice that these are really both *attitude* objectives, which are most effectively met through self-discovery. Lecturing on attitude is not received well unless the trainer has a phenomenal amount of experience and respect.

The simulation involves building a bridge. The teams are given all the supplies they need, including a blueprint. They are asked to take three minutes to estimate how long it will take them to build the bridge and how many people they need. They don't have to use all the people on their team. The estimates are collected on a flipchart before the simulation begins. As the teams finish, their bridges are tested for quality and their final times and resources are recorded on the flipchart. As usual, most of the learning occurs in the reflection and debriefing. The learners discuss what contributed to project success and failure.

Here's how the intelligences map to this simulation:

Intelligence	Aspect of Simulation
Interpersonal	The simulation is done in a team.
Linguistic/verbal	The simulation requires talking and listening.
Spatial/visual	The simulation requires interpreting from a blueprint and creating a visual model.
Musical	Quiet, instrumental music plays during the simulation.
Logical/mathematical	Planning requires a step-by-step approach.
Intrapersonal	Each individual has to deliver her part for team success.
Bodily/kinesthetic	The bridge building requires physical movement.
Emotional	The implied competition of the simulation adds excitement.
Naturalist	Weak; this simulation could be done outside, though.
Existential	Individuals need to be clear about their personal role for team success.

Through their actions, the learners see the role their initial planning plays, and how necessary it is to consciously change the plan as the situation changes. They remember what makes projects successful because of the many links that occur as they self-discover using all intelligences.

UNDERSTANDING YOUR MEMORY

Memory can be influenced by factors beyond your control, such as age and other people. This section explains some of these factors.

Age and Memory

Adults don't have to lose their memory and brain abilities as they age. Dr. David Snowdon, professor of preventive medicine at the University of Kentucky, has studied the brains of seven hundred nuns from the School Sisters of Notre Dame in a large-scale, long-term, ongoing research project. One of his exciting conclusions was that the subjects who continued to challenge their minds lived longer than their peers who did not. His findings show:

• Overall brain mass declines by 5–10 percent during our sixties and seventies. Younger people generally outperform the elderly on speed tests that gauge storing and retrieving abilities, but the differences are minor.

• Unless you develop a condition such as Alzheimer's or a vascular disease such as high blood pressure, age alone won't ruin your memory. The worst it will do is make you a little slower and less precise.

• Other things that can negatively affect memory include too little sleep, too much alcohol, depression, anxiety, lack of stimulation, stress, and a dysfunctional thyroid gland—all more common with age. Common misperceptions about memory and age must be eliminated in the corporate classroom. Everyone can learn, and remember. Exercise, sleep, plenty of water, and healthy eating habits help prevent memory loss.

Memory and Other People

Memory researchers are now acknowledging that memories are not always "true" in the sense that they are accurate and factual. They are based on facts as people perceive them to be, which may or may not be what really happened. Two things create this phenomenon; one is filtering and the other is that memories change over the years. Every time the memory is recalled, new context is added from what is happening at the time of recollection. These new memories and links are kept when the memory is re-stored.

Psychologist Ulric Neisser did a study with his freshman psychology students. When he quizzed them about the space shuttle *Challenger* disaster three years after it happened, he found that their memories varied a great deal. Comparing their quiz answers to the journals they were keeping at the time of the explosion, he found that 65 percent of the learners had memories that were partially true, and 25 percent were completely wrong. Only 10 percent recalled things accurately (as quoted in Jensen, 1995). This explains how those big-fish stories get better and better. It also explains why your colleague's story and yours of what happened when you were both on that big business project differ so much. It also explains why participants remember learning different things from the same workshop. It may be that all the memories of the learners—or none—are completely factual.

The Zeigarnik effect is the name for a surprising phenomenon: learners remember more about uncompleted tasks than about the tasks they actually complete (Rose, 1997). This line of reasoning suggests that good trainers would, within limits, allow students to leave each class with some unanswered questions.

People have survival reasons for remembering or discarding new information. Their brain is trying to protect them. The Masie Institute study that was cited in Chapter Two found two factors influencing long-term retention. The most influential factor, discussed in Chapter Two, was that learners had a learning objective. The second was that the learner's boss acknowledged the learner had attended the training. The boss didn't have to quiz the participants on content, or demand a full report, or formally ask for anything. All the boss needed to do was notice that the learner had attended the workshop. This "noticing" rewarded the learner for attendance and thus indirectly rewarded learning. It reinforced the learner's recall (Masie Institute Newsletter, 1995).

LEARNING POINT

In today's chaotic business environment, bosses may never see their staff. As facilitators, you need to fill the shoes of the missing boss by encouraging and noticing when your learners learn. This can be done by:

- Asking learners to share something they've learned at the end of each session (see review exercises in the Appendix).
- Checking on learners with an e-mail, or calling after they've returned to their desks.
- Creating a focus group with the learners to continue sharing the learning after class.
- Sending a follow-up letter to the learners' bosses about the success of the workshops. This is not a report card, but a reinforcement to encourage the bosses to notice the learning.

Short-Term and Long-Term Memory

In the late 1950s and early 1960s, psychologists started to differentiate between short-term and long-term memory. Short-term memory is just what it says: it lasts only about twenty seconds. Try this experiment:

1. Open the phone book.
2. Locate anyone's phone number, and memorize it.

3. Wait twenty seconds. Can you remember it? Can you remember their name? Their address?

Short-term memory is very limited in the amount it can handle—usually about seven items, plus or minus two (see "Information Chunking" above). As new items enter short-term memory, older items get pushed out to make room. In addition, short-term memory is so transient that stuffing it very full or very fast will hurt retention. Therefore, rather than inundating learners with lots of facts and information in a short time, provide a bibliography and glossary so that those who are especially interested in the details can continue collecting knowledge after the learning event ends.

Long-term memory is where learning needs to end up, and the techniques in this book are designed to achieve that purpose. Scientists believe today that long-term memory is essentially unlimited. There is some disagreement about whether people ever forget memories that have been written to long-term memory, or whether they just lose their ability to find them. Often, a sensory link—a smell, a song, a color, or a person—brings up a memory that might have seemed lost. That's why engaging the senses, as well as all the intelligences, is so important in AL.

Sleep and Memory

There is some evidence that memories are moved to long-term storage during sleep. Learners who cram and sleep seem to outperform learners who cram and test without sleep. Many accelerated learning practitioners lead their learners through relaxation exercises, hoping that this will offer the brain a pause in which to write its memories in long-term memory. Chapter Nine covers this process, called "passive concert," in more detail.

For the same reasons, listening to tapes while sleeping doesn't work. Sleep is when the brain moves things from short-term to long-term. When the brain is sleeping, short-term memory is turned off, so there is no place to put new information.

LEARNING POINT

A carefully planned workshop schedule can help use sleep to create better learning.

For a one-and-a-half day workshop, start at 1:00 P.M. the first day, and have a full day the second day.

For a one-day workshop, consider 1:00 to 5:00 P.M., then 8:00 A.M. to noon the next day (transportation and such considerations permitting).

Experiment for yourself—the energy level and retention differences are noticeable.

CONCLUSION

The retention of lessons learned is key to business success. Business needs are constantly changing, and employees must be able to learn quickly and retain thoroughly. Efficiently receiving, filtering, storing, and recalling are core competencies of a productive employee.

The importance of quick learning and thorough retention is nowhere clearer than in the field of computers, where the software being used changes as often as twice a year. No sooner does a manager feel comfortable than the software needed to be effective on the job changes again. Interesting work has been done recently on retention of computer skills. People who take personal computer workshops in a monotone, quiet corporate classroom using a repetitive Microsoft PowerPoint or overhead-based lecture have very poor retention. This classroom environment is completely unlike the chaotic environment in which the learners apply the new skills: at their desks. Thus, weak memory links established by the bland corporate classroom are not accessible when the memory triggers at the learners' desk are varied and ever-changing. If the workshops are integrated with more variety through color, music, simulations, attention-getters, and analogies, the retention increases.

LEARNING POINT

Use this memory concept about context to explain to your learners why you will ask them to change teams, and even seats, during the workshops. Most people feel safer staying right in the same spot, until they hear that this habit (1) short-changes the indices that are being built into the memories and (2) limits their effectiveness. Selling them on the movement ahead of time helps ease the discomfort of change and keeps them safe.

Here are some additional ideas for maximizing retention through effective memory management:

- For each learning objective, think about what types of learning will be required (skill, knowledge, or attitude). Think also about the depth of learning—how much the learners will need to remember and how much they will just need to be able to look up when it is required.
- For each learning objective, use the multiple intelligences to ensure strong linkage.
- Plan and implement a variety of techniques for gaining and keeping attention, including surprises such as colored markers and prizes (see Chapter Eight).
- Help learners chunk information by using mnemonics or other organizing strategies. Even better, ask them to construct the mnemonics or organize strategies for themselves.
- As much as possible, stress the *why* behind the learning. Establish the motivation that will help motivate the learners to open their filters to remember.
- Ask about the existing knowledge in learners and plan ways to help them hook to it and relearn.
- Take a little time to demonstrate to the learners ways to maximize their own learning style to maximize memory. Help them value and honor the limitless variety of their own learning and that of others.

To improve your memory and that of your learners, bear in mind the mnemonic "**R**emember **f**or **S**uccessful **R**etention."

Mnemonic	Memory Process	Explanation
R-	Receive	Exposure to learning from outside of yourself
F-	Filter	The unconscious or conscious choice of whether or not you will allow the learning in
S-	Store	The process of putting the new learning in memory and creating paths to access it
R-	Recall	Remembering learning by accessing the paths to it in the brain

Building proficiency in all four will accelerate learning.

 ## PERSONAL ACTION PLAN

Please look back through this chapter, and jot down your thoughts below: insights, things you want to do, things you want to remember, games, and quotes. I've added a list of my own to supplement your list. It is better for your learning if you make your own list before you look at mine.

The learning objectives of this chapter were to

- Adopt specific improvements in how you communicate new learning to learners
- Identify how you learn best
- Identify and rethink those personal beliefs of yours that block learning
- Maximize memory in self and others for long-term retention
- Develop classroom learning events to meet a specific learning need
- Create a personal action plan to increase personal learning and the effectiveness of your delivery of learning events

Your thoughts:

_____

_____

_____

_____

_____

Here are my thoughts:

- Memory is the process of four actions: receive, filter, store, recall.
- Mnemonics are linguistic or other techniques that help you remember.
- Memory consists of short-term and long-term memory. Although many people have successfully stored new knowledge in short-term memory temporarily (cramming for a test, then immediately forgetting it all), true learning occurs when memories are stored and recalled from long-term memory.
- Techniques that can be used to improve learners' retention include:

  Identifying the rules they are creating for themselves, and freeing them from those rules
  Helping them chunk information into manageable pieces
  Adding positive emotion to the learning
  Using visual or kinesthetic images
  Using primacy and recency, and having many breaks to increase both
  Using bizarre or unusual words or things (such as *orts*) to create attention

PART TWO

How Successful Learning Is Delivered

Business Success

**THE LEARNING
OBJECTIVES OF
CHAPTER 7**

After reading this chapter, you will be able to

- Identify times in a learning event when you play the roles of facilitator of learning, trainer, and learner

- Adopt specific improvements in how you communicate new learning to learners

- Identify and rethink those personal beliefs of yours that block learning

- Create a personal action plan to increase personal learning and the effectiveness of your delivery of learning events

You Are the Deliverer

Teaching, like any truly human activity, emerges from one's inwardness, for better or worse.

—Parker J. Palmer, *The Courage to Teach*

You have probably overhead two of your learners on a break, as one asks, "What training are you taking today?" Your ears perk up to hear not only the words but also the emotion. How she describes the use of her time to her friend defines how well you are performing as a learning facilitator.

PRACTICE

On a blank piece of paper, draw yourself teaching (stick figures are fine; you are the only one who has to see this). If you have a strong visual/spatial aptitude, consider using multiple colors as you draw. Think about what's surrounding you as you teach, and sketch that in. Sketch in clues that indicate what time of day it is. What does the physical space look like? What are you doing? What can you hear? Work on this for about three minutes.

Now flip the paper over on the other side and draw yourself *learning*. Again, sketch what's surrounding you as you learn. What time of day is it? What does the physical space look like? What are you doing? What can you hear? Work on this for about three minutes as well.

Reflect on these pictures and what they tell you about how you like to teach and learn:

- Is one picture happier than the other? Why?
- Are you more confident in one picture than the other? Why?

- How is the environment in your trainer sketch different from the environment surrounding you as learner? Why? How are they similar? Why?
- In the ideal setting, what do you need to be a great learner? A great trainer? How are these two roles connected?

When teaching, you may be carrying rules unconsciously that limit your ability to meet the learning objectives of your learners. If you are not comfortable with how you learn (the picture seems negative), you will tend to create a negative learning environment for your learners. In contrast, being a happy learner can be the building block for becoming an effective learning facilitator. You are the candle that illuminates learning for your workshops, as you will read in Chapter Eight.

Accelerated learning challenges practitioners to rethink their labels and redefine their roles. Everyone assigns labels to things to create stability and order, similar to creating mnemonics (which you read about in Chapter Six). Labeling is a way of filtering input by minimizing information overload. Labeling can also have a dark side. It can carry with it a set of values and beliefs that may be unconsciously but strongly coloring behavior. Business labels drive communication and carry the beliefs and values of the corporation.

 LEARNING POINT

Learning and teaching are intimately connected. If you believe learning is limited, you limit your teaching. If you believe that to learn you must be in pain, you will teach with pain. If you believe that learning is liberating, your teaching will liberate others.

Up to this point, I have been selling you on AL by proving or reconfirming through research how learning occurs. In Chapters Two through Six, you read about how learners set objectives; how they prefer to take in new information; and how they process learning, including research about multiple intelligences, brain dominance, and the triune brain. You finished Chapter Six with information about building reten-tion. If you overhear a learner talking about an accelerated learning workshop where her diverse learning needs are met, she will be enthusiastic.

In the next three chapters, you will read how to create the best environment for maximum learning in the corporate classroom. The most critical part of this learning environment is you as the learning facilitator. I hope this chapter provokes you to think and learn about how your behavior in the classroom and in course development (covered in Chapter Ten) drives the success of your learners.

It's up to you. You must choose whether to continue to teach and learn as you have been or whether to continue the journey toward accelerated learning. The next chap-ters will help you enhance your toolkit for delivery and course development. The first step, in this chapter, is to look carefully at your own labels. You will then read about the roles you play in the classroom.

 ## PRACTICE

This exercise is more useful if you find some others who do the same kind of work and do this together, but alone will work fine. For each of the two words on the left, brainstorm word associations that go with each. Here is an example of a word association:

Word	Associations
DONUT	*junk food, sugar, messy, cushion*
TRAINER	
FACILITATOR	

Words are neutral on their own. The meaning you add to them colors your behavior. Use the following debriefing questions to uncover learning about your labels:

- What is the title on your business card? Considering your brainstorming above, what meaning do you associate with the title?
- What words do you use to tell others what you do?
- What behavior may be indicated by your definition of these words? What are you going to do about it? Is there a better word that you can use to describe your role?

LABELS

My business card used to say "Trainer"; that is the word I would always use to describe my line of work to others. Then I attended a one-day workshop on accelerated learning. I admit now to thinking, "What could I possibly learn here?" but in retrospect, that single day changed the future of my teaching and my learning. It was there that I first understood the difference between learning and training. Training focused on the person teaching, while learning focused on the learner. Learning is always changing, always growing. Training can stagnate and remain constant. Learning is my vocation and my avocation.

One of the first things I did was change the title on my business card to "Learning Facilitator." I don't own a training company, I own a learning company. Learning is the service we provide to our customers. Training may be one of the ways we do that, but it is not the only way and it is not the end-deliverable. Put another way, training events may be the feature we provide, but learning is the benefit that our customers need and get. Consider carefully what you think you deliver and how you deliver it every time you enter a learning event.

 PRACTICE

Take a close look at your business card. If you don't have one, get one. If your company won't change your title on your business card, make new business cards for yourself and pass out both.

ROLES

As you read in this chapter about the roles played in the classroom, the generic term *instructor* will be used to mean the person leading the learning in the class. In future chapters, the term *learning facilitator* will be used.

In a classroom, an instructor actually plays multiple roles. Figure 7.1 shows these roles along the outside of the triangle: trainer, facilitator, and learner. In parallel to this

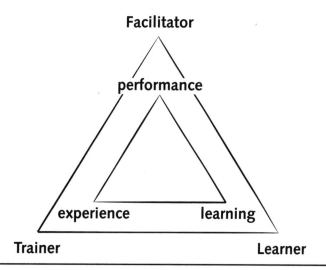

FIGURE 7.1. **Classroom Roles.**

model is one developed by Tim Galway and described in Senge's *The Fifth Discipline Fieldbook* (Senge and others, 1994). Galway shares a model for organizational learning that contains the words inside the triangle in Figure 7.1: experience, performance, learning. As he relates, specifically to the learning organization discipline of personal mastery, people must grow in experience, grow as performers, and grow their internal learning.

When a class begins, the accelerated learning instructor plays the role of trainer, bringing to the learning event a plan, structure, experience, and objectives (introduced in Chapter Two). As she asks her learners to prioritize the objectives, she slowly releases control of the learning event, inviting the learners to become partners in their own learning. As the instructor moves into the facilitator role, the objectives are the contract between the instructor and the learners for the learning facilitation. Little by little, control is released to the learners to find how they learn best.

Sometimes the pendulum swings too far, and the learners begin to have so much fun that they start to move away from the learning objectives. This can shift the workshop flow toward entertainment rather than education (the middle ground is sometimes referred to as edutainment). At this point, the learning facilitator must swing the pendulum back a bit, returning to the more control-oriented role of the trainer. Control is introduced just enough to ensure alignment to the learning objectives. Throughout the entire workshop, the AL instructor is balancing flexibility (facilitation) and structure (training).

But there is a third role that all great AL instructors play in the classroom: the role of learner. If you are open to it, you can learn many new things whenever you are in class. The two most common things you learn are content and how people learn.

Content Learning

Content learning is what occurs when you learn something new about the subject matter that you're teaching. Many people put word associations around the word *trainer* that have a flavor of "expert" to them. Being an expert is a very precarious place to be: you are standing out in the open by yourself, and it is pretty simple for others to take a clear shot at anyone out in the open.

If you believe that you have to be an expert as an instructor, you will not be very effective. Experts cannot risk being learners in their own classrooms. Instructors teaching technology workshops today know this all too well. Even with more preparation than seems humanly possible, it never fails that there is a learner in class who knows something about a technological feature that the instructor doesn't. Instead, focus on the fact that you, as the instructor, know the most about the content related to *all the learning objectives.* It is very possible that individual learners know more about a specific topic. It is helpful to your learning and the learning of the participants if you honor and encourage the sharing of this expertise and don't shut it down in your insecurity. Expertness can block learning for the instructor and for the learners.

This is not to say that it's all right to be ignorant of your topic, or to enter the workshop with only superficial knowledge and skills. Preparation is hugely important and cannot be downplayed, even with instructor guides written so that any one can teach. Reading the material to learners is not accelerated learning. You learn very little about content, and so do they. Facilitating learning requires commitment and passion to remain a full-time learner, a concept this chapter started with.

Learning How People Learn

Learning how people learn is what I crave in class. Just learning about content is fine if you are a practitioner or a researcher, but a learning facilitator needs to continuously polish her delivery technique for learning to be accelerated. The preface of this book acknowledges a small number of the people who have taught me about learning. Here are a couple of additional nuggets that learners have taught me about how people learn.

First, a learner who is an ordained minister said in response to learning about intake styles, "There is an intake that comes from outside of us, but not through those three." He was referring to spiritual messages from God. That was dangerous ground for a corporate workshop, but as the class talked about it openly, it made a huge impression on everyone there. First, he very wisely interjected his thoughts without threatening or evangelizing anyone, and second, he gave me a new thought.

Second, in one AL presentation a learner noticed that the kinesthetic learners were all sitting in the back of the room, the auditory learners were sitting in the front, and the visual learners were primarily in the center. I have since observed that this pattern holds true in most places.

Third, at an AL workshop for trainers, a participant asked how many people were first-born children. About 80 percent of the participants raised their hands. As I've asked the question again in other groups, there seems to be a correlation between oldest child and trainer. Being the oldest child can indicate a preference toward control which you may have to fight in the classroom (I know I do).

How do you feel about learning from your learners? Revisit the pictures you originally drew of yourself learning and teaching. Is your learner happy? Why or why not? Can you create an environment for learning in the workshops that you are facilitating? Is your teaching picture one of partnership, control, or both? Which roles do you need to practice?

The next Practice Box is an exercise that will allow you to reflect more deeply on your views about learning and teaching.

PRACTICE

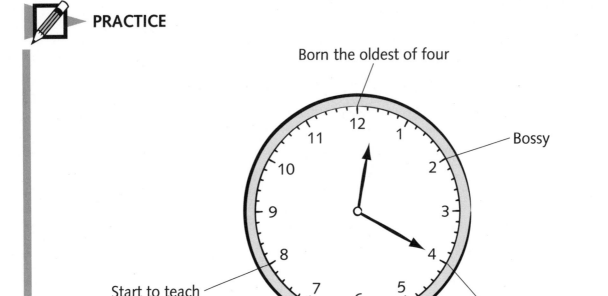

In this reflective activity, think about what life events have influenced your beliefs about how you learn and how you teach. On the clock below, mark 12:00 as the "time" of your birth. Now follow the clock around until you return to 12:00, which is today. Think about what has happened at different points in your life up to now, and add the events to your clock of learning. I have written four comments on the clock as an example.

Share this clock with someone you love and trust. As you express this personal journey to that person, you will learn more about yourself. Make notes about what you've learned as to what you believe regarding learning.

CONCLUSION

To bring your thoughts together, consider creating a personal mission statement about your role as a facilitator of learning. The next practice will lead you through this process.

PRACTICE

Step 1: pick your three favorite verbs to go with the noun *learning* to complete the phrase:

I _____, _____, and _____ learning.

Here is my own example—Lou's Personal Mission for Learning—as a guide:

I ignite, affirm, and sustain learning.

So, what's it going to be? Are you ready to take the material in this book and continue to grow learning in yourself and others? Can you get passionate about the infinite ability of people to learn? Are you willing to invest your energy in getting better at helping people learn? If you are, continue to the next chapters on learning event development and delivery. If you aren't yet convinced of the importance of this endeavor, then it's OK to set this book aside—perhaps, I hope, for another day.

PERSONAL ACTION PLAN

Please look back through this chapter, and jot down your thoughts below: insights, things you want to do, things you want to remember, games, and quotes. I've added a list of my own to supplement your list. It is better for your learning if you make your own list before you look at mine.

The learning objectives of this chapter were to

- Identify times in a learning event when you play the roles of facilitator of learning, trainer, and learner
- Adopt specific improvements in how you communicate new learning to learners
- Identify and rethink those personal beliefs of yours that block learning
- Create a personal action plan to increase personal learning and the effectiveness of your delivery of learning events

Your thoughts:

_____

_____

_____

_____

_____

_____

_____

_____

_____

_____

_____

Here are my thoughts:

- Seek to clarify daily those beliefs that limit your ability to learn, and therefore to teach.
- Learning is a gift for you, and from you, to others.
- Choose carefully what you call yourself and what you call your outcome.
- Clarifying your purpose can help you better honor your roles in a learning event.
- If you can't accelerate learning with passion, don't.

Business
Success

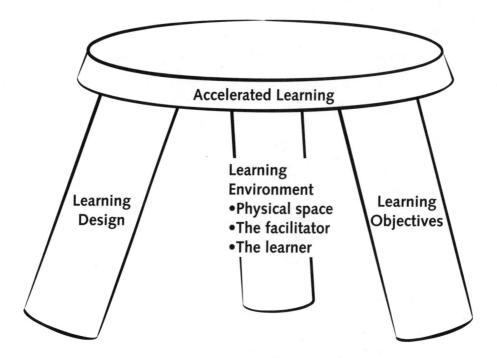

Accelerated Learning

Learning Design

Learning Environment
•Physical space
•The facilitator
•The learner

Learning Objectives

THE LEARNING OBJECTIVES OF CHAPTER 8

After reading this chapter, you will be able to

- Identify times in a learning event when you play the roles of facilitator of learning, trainer, and learner

- Adopt specific improvements in how you communicate new learning to learners

- Maximize memory in self and others for long-term retention

- Develop classroom learning events to meet a specific learning need

- Create a personal action plan to increase personal learning and the effectiveness of your delivery of learning events

CHAPTER 8

The Environment Delivers Learning

The most demanding endeavor can be leavened by a playful spirit.

—Charles Toll, "Creating Environments for Successful Learning"

One day several years ago, I passed by a corporate classroom. Intrigued by what I saw and heard, I passed by a couple more times. Finally, I paused and took a better look. There was a large screen in the front of the room, showing a video of a fish tank, accompanied by some calming music. No plot, no people, just a video fish tank with fish swimming around. The tables were arranged in small groups, with six chairs around each. On each table sat a red plastic cup with colored markers and colorful licorice sticks. The walls contained a few colorful motivational posters, some art work, and some other flipchart sheets with acronyms and terminology I didn't recognize. Beautiful kites were strung along the ceiling. The facilitator was bustling around setting up a few other things.

I asked her what she was teaching. Of course, I expected her to say she was teaching stress management, customer service, or something that is more normally taught with a lighter tone. To my surprise, she told me that she was teaching a "service representative acronym class." New service reps had to learn hundreds of cryptic acronyms to use the computer systems to process customer orders. This was not a workshop most learners would look forward to.

I continued to check in on the workshop over the two days it was held. The energy level of the learners and their attention was astounding. I was not surprised to hear that this facilitator had been coached by David Meier (see the Resources section, p. 311) to create this wonderful learning event.

In accelerated learning, the entire context of a learning event influences the learning of the participant. You already know how important rich context is to memory and retention, and in the next chapter you will learn about how music can accelerate learning as

149

well. Combining attention, learning theory (Chapters Three, Four, Five, and Six), learning objectives (Chapter Two), and environment maximizes the amount that people can effortlessly learn in small chunks of time.

My approach is used as an illustration, but only as that. It is critical that you create your own variation of a learning environment that works in your unique business context. Think about how your company greets an honored guest, such as the chairman of the board, to a meeting. Nothing is left to chance to ensure that the chairman is welcome. The same can be true in your classrooms. The environment speaks a clear message to the people entering it.

In this chapter, you will read how to maximize learning through these environmental factors:

- Color
- Visual impact
- Seating
- Equipment and supplies
- Refreshment
- The rhythm of learning
- You

COLOR

The brain pays attention to things that are bright, moving, and unique. Because it is always preoccupied with surviving, anything bright or moving or unique gets its full attention in case it's a threat. Color taps the emotional power of the limbic brain, which means it can significantly increase long-term retention. Used incorrectly, color can also trigger the reptilian component, if the brain relates the color to an unpleasant emotion.

How color affects a learner depends on the individual's (1) personality and experiences, (2) state of mind at that moment, and (3) cultural background and upbringing.

PRACTICE

Here's a list of emotions. Find some markers in several colors. On a plain piece of paper (not this page), write and then circle an emotion with the marker color that best represents it to you. Write and then choose a color to circle another one. And so on through the list given here.

happy	angry	sad
neutral	confused	tired
anxious	excited	loving

Now, find a friend and ask that person to do the same exercise, without revealing your results. Discuss why you picked the colors you did and why the choices are different from your friend's, or the same. What historical experiences did you tap into in choosing the colors? What experiences did your friend tap into?

Think about the ramifications in the classroom. Using a color that triggers a negative emotion can work against learning. What if your worksheet color creates anxiety? What if the evaluation form creates anger? How are you currently using color? Random use of color can be a dangerous proposition. Because reaction to color is very individual, it is best to stay with colors that show milder reactions in people. Some color tips follow.

Here are some thoughts about color from Eric Jensen's book *Brain Based Learning and Teaching* (1995, p. 57):

Red	Engaging and emotive; disturbing to anxious learners, exciting to calm learners
Yellow	Stress, caution, and apprehension; first color a person decodes in the brain
Blue	Most tranquilizing universally, increases feeling of well-being, lowers stress
Green	Calming
Brown	Promotes a sense of security, reduces fatigue
Gray	Most neutral
Darker colors	Lower stress, increase feelings of peacefulness
Brighter colors	Energy, creativity, but also aggression and nervousness

Notice the positive and negative possibilities of each color. Some researchers have drawn universal emotional conclusions about color, but I have found that color reaction in class is far from fixed. Assuming that everyone views a color the same way emotionally is dangerous to learning success. Watch and learn as you apply color to your presentations and environment, staying close to blues, greens, grays, and browns.

Here are some pointers for using color:

• Consider color coding learning objectives or corresponding parts of a concept you teach. The words with the color speak strongly to the brain, so make sure that the colors support your key learning points. Using colors that don't make sense for a learner can hinder learning—for example, green to indicate fire. A better example (using a learning point from fire safety training) might be

Stop	Color-coded in *red*
Drop	Color-coded in *brown* (for the ground)
Roll	Color-coded in *black* (for putting the fire out)

The facilitator should explain the color significance to help learners link the new knowledge to existing knowledge of colors.

• Avoid using red and green together, as people who are colorblind cannot differentiate between these colors.

• Use primary colors for safest results. Consider using blue or gray paper for tests, assessments, and evaluations; consider using white for new material.

• Watch out for PowerPoint (or other software) presentations. The templates that come with those packages tend to be overwhelming and anxiety-creating in their use of color and graphics. Consider the safer use of black type on clear background, with color only for emphasis. It may look a little old-fashioned, but it is easier to read. Other benefits are that simplicity does not distract from the content and is less expensive to reproduce.

Color can be used to help people consciously; for example, color can emphasize or tie in to a learning point. If you are teaching a four-part checklist, color coding the four parts in the learner materials, on the overheads, on the flipcharts, and on job aids will increase the speed of learning and improve retention. Color helps to align the right and left brains and also triggers a strong emotional link to the neocortex.

VISUAL IMPACT

In Chapter Six, you first read about the idea of peripheral learning, which means putting visuals on the walls (peripherally) with material that you will cover in class. Lozanov, Nadel, and Rosenfield (as cited in Jensen, 1995) have verified in their research that learners pick up material not only from facilitated, conscious activities but also subconsciously from the things they see, smell, hear, and touch. In their research, learners taught with the use of peripheral learning in the classroom had more retention of the material than learners taught in classrooms with no peripherals. The visual impact of the room can teach, too.

Here are some guidelines for planning peripherals:

• Plan to put up 30 percent motivational, 30 percent learning objective-oriented, 10 percent logistics, and 30 percent learner-generated materials. I break it down like this:

Motivational: hang quotes pertaining to the subject (a few on the door as learners come in).

Learning objective: create visual, colorful flipchart posters highlighting (teaching) the main points relating to the learning objectives.

Logistics: create agenda and logistics posters. They eliminate any questions about class hours, lunch, breaks, spelling of your name, and content flow.

Learner-generated: as soon as possible, give teams the opportunity to do something on a piece of flipchart paper and post it, helping create an environmental sense of community for the learning. These posters also serve as a peripheral review for the learners, especially the people who drew them.

 LEARNING POINT

Never take down the learners' work until they have gone. Having someone remove, rip up, or appear to devalue work activates the reptilian brain, causing learning to cease immediately.

• Move the peripheral learning material from one part of the room (for new) to another part (for old) after you have gone over it. Some AL practitioners believe that the eyes of a learner look to the left when processing something new and up to the right when remembering. If you use that approach, things as yet uncovered should start on the left and move right when they have been covered. This pattern is not possible if your seating is at round tables. For this type of seating, move the covered material to a specific location, such as the back of the room, to keep it all together.

• Moving the peripherals bothers some learners; remember, memory depends on the context of the learning. You might have seen learners look right at the spot where a poster was when they learned it as they try to recall. It's important to manage the expectation of the learner and explain to them the importance of change. As you remember from Chapter Six, moving the materials adds variety to the context and creates new links to memory, but the facilitator can help the learners by moving posters while they're watching the action.

• Group together pages that have been covered with learner-generated work that is all about the same thing. The grouping minimizes visual confusion, especially in classes without much wall space.

• Watch out for the walls. Buy some good masking tape so that it comes off without messing up your customer's walls. Never use transparent or shipping tape. If possible, tape to wood or glass instead of paint or wallpaper.

• For variety, add a couple of new quotes every morning or after lunch. The learners notice and appreciate the addition. This also prompts them to scan the room often, looking for changes.

Visual impact comes from the use of peripherals in the room, but it also comes from the learning materials. Here are some tips for strong visual impact:

• Use vivid graphics in learner materials, on overheads, on the walls, on job aids—everywhere.

• Add structure by using the same vivid icons repeatedly to emphasize a topic. For example, use a magnifying glass to represent the analysis step of problem solving.

• Ask learners to create symbols to use during review. This is especially helpful for learning objectives that are not easily tied to existing knowledge. For example, an object in object-oriented workshops might be remembered as a puzzle piece.

• Ensure that every graphic is consistent with the learning objective it is supporting.

Another component of the environment that strongly influences what the learner sees visually is the seating.

SEATING

The seating pattern of the workshop can drive the role the learning facilitator will play. Put simply, the learners' faces go toward the most important element in the room. For this reason, have learners face each other as much as possible, while still having a clear view of the facilitator. This arrangement keeps the focus on the learners. Here are some other tips:

• People need their personal space. If you pack them too close together, you increase their anxiety and decrease their ability to learn. Likewise, they don't like to sit with their knees straddling a table leg.

• People like choice. If there are different options for seating—breakout rooms, refreshment areas, picnic tables outside—they learn better. Even if they spend the majority of the time in the same room, don't underestimate the power of a field trip.

• Seating patterns mean a great deal. Each has its own strength, so the choice of seating pattern should be driven by the topic and learning objectives. If possible, limit groups to three to five people. Odd numbers work best to avoid fighting teams. Assign a leader to the team, so learners don't have to worry about jockeying for position. Use fun criteria such as "The leader is the person born farthest from this room." Here are some seating examples:

Type of Seating	Seating Focus	Seating Message
Lecture hall (chairs in rows, no tables)	All focus on speaker, no interaction, no notes.	"Boss is speaking, FYI, not detailed, no need to write down anything."
Lecture hall (chairs in rows, behind tables)	All focus on speaker, no interaction, notes.	"Boss is speaking, lots of detail, write it down, but don't talk."
U or V shaped with tables	Teacher is still the main focus, but can also interact with the whole class (size of class may intimidate and lessen interaction).	"Expert is teaching, you may ask him questions and talk some to others."
U or circled chairs only	Focus is on discussion, facilitation.	"No expert, honest discussion, no need to take notes, informal."

| Chairs around square (or, less effective, rectangular) tables | Focus on team, interaction easy, small groups. | "Facilitated team, learning encouraged." |

Figure 8.1 shows two options: chairs with round tables or rectangular tables. With rectangular tables, "fishbone" them so that they point to the screen as shown. In this pattern, participants are not sitting with their backs to the facilitator or the projection. Few corporate trainers have much choice about rooms, so they often have to make-do. Lecture halls or lecture seating can still work in a pinch; for example, during group work, ask pairs of people to turn around from one row and group with the pair sitting directly behind them.

Software computer training rooms require some special thought. Software training experts such as Bob Mosher and Elliot Masie encourage the configuration in Figure 8.2. The computers are on tables around the outside of the room. The learners turn to them when trying the software, but they work at the center table, facing the facilitator, during demonstrations. The benefits of this arrangement are that

- Learners aren't typing or jumping ahead while the facilitator is explaining something.
- The facilitator can easily view the screens of the learners from the front of the room and when walking around.
- Learners can use the center table to store their things, keeping the computer space clear for using the mouse and keyboard.
- The computer plugs and cables are safely away from the walking space.
- The changing context increases retention (see Chapter Six).

EQUIPMENT AND SUPPLIES

Here are some additional tips that have to do with the equipment in the room and the supplies needed:

- Keep the lights on as much as possible. Open the blinds and let the outside in. It doesn't distract; it adds context and feeds the naturalist intelligence.
- Don't hide behind the instructor's equipment. Get rid of lecterns because they are a physical barrier between you and your learners. Turn a table perpendicular to your learners for your AV equipment so you can easily access it without putting a barrier between you and your learners.

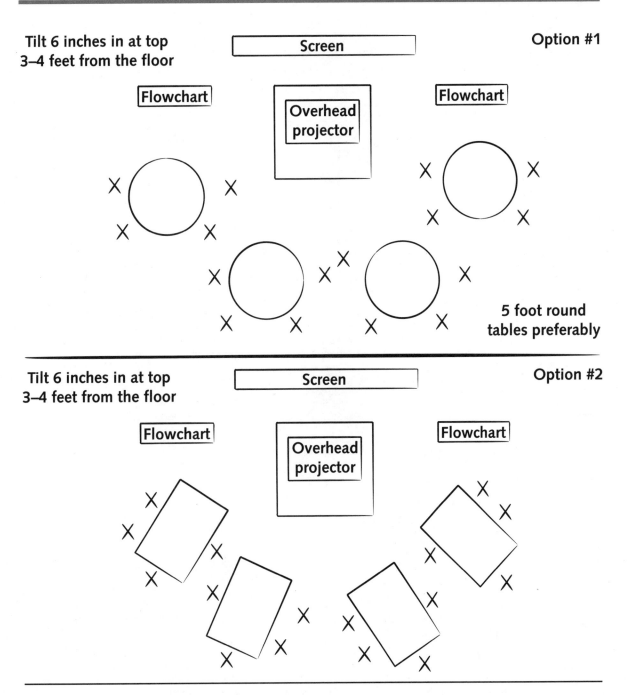

FIGURE 8.1. **Two Room Setups for Team Learning.**

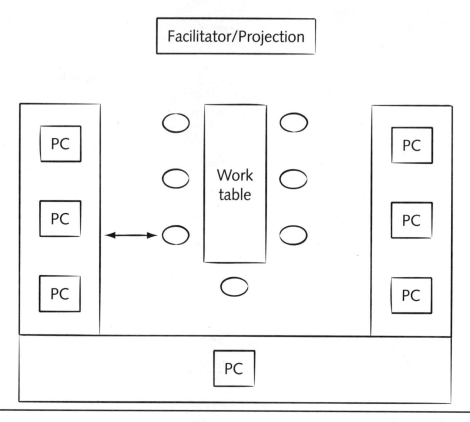

FIGURE 8.2. **Room Setup for Computer Training.**

• When turning over flipchart paper, hold a bottom corner to flip each page over easily, without tangling the paper up. Write while standing perpendicular to the flipchart to minimize the amount of time your back is to the learners.

• Never stand in front of an overhead projector. When learners see the projected image on you, it is very distracting. Point at the overhead, not at the screen, using a small pointer. This keeps you from turning your back on the learners, which would create another barrier.

• Tape any extension cords down to the floor. This protects you and your learners from tripping and having a humiliating (and reptilian) experience.

• Get plenty of flipcharts, paper, pens, and wastebaskets before the class starts. Try out all the equipment you need to make sure it works. Check these supplies often.

• If you are able to, put about four to eight small plants or two large ones in the classroom. NASA uses this strategy to better the learning environment for astronauts during their training. It increases the fresh oxygen level in the room, is visually pleasing, and honors the naturalist intelligence in the learner.

• Recent research on aromatherapy indicates that the scents of peppermint, basil, lemon, cinnamon, and rosemary encourage mental alertness. These scents are useful before and after lunch. To calm, use lavender, chamomile, orange, and rose—for example, during the final review at the end of the day. Oils and sprays are available at many stores. For safety reasons, avoid burning candles or incense. Some companies may have strict policies against burning anything.

• Watch and learn from your learners what you can improve in the environment. Pay attention when a learner asks for something, and learn from it.

Controlling the environment down the hall is easier than controlling the environment across the country. If you travel to teach at other locations, the benefits of a learning environment have to be balanced against the cost and energy required to ship things to the location. Here is a suggested shipping list and how each item is used in class:

Item	Use
Blank overheads	Impromptu illustrations, group exercise results
Overhead pens	To highlight overheads or create illustrations
Pencils (one per learner)	Place on tables for the learners
Colored (or scented) markers (one per learner)	Place on learners' tables
Red plastic cups	To hold pencils and markers on tables
Post-its (two small pads per learner)	Place on tables for use during exercises
Small pads of paper, two per grouping	Place on tables for learners' note taking
Stickers, four sets of four different stickers	For breaking into groups (see Appendix, p. 285) and for diplomas
Diplomas, one per learner	To celebrate learning
Mixed hard candy, one bag per day of learning	For kinesthetic learners, quick energy, and for color
Sugar-free hard candy, one bag	For kinesthetic learners sensitive to sugar
Four Slinkies	For large rewards (for example, end-of-class review)
One roll masking tape	To hang peripherals
One roll shipping tape	To pack boxes for shipping (if necessary)

Item	*Use*
Shipping label for return	To return boxes (if necessary)
Learner guide	Copy of presentation and resources

Our facilitators carry their own music and players with them. I prefer a small CD player with small speakers. My company used to ship every box of supplies to and from the customer's site but found the expense of shipping it back was often more than the savings from getting the extra supplies back. Now we ship back only course supplies that are reused, such as simulation props.

The favorite equipment of most learners is the coffee maker. The favorite supply is the food. In the next section, you will learn the benefits—and drawbacks—of food.

REFRESHMENT

You may have been raised the same way I was: if you are having a dear friend over, it is sacrilege not to provide food. The budget battles over food in the corporate classroom continue. These battles do not change the fact that providing learners with food and drink in class is very comforting and creates a state of anticipation, relaxation, and enjoyment that opens the learners to new thoughts. Besides, hunger distracts attention from the learning.

A study by Jenkins in the *New England Journal of Medicine* (cited in Jensen, 1995) found that learners who ate three traditional meals per day had less brain function in comparison with learners who ate seventeen snacks through the day. Less cognitive functioning can easily lead to more discipline problems and less self-esteem in class. The learning from this research is that, biologically speaking, snacks help you learn.

Although the typical coffee and donut tray with its caffeine and sugar is certainly not the best nutritional fuel for a learning body, it is a strong cultural comfort. Learners should be allowed to make the choice of what they eat, just as they make the choice about what they want to learn. I have had learners get very angry about not having coffee or donuts because someone else has decided to regulate their nutrition for them with fruit and juice. If you try to decaffeinate people who are used to caffeine, they can get headaches. The classroom is no place for detox.

Use trays with a variety of breakfast items: donuts, muffins, bagels, and fruit, with coffee, tea, water, and juices.

In the afternoon, it is fun to have pretzels, cheese, soft drinks, juice, and water. Cookies are a good reward as well. Even if the corporation has eliminated the snack budget, consider bringing in snacks on your own, on at least one of the learning days. It's well worth the $15 investment.

As you noticed in the supply list in the previous section, you can put hard candy on all the classroom tables. It adds color and gives people something to do to feed their kinesthetic needs without encouraging them to overdo it. Eating hard candy allows the learner to move in a small way for a bit of time, which is useful to a kinesthetic learner. Lollipops can work nicely as well. People will be appreciative when you also bring sugar-free hard candy. For sanitary reasons, make sure the candy is individually wrapped, even though the paper can be a little noisy.

Wrapped red licorice or licorice sticks in multiple colors are a great diversion. You can place them in colorful plastic cups on each table to perk up the energy in the afternoon. Adult learners also love silly candy that they remember from childhood, including bubble gum, lollipops with gum centers, and jawbreakers. Save this type of thing for late-in-the-day energizers because some noise may be generated. Be careful not to encourage too much sugar consumption.

THE RHYTHM OF LEARNING

Everything has a rhythm. Your heart has a beat, your brain waves have a flow, and your energy peaks and wanes, just as the ocean's tides come in and out. AL professionals such as Ole Andersen, Don Campbell, and Chris Brewer have studied the optimum use of rhythm in learning events.

Our levels of minerals, vitamins, glucose, and hormones are highest in the morning, and lowest (rendering us least effective) in the afternoon. Here are some tips to increase energy for learning:

• People need sleep to learn well. Don't add to the activity level of today's businessperson by assigning lots of homework. Research from the University of Lille in France shows that reducing sleep time not only diminishes the learning energy the following day but also interferes with the storage of long-term memory from the learning the previous day (Jensen, 1995). Consider scheduling a one-day workshop as two half days, with an overnight in between for sleep for long-term storage.

• Laughter has been proven to increase white blood cell activity, which may improve alertness and memory. Many people are practicing laughter as a healing therapy because of its ability to enhance the body's immune system. Encourage safe humor in the classroom by laughing often and sharing humorous analogies.

- Stress impedes learning, and learners sometimes come with a bucketful. Consider slow stretching, laughter and humor, games, unstructured sharing, discussion, and reading to music tied to a learning objective as ways to slow and relax the learners. These activities are especially critical whenever they return from the so-called real world (such as first thing in the morning or after lunch).

Our learners have been living in an overshocked world of high contrast and stimulation. Trying to keep up with or exceed this level to hold the brain's attention is not productive. Instead, such unique influences as prizes, colored pens, posters, and music offer a subtle and gentle contrast, promoting retention but not creating so much visual noise that retention is blocked.

In their book *Rhythms of Learning*, Campbell and Brewer (1991) share research and techniques to help trainers maximize learning energy in their classes. Although the book is directed toward grades K–12, corporate AL professionals find that this research is pertinent to the adult learner as well.

Campbell and Brewer's graph of the typical rhythm of the day shows that most people reach their highest energy level at 10:00–11:00 A.M. (Figure 8.3). However, there are morning-active people and evening-active people, so again, the unique characteristics of a specific learner may cause deviation from this rhythm. The generalizations below support the best interventions for the greatest number of learners.

For almost everybody, there is a sudden drop in energy between 1:00 and 2:00 P.M. Corporate trainers are very familiar with this after-lunch droop. This is where the traditional training rule "never show a video after lunch" came from. Campbell and Brewer assert that moving the meal or changing the food in the meal makes little difference. The drop still occurs.

So if you can't beat 'em, work with 'em. During this energy lull, learners do best with repetitive tasks that don't take much learning energy. Simple paperwork, easy review work, movement games, and other tasks that don't require learning new things or creating new thoughts are good during this period.

Short-term memory processing, or taking in new learning, is best done in the morning. Don't waste too much time getting the class started. Between 9:00 and 11:00 A.M., the brain is 15 percent better at short-term memory than at any other time before 5:00 P.M. (Campbell and Brewer, 1991). Consider starting the classes at 8:30 A.M. instead of 9:00 to maximize learning energy.

Moving the new learning to long-term memory is better done in the afternoon. Processing the meaning of new information, sometimes called *semantic processing*, gets better as the day progresses and is highest in the afternoon. Spend afternoon time on

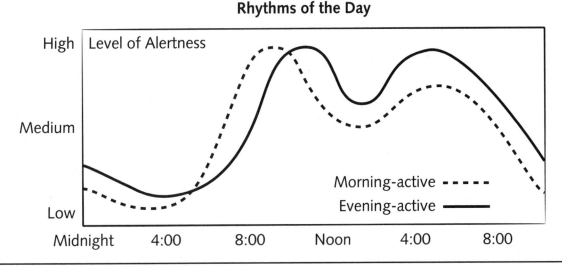

FIGURE 8.3. Alertness Levels of Morning-Active and Evening-Active People.

Source: Campbell and Brewer (1991). *Rhythms of Learning* © 1991 Zephyr Press, Tucson, AZ. Used with permission.

reading, evaluating, practicing, and moving the items learned in the morning into long-term memory through review and practice.

Here's a comparison of a high-level daily flow on the left and, on the right, a specific flow for a typical corporate training day (but remember that no two people have exactly the same rhythms):

9:00 to noon: short-term memory work. Rote learning: terminology, theories, background, facts. Abstract reasoning: problem solving, projects.

8:30–9:30: Open; prioritize objectives. 9:30 to noon: short-term memory work (see Campbell's suggestions).

noon to 2:00 P.M.: repetitive, review-oriented, and simple tasks: movement, paperwork, computer work, drawing.

noon to 1:15: lunch and message checking. 1:15–2:00: repetitive rehearsal (creative review games here).

2:00–5:00: long-term memory work: review, practice, application. Manual (moving) practice and application.

2:00–4:00: long-term memory work (see Campbell's suggestions). 4:00–4:30: review of the day, lessons learned.

Creating opportunities for review is critical to long-term retention (see Chapter Six). Campbell and Brewer's model suggests that review is best in the afternoon, but even in the morning when presenting new information it is important to get immediate feedback from the learners to ensure that the message was heard. Review can take many forms and is not limited to the day of learning. Here are some ideas for review in a corporate training session:

When	How long	Activities
Initial learning	Thirty minutes	Keep lecture under thirty minutes.
Ten minutes later	Five-minute review	Ask open review questions, such as "What are the five key issues?"
Afternoon	One-hour review	Use simulation or applied learning exercises.
One day later	Thirty-minute review	Play Jeopardy for review (see Appendix).
One week later	Three-minute review	Send the learners e-mail—for example, a word scramble on terminology.
One month later	Three-minute review	Send the learners e-mail—for example, a content trivia quiz.
Six months later	Three-minute review	E-mail the learners a Website article on the topic.

The rhythm of learning is a powerful component of the learning facilitator's toolkit. Simply adjusting your delivery to allow learners to honor their natural biological energy levels ensures that learning will be accelerated. Instead of talking faster whenever learners' eyes glaze over, consider not talking at all and substituting a review exercise.

YOU ARE THE ENVIRONMENT

Much of the time the learners are in class, they are watching you as the facilitator. Everything you say, do, and wear influences their learning. In fact, you are the most important and influential part of the environment. In this section, you will read about controlling the environment that you create through

- Your fame
- The Pygmalion effect
- Your spoken word
- Your clothes
- Your reaction to difficult learners

Your Fame

The "famous instructor effect" is very powerful. It is a common perception both in companies and outside them that business learners listen to facilitators more if the presenter flies in from somewhere. Likewise, learners are less likely to listen as well to facilitators who work with them (or who even are from the same city). The geographic distance the facilitator travels to get to the classroom usually has no real bearing on the effectiveness of the training, but it is influential on the learners' perception of authority. Often the material learners get from outside folks is something that inside folks have been trying to get through to them for months. What makes the difference?

It may be a placebo effect, but learners want the facilitator to be "superior" to them in the topic—to help make the learners superior. This dynamic gives each facilitator a window of power that, unless abused, can truly maximize the learner's learning. It also makes it more difficult for an in-house trainer, perceived as a peer, to teach fellow workers.

In Chapter Seven, I cautioned you about playing the role of the expert. It is a delicate balancing act to walk the line between being an all-knowing expert and a person with authority in the subject. This balance is achieved whenever you are continuously learning in the content area yourself, and you are eager and able to help others learn. On the one hand, you are trying to convince the learners that you have what it takes to teach them, while on the other, you are reminding yourself that there is always room for more knowledge.

On a market research survey that my company did, the top factor that influenced the purchase of training workshops was "expertise and experience of instructors." Here are some tips for things you can do to maximize and communicate your expertise:

- Make sure that you are prepared. Do your homework, prepare for each class, get to know the needs of the learners before you get there if possible, and be flexible. Don't fake it—the learners will know. Watch out for burnout, because when you get tired you tend to underprepare.

• Affirm to yourself that you are an expert. Many people don't like to consider themselves experts, especially women. Give yourself permission, and congratulate yourself on your success and knowledge.

• Don't start the class with a long-winded introduction of how amazing you are. Don't have the first page of each guide contain a one-page diatribe on your greatness. Remember Shakespeare's phrase (if I remember it correctly!): "Methinks the lady doth protest too much." You've got to have hype, but be subtle with it. Instead of doing traditional introductions, consider the humbler alternatives in the next two bullets.

• If the customer insists on introducing you, let it be a reading of four facts to the learners, explaining that one of these facts is a lie. You can brag with the three facts and have a fake, wild brag with the lie, but it's OK because that's how the game is played. Reveal the lie at the end of class to create another example of creative discomfort.

• If no one else is introducing you, simply share your name and move on. Better yet, introduce yourself to each of the learners as they enter and then there is no need for a formal recitation of your name. As the learning event progresses, shore up your authority by dropping little tidbits into your stories that tie your experience to a learning objective. Here's an example, assuming you are facilitating a learning objective on project management or systems thinking: "When I was at the Project World conference speaking on systems thinking, one of my participants had an insightful thought that I'd like to share with you. . . ." (Contrast that with another intro: "I was invited to speak at the Project World Conference on Systems Thinking a couple of months ago.") You can share

> How long you have been working with this topic
> University and degrees
> Other companies you have worked with and lessons learned
> Books, articles, or training materials that you have developed
> Conferences where you have spoken

• Even if you hate it, have someone videotape your teaching at least once a year. Then hide in a room by yourself and critique your nonverbal communication. Your voice and your body language communicate a large part of the message to your learners, so the time and pain are worth the return. Manage your learners' expectations by briefly explaining that you are videotaping your presentation—and not their participation—for future use, but don't go into a great deal of detail explaining that you will be reviewing your flaws. Learners want to believe that you are perfect. If this proves difficult, videotape yourself presenting without learners in a staged environment. You can improve a lot by looking at even fifteen minutes of material.

• Use the magic tool of *silence* often. Learn to keep quiet after you ask a question long enough for someone to answer—no matter how long it takes. This is hard, and it takes practice. It is also important to use silence when you are speaking to give learners time to process before moving on to something new. Corporate poet-philosopher David Whyte is exceptional at this technique. As he speaks, he pauses for what at first seems like minutes (but it is only seconds) to let his audience process. It is startling, at first, because it is unusual, but before too long I was looking forward to the pauses and using them effectively to learn more from his words. As a highly kinesthetic learner, I was impressed by the way this technique helped me remain focused.

• *Never, never, never* tell sexual or racist jokes, use derogatory language, or talk about someone negatively, especially other facilitators or experts. Because it's negative, it affects all learning; you come off looking like a jerk.

• Strive to balance

Learning that is challenging: not too difficult but not too easy
Learning that is low-stress but not trivial
Learning that is flowing naturally: learner, skills, attention, environment, and
   facilitator aligned to task

As a person with authority, you have the ability to predict exceptional behavior in yourself as well as others. This phenomenon, called the Pygmalion effect (after a Greek myth by that name), is an important tool in controlling the environment of you.

The Pygmalion Effect

It is a given in educational research that learners learn better if they believe that they can. I call this phenomenon "magic powers"—everyone has them, but not everyone uses them. If you believe it, you can achieve it. In addition (with frightening evidence all around us in corporate training classes), if you don't believe it, you can't achieve it. For example, many learners have a difficult time acquiring personal computer skills because they don't believe they will ever be able to learn about computers.

The Pygmalion effect is alive and well in the corporate classroom. The facilitator makes of the participants what he or she expects them to be. Educators often refer to the research study where the elementary teacher was told the IQs of the children in the class. But the IQs were intentionally backwards; the high IQ kids were said to have low scores, and vice versa. At the end of the year, when they were retested, the learners' test scores aligned with how they had been treated by the teacher. Her belief had created a self-fulfilling prophecy. As corporate learning facilitators, we wield the same power.

The facilitator, representing the authority in the classroom (see Chapter Seven) plays the significant role in setting this positive learning expectation. As in the Greek tale of Pygmalion, where a man's love for a statue brings it to life, our passion has the power to change our frozen-statue students into live learners. The facilitators who do the following things naturally are gifted indeed. If you are not gifted in this way, you can nevertheless begin consciously adding these to your skill set:

- The facilitator shares how much she enjoys this material. These statements set a positive expectation.
- The facilitator shares stories of other people in the company, or in other companies, and how they have benefited from this material. The stories provide evidence that the learning experience will be successful.
- The facilitator allows learners to vent all their anxieties about the material and honestly addresses each one, sharing both the dark and the light side of the learning when necessary. The sharing can help turn around any negative assumptions of the learners.
- The facilitator acknowledges every question and comment as important to learning. This behavior gives the learners the message that the facilitator is dedicated to each learner's experience.
- The facilitator does not allow put-downs, sarcasm, or teasing in the room. This attitude is made clear from the start, modeled by the facilitator and enforced according to preagreed rules. Such an approach keeps the negative Pygmalion effect neutralized for learners, keeping learning safe.
- The facilitator welcomes each learner to class and says goodbye to them individually as they leave (as you would treat honored guests). This kind of attention indicates that the facilitator values the experience as well as the relationship with the learners.
- The facilitator is cautious with compliments. If you are always saying "Great job!" no one will believe you after a while. Make your compliments specific, as much

as possible, so they are real. For example, instead of "Great job on that!" say, "I like the way you worked conflict resolution into that solution." Be mindful that you can encourage the learner ("You are on the right track . . .") even while letting his performance fail and helping him learn from the mistake. Learning happens from mistakes, so the mistakes need to be honored, not ignored. This integrity will show the learners that learning is not always painless, but that it is still very possible.

Your Spoken Word

Lozanov said, "There is no suggestion without desuggestion, without freeing the paraconscious from the inertia of something old" (letter from Lozanov to AL practitioners, January 1999). In fact, he now calls his approach "desuggestopedia." You will read more about his work in Chapter Nine. Lozanov found that the facilitator influenced the three factors that are critical to conscious and unconscious learning:

1. If the learner is confident, the learning goes up.
2. If the learner believes in the trainer, the learning goes up.
3. If the learner believes it will be fun and valuable, learning goes up.

Your learners are entering your learning event influenced by historical events that have changed their perceptions of their ability to learn and your ability to teach. Here are some phrases that may be slipping from your mouth that inadvertently trigger these blocks to learning. Think about the Pygmalion effect of the message to the learner:

Facilitator Says	Learner Thinks
"Pay careful attention to this part. . . . "	I'm in trouble for not paying attention.
"This part is a little harder. . . . "	I'm not going to understand this part.
"I'm new to this material. . . . "	She doesn't know what she's talking about.
"I didn't get enough sleep last night. . . . "	She's going to be an awful trainer.
"Don't forget to bring in . . . "	I will forget to bring it in.
"Don't worry if you're wrong. . . . "	I will be wrong; I'm worried about it already.
"The test won't be hard. . . . "	The test will be hard.
"Some of you may find this boring. . . . "	I will find this boring.

Compare those phrases with better ones:

Facilitator Says	*Learner Thinks*
"This part you will find exciting. . . . "	What is this about? (paying attention)
"This part will be easy for you. . . . "	I may be successful at this.
"I've read a lot about this material. . . ."	She prepared for my learning.
"I'm looking forward to this class. . . . "	She seems excited about this, so I might be, too.
"Bring in . . . "	In my head I picture myself bringing it.
"There are only right answers for this. . . . "	If nothing's wrong, I can try out some new thoughts.
"The review will be a Jeopardy game. . . . "	Huh?!? That sounds interesting.
"This afternoon will fly by. . . . "	This material must really be something.

Your verbal message can be a powerful ally or an insidious saboteur. Not quite as influential, but similar in effect is the message spoken by what you wear.

Your Clothes

What should you wear? This has become a challenging question for men and women, because the variety of dress codes in companies is increasing. While some are going business casual, others are returning to more formal attire.

The most important step in managing your clothes is to always call before the event and ask what the dress code is. Clothing requires a little planning. Ask your customer what the learners will be wearing so you won't feel out of place when you get there. Some occupations demand different dress codes. If you are teaching engineers, they will have a different dress code from graphic designers or accountants. The regions of the country find people dressing differently, and this is likely to be the case between countries as well. Find out ahead of time.

After you've asked, here are some guidelines:

• If the dress code is less formal, wear colors you feel comfortable in, that are uplifting, and that draw attention to you. Women might consider wearing primary or muted pastel colors. Men might consider less bright colors, and move toward earth tones. Both men and women should avoid black and navy because of the seriousness. These colors speak "control."

• While teaching, I saw a man in a very expensive suit walk by and asked my learners who he was. They looked at his clothes and said with disdain, "Oh, he's a *vendor*!" Wear clothes that are a little more professional than the culture you are teaching in to help you when you play the role of trainer (see Chapter Seven), but not so far beyond their culture that it makes the learners distrust you. For example, at a conservative insurance company where the dress code is black or dark navy two-piece suits with white shirts (with skirts for women), you could wear a simple dress or monotone suit in a lighter color. At a very casual athletic shoe company filled with young people, you could wear pants and a colorful shirt—with their shoes, of course. The clothes you see at Harley Davidson in Milwaukee are very different from the clothes you see at Goldman Sachs on Wall Street. Consider a little more color and formality than the business culture at the company to communicate to your learners "I'm not from here, but I'm in tune with you," which creates respect, from you to them and them to you.

• Avoid distracting jewelry, scarves, ties, or patterns. It's fun to accent to communicate your uniqueness, but it is visually distracting in a class. Don't let what you are wearing interfere with the content of the learning for the learner. Remember: it's likely that more than half of your class is very visual. Look and be successful, together, approachable, and intelligent.

• Photos are often included in preclass course mailings and brochures, and they send a message about your expertise before you get there. Consider paying the money to get a good photographer who can capture your essence in a head shot. Photography shops in malls, which are easy to find and deal with, often produce results that send the wrong message; it is not appropriate to appear seductive in corporate training. Getting pictures taken by your friends in the back yard with trees appearing to grow out of your head is careless enough to do serious damage to your image. Likewise, the typical corporate pictures created through the public relations areas are dull and lifeless. That is not what a learning facilitator should be perceived as being.

• Let your personality come out through your choice of what you wear. Don't try to dress just like anyone else. Even with these guidelines, it is most important to be yourself.

After all is said and done, only you can judge how well you've accomplished this balancing act. You must be comfortable. Don't lose yourself. In addition to what you look like, learners are carefully studying what you do to interpret what you say. Your gestures, choice of words, intonation, and facial expressions can accidentally change the meaning of your message in responding to them. All facilitators will run into a difficult learner at some point, and how you handle these participants shows how committed you are to accelerating learning.

Your Reaction to Difficult Learners

Difficult learners cover quite a range of types: from participants who are dead set against learning, to learners who have just been momentarily sidetracked. The level of interruption determines the intervention. The goal for an AL facilitator is to walk the fine line between learner-directed learning and total chaos. In most cases, clear, direct statements move learners back to the learning objectives without any problems, as long as the statements do not threaten the safety of the learner. Anger from the facilitator is never appropriate, especially in front of an entire classroom.

If restoring order is necessary, consider the "SAT method." Using this approach (practiced by accelerated learning facilitators in grade schools), a facilitator consistently applies an escalating sequence of three steps to regain alignment to the learning objectives.

Assume a group is busy talking about a party last week instead of working on the exercise. Here are the three steps:

1. S for suggest: "If you'd like, you can use those colored markers for working on that poster."
2. A for ask: "Can I answer some questions about the exercise for you?"
3. T for tell: "Please start working on the exercise now because there isn't much time left."

Suggest allows the learners some pretty broad choices in hopes that they will catch themselves. *Ask* is slightly more direct, bringing the learners back to the learning. *Tell* is used when the learners have not taken the hints up to that point.

Notice the use of the word *because* in the final, direct statement. Naomi Karten explains in a newsletter article that research by Robert B. Cialdini has shown using the word *because* increases motivation to honor your request (Karten, 1995). Here are some other ideas for keeping learners focused on the learning objectives:

• To control a rowdy group, consider passing a microphone for people to speak. If a microphone is impractical, use another object like a pointer or a pen to be a "talking stick." This Native American technique suggests that only the person with the talking stick can speak. Exchanging the talking stick gets learners to think through what they want to say very carefully before they speak. If you use this technique too long, people will get accustomed to it, but it works well in small doses.

• If you facilitate learning with the same people over and over, consider setting up some consistent rules of behavior before you need them. A few suggestions:

If a learner needs to ask for a break, establish a hand signal that is subtle but that you can obviously see. A suggestion might be for the learner to hold a pen up.

Another signal could be used for having a question. This is useful so that you can continue but come back and take the question without damaging the flow.

Coach the learners to manage their self-talk. Many people are so busy practicing what they are going to say next that they don't hear what is being said. Getting learners to release these thoughts, even by writing them down, helps them focus their attention on others.

Coach the learners to ask genuine questions—those that the learner truly wants to know and that are not motivated to make the inquirer look intelligent or to trip up the speaker.

• Avoid these negative words: *should, have to, don't, can't.* They can leave a negative Pygmalion effect.

 LEARNING POINT

The first time I hear someone being sarcastic toward herself or others, I squeeze a stuffed dinosaur I carry with me, and it screeches. I then give "Negasaurus" to the learner and encourage her to catch the next person being negative.

Many people use guns for this—squirt guns, toy laser guns, Nerf guns, and the like. I did so as well—until a group of elementary teachers pointed out the negative, unsafe image that using a gun carries.

CONCLUSION

So, what is the perfect environment for accelerated learning? There is no one answer because it is dependent on your facilitation style, the limitations of the physical space, the learning needs of your participants, and your budget. As you grow in your knowledge and skills, you will learn to create an optimum environment for yourself through experimentation.

Don Campbell is renowned in the field of music and learning. He has a test for delivering learning that he calls triple-coding (1992). These questions ensure that your environment—composed of the physical space, you, and your learners—is a place where the learning objectives can be *seen, heard, and felt* (visual, auditory, kinesthetic):

- Did the learner hear me? (auditory)
- Did the learner see what I meant? (visual)
- Could the learner repeat what I said in his imagination? Could he write it down? (auditory, kinesthetic)
- Did I present the material with visual clarity? (visual)
- Did I speak clearly the information I was teaching? (auditory)
- Did I review the information while the learner was relaxed? (kinesthetic)
- Did I review the information in an alert, active, style? (kinesthetic)

Having read this chapter, you now know the importance of the learning environment and how, in combination with the learning objectives (Chapter Two) and the learning preferences of the participants (Chapters Three through Six), you can use the environment to maximize learning in your workshops. The next chapter details how music enhances this learning environment. Following that, you will learn a systematic approach for building, assessing, and marketing accelerated learning.

 PERSONAL ACTION PLAN

Please look back through this chapter, and jot down your thoughts below: insights, things you want to do, things you want to remember, games, and quotes. I've added a list of my own to supplement your list. It is better for your learning if you make your own list before you look at mine.

The learning objectives of this chapter were to

- Identify times in a learning event when you play the roles of facilitator of learning, trainer, and learner
- Adopt specific improvements in how you communicate new learning to learners
- Maximize memory in self and others for long-term retention
- Develop classroom learning events to meet a specific learning need
- Create a personal action plan to increase personal learning and the effectiveness of your delivery of learning events

Your thoughts:

_____

_____

_____

_____

_____

_____

_____

_____

_____

_____

Here are my thoughts:

- Short-term memory processing is best done in the morning; moving the new learning to long-term memory is better done in the afternoon.
- Snacks help. Consider treating your learners like honored guests with candy, snacks, and drinks.
- Color has the power to tap into the limbic brain, which means it can significantly increase long-term retention. Used incorrectly, it can trigger the reptilian brain.
- The retention of the material absorbed from peripheral learning is a strong ally in accelerating learning. Let the classroom teach, too.

- A seating pattern has its own strengths. Choosing the right one should be driven by the topic and learning objectives as closely as possible within the restrictions of the physical space.
- For much of the time that the learners are with you, they are watching you. Everything you say, do, and wear influences their learning. In fact, you are the most important and influential part of the environment.
- The Pygmalion effect ensures that positive words and actions will increase learning.

Business Success

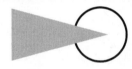

THE LEARNING OBJECTIVES OF CHAPTER 9

After reading this chapter, you will be able to

• Adopt specific improvements in how you communicate new learning to learners

• Identify how you learn best

• Identify and rethink those personal beliefs of yours that block learning

• Assess your preference for processing new learning to Gardner's multiple intelligences

• Use the multiple intelligences to design the logistical flow of a learning event

• Balance the use of both the left and right sides of the brain for learning

• Maximize memory in self and others for long-term retention

• Use music to create focused learning environments

• Create a personal action plan to increase personal learning and the effectiveness of your delivery of learning events

CHAPTER 9

Music to Deliver Learning

Music has the unique quality of integrating the emotional, cognitive, and psychomotor elements that activate and synchronize brain activity.

—Zephyr Press Website

'd like to take you on a trip to visit two very different stores at a typical American mall. Imagine yourself walking through the mall. You are stopping in a shop that has gifts for adolescents: lava lamps, black lights, and suggestive T-shirts. You feel the pulsing of strobe lights, watch the lava lamps blobbing, take in the strange fluorescent colors created by wild psychedelic posters under black lights, and marvel at the nervous energy of teenage shoppers. The music is loud, fast, intense, rock. The music parallels the message of the store; you are entering a slightly forbidden and rebellious land, something parents would find fault with.

Now walk down the mall a little to an upscale lingerie and beauty products store. As you enter, you notice that the entire store feels pink, even though it isn't. You are affected by the entire experience as you walk in: it is soft, subtle, warm, romantic, feminine. You notice the music, which is slow, classical, instrumental, and calming. More than notice the music consciously, you are aware of the "feeling." The music parallels the message of this store—you are entering a boudoir, a soothing place to be.

Music completes, perhaps even creates, mood. As you imagine these two contrasting shopping experiences, you may distinctly remember the feelings you got from each one in your own life. These feelings were strongly influenced by the music being played at the time.

The same effect can take place in a learning event. We have the power through music to create a powerful learning environment. Using music as a catalyst, we can set a tone of anticipation, alertness, humor, energy, focus, and reflection. From Albert Einstein to Charles Schulz ("Peanuts"), creative thinkers have recognized the value of music and its role in creating an environment of free thought.

Hideo Seki of Tokyo used music to teach a semester course on electricity and magnetism to his computer science learners. The first day was devoted to goal setting and positive suggestions by and for the learners. The rest of the program was sequenced like this:

- Ten minutes of mood-setting music as learners walk in
- Presentation of new material through lecture with no music
- New material presented visually with an overhead projector, with more active music and learner involvement
- The same material presented with slow, instrumental music, with the learners just listening
- Energizing music as learners leave

The learners attended a sixty-to-ninety-minute class once a week. At the exam, three times as many learners than in previous classes of similar size achieved scores better than 80 percent (Ostrander, Schroeder, and Ostrander, 1979). Music can be a powerful tool to increase learning and retention when used well. This chapter gives you enough research and techniques to ensure that you are gaining all the learning you can from the use of music.

In the first part of this book, you learned about how diverse learning experiences and learners are. Music was discussed briefly as one of the multiple intelligences and as a powerful way to align the right and left brains. Moving into the second part, you learned about the influence of your own beliefs regarding learning and teaching and then the power of the learning environment. Finishing up Part Two with Chapter Nine, you will now read about the specific influences of music on learning.

Music is such a significant part of the accelerated learning environment that people often mistakenly believe that playing music in class means you are doing accelerated learning. It is an obvious difference between AL and traditional instruction. Accelerated learning practitioners have been studying and experimenting with music in the classroom because of the amazing power it has to increase learning. But like all the ideas you have read about, music works better or worse depending on the learner.

In this chapter, you will read about the current theories as to how music works. These theories have been implemented in the CD that you receive with this book. In Chapter One, you read how to use the CD to maximize learning while reading this book. In this chapter, you will read about how the composer and producer, Marty Morrow, approached the design of the pieces to create learning music.

The sections of this chapter are as follows:

- How music works
- The use of music in learning
- Making the transition to music in the classroom

HOW MUSIC WORKS

In this section, you will read about the music research and theories as to how music influences learning, including the benefits of music to the learner, how the physiology of the brain is influenced by music, and the use of music in the classroom.

The Benefits of Music to the Learner

At the Center for the Neurobiology of Learning and Memory at the University of California's Irvine campus, the impact of listening to Mozart while taking a standardized test was studied. Learners took spatial intelligence tests after listening to music for ten minutes. Some learners listened to other music, and some took the tests in silence. The IQs of the students who listened to Mozart went up 9 points, while the control group's IQ scores did not increase (Anderson, Marsh, and Harvey, 1999). The researchers theorized that music could help learners relax and focus while learning, increasing the test scores.

This often-cited study was the trigger for the phrase "the Mozart effect," creating some mistaken beliefs in practitioners that only Mozart's music could increase learning—and that all the compositions by Mozart do so. As you will see, neither of these beliefs is true.

Although music was once thought to activate the right brain, researchers now believe that certain music actually crosses both sides of the brain. More importantly, music activates the limbic area. Because the limbic brain is so crucial to long-term retention, music can help make long-term retention more efficient. As you read in Chapter Six, music adds another dimension or strand to the link to memory, strengthening the context.

Some researchers also believe that music has a physiological effect. Your pulse tends to become synchronized with the beat of the music. This explains how slower music has the effect of slowing down the pace of a workshop, allowing the learners to focus. AL facilitators believe listening to music while learning can also have these benefits:

- Relax the learner and reduce stress
- Increase learning energy
- Improve concentration and attention span
- Improve the amount of new information that can be acquired
- Improve the time it takes to acquire new information
- Strengthen learners' memory retention
- Foster creativity by stimulating both the right and left brains
- Foster deeper thinking by stimulating both the right and left brains
- Focus and align a group to a common purpose
- Give individuals a feeling of time expansion—time stands still
- Improve feelings of positive self-esteem
- Reduce fatigue, attention problems, and discipline problems
- Settle the kinesthetic, attention-deficient, or hyperactive learner
- Mask distracting background noise

Here are a few examples of the practical uses of music to achieve such results. Music can be used to establish a state or change the environment. When the class plays a Jeopardy-like game (see the Appendix) for a review, play music that sounds like game show music. In a conflict management workshop, the different steps of conflict resolution can be emphasized by playing music that sounds like the steps, each unique in its mood.

A little later, you will read about copyright restrictions on music. Despite this consideration, there is a great deal of choice in music created specifically for classroom use.

Another example, the concept of time expansion, is an interesting one. Two doctors, Lynn Cooper and Milton Erikson, set 60 beats per minute (bpm) clicking on metronomes. They found that people felt as if time had ballooned, accelerating their thinking and creative skills. In small amounts of clock time, they were able to create comprehensive designs, thinking they had been working on them for an hour (Ostrander, Schroeder, and Ostrander, 1979). Using music to slow learners down actually accelerates their learning productivity.

Keeping learners aligned to the learning objectives is another example of practical use of music. The focusing power of music seems to minimize getting off track. I personally find that playing slow instrumental music while I am developing new workshops helps me manage my naturally short attention span and kinesthetic nature.

TABLE 9.1.   **Brain State and Rate of Heart or Music Beat.**

Brain State	Rhythm of Brain Waves	Heart Pulse/ Music Rate	Description
Delta	0.5 to 3 cps	resting rate	deep, dreamless sleep, no outer awareness
Theta	4 to 7 cps	resting rate	unconscious, light sleep, deep meditation
Alpha	8 to 12 cps	60 to 80 bpm	aware, relaxed, calm, high suggestibility, daydreaming
Beta	13 to 40 cps	80+ bpm	normal waking, consciousness, alert, active

Note: cps = cycles per second; bpm = beats per minute.

The Physiology of the Brain Influenced by Music

Take a look at how music influences the physical brain. Brain waves associated with a specific brain state have a brain pulse that identifies them. Being in the right-brain state is important for maximum learning; there are times in learning to be active and times to be relaxed. Table 9.1 gives the brain states and their associated pulse rates.

The alpha state is good for learning facts, synthesizing new knowledge, strengthening long-term memory, and nurturing creativity. You may have found you go into the alpha state automatically when you are running, walking, driving, or riding. It is being in this alpha state that causes you to get home without remembering any of the trip. It is also in this state that your brain can create those a-ha experiences so critical to creative learning—for example, you suddenly solve a business problem or you have a great idea for a new learning event while driving home. You might find it interesting that the rhythm of ocean waves, as with music at 60–80 bpm, can stimulate alpha brain waves for some people. This is why many find the ocean so relaxing.

Researchers have seen that music at 60–80 bpm calms breathing, reduces the heart rate to a similar pulse, and sets the stage for a brain rhythm of 8–12 cycles per second (cps). Researchers are really not sure how music does what it does, but they theorize that as both sides of the brain synchronize to this rhythm, the brain moves from an active beta state to a more relaxed beta state and then toward an alpha state. Both alpha and beta brain waves can be in the brain at the same time, and because alpha tends toward an inner focus, most learners in a learning event with others will rarely move to a complete alpha state. Instead, the music will slow them to a relaxed beta state, lowering their beta brain waves while increasing their alpha, settling them down to focus. This effect, influenced by music, is most pronounced on kinesthetic learners and least pronounced on auditory learners.

"K complex" is a specific brain state within the alpha state, where the a-ha experience occurs. The K complex is every facilitator's dream—there is no better reward than to see that a-ha expression cross a learner's face. Research has shown that you can help learners get to the K-complex state more effectively by ensuring that they have time to reflect on what they have learned. Relaxing allows incubation and is accelerated through quiet instrumental music at 60–80 bpm. It is an interesting paradox that accelerating learning sometimes requires slowing down.

To better understand how to match the right pieces of music with the right effect will require a little side trip into music appreciation class. This information will help you make the right choices when selecting and investing in music for your learning events. After you read a little about music history, you will learn about two renowned researchers in the field of accelerated learning: Georgi Lozanov and Alfred Tomatis. Through their work, you will begin to see ways to incorporate music and learning. In the following section, you will learn more detailed processes for applying music to your learning events.

Music History

As you begin to experiment with music and learning, you may become confused with the terminology. All of a sudden, everyone is talking about baroque, Mozart, and Vivaldi. Maybe you did not have music training (or didn't see any reason for the music training you had); this could make it an unpleasant reptilian learning experience.

Gregorian music (A.D. 600–1400) was first codified during the time of Pope Gregory I (540–604) to facilitate prayer. Chant was the basis for the music. You may have heard some of this music in 1994 when the Benedictine monks of Santo Domingo de Silos in Spain had a best-selling CD entitled *Chant*. This music is wonderful for personal reflection because it is soothing and inspirational.

Renaissance music (1400–1600) reflected the creativity of the music, art, architecture, and thought of the Renaissance. This type of music can stimulate creativity and inspiration.

Baroque music (1600–1750) has more variety of sounds, instruments, and rhythms than the previous two. Slow movements of baroque music, which tend to be at 60–80 bpm, are very popular in AL circles for studying, listening, and concentrating. Handel, Bach, Pachelbel, Telemann, and Purcell are composers from this era. Be warned that there is also a lot of dark, fast, fiery, and celebrational music in the baroque period, all of which is distracting when learning. Put another way, contrary to some beliefs not all baroque music will work.

Music has been used to improve learning in foreign language classes. In foreign language learning, the number of words a learner retains can be readily tested, making it easy to quantify improvement. Many have successfully used baroque music to accelerate foreign language retention.

Classical music (1750–1820) identifies a period in history in addition to being the nickname many people use for all music written over a longer period of time. It is music that is clear, elegant, and easy to predict—all of which makes it good for stimulating learning. Mozart composed during this period. Because much research has been done on Mozart and learning, some people mistakenly believe that Mozart is from the baroque era. Like baroque music, some classical music can be very dark; Mozart himself wrote many sadly emotional compositions that are inappropriate for learning. Haydn and Beethoven also wrote music during this period.

Romantic music (1820–1910) is more expressive and emotional. This music varies in form and style, but when carefully chosen to inspire the imagination it can be very useful. Chopin, Tchaikovsky, and Schubert are among the most popular romantic composers.

After the beginning of the twentieth century, music began to integrate the sounds and rhythms of the global community as people traveled more. Debussy and Ravel created some beautiful music for learning. Today, composers continue to experiment with unique sounds; many are useful for learning, including some pieces by Gershwin, Copland, Stravinsky, and Shostakovich. Pop, rock, and rap continue this experimentation. New age music—characterized by ambiguous melodies, little predictable rhythmic design, and lots of different sounds—can be used for relaxation, meditation, and imagery. Surprisingly enough, country and western and Middle Eastern music share many similar elements, styles, and moods, and create a nice sound break. Jazz (which has been influenced by African music), opera, and the new "sports" music are good ways to set an upbeat mood, especially for breaks. Much music has been recorded for legal use in learning events (more on this later).

Accelerated learning researchers have compared baroque and certain new age music and found no statistical difference in their effects on learning. However, rock music—although it is largely from the same era as new age music—does not work as well for learning. In fact, the low frequencies prevalent in rock—organ, bass guitar, drums—may trigger anxiety in some learners. Learners may think that rock works for them because they have conditioned themselves to it (by playing it during homework), but its effect on learning is relatively unpredictable.

As always, the specific piece strongly influences the results, and there is no style of music that is universally good or bad for learning. In general, though, music with vocals—a characteristic of most rock—does not work well.

Baroque and classical music are the kinds that researchers focused on as they began looking at how music and learning combine to accelerate learning. The person most people credit with the first music and learning research is Lozanov, whom you read about briefly in Chapter Eight.

Georgi Lozanov and Suggestopedia

After World War II, the Soviet Union was determined to create superlearners. By retraining, the country hoped to leap ahead of other countries after the costly material and human expense of the war. Continuing into the cold war, well-funded learning labs in the USSR tried to find ways to improve human learning. One of the things looked at was how gifted people differed physiologically from others.

Researchers found that people who were very good at remembering were able to calm their brain pulse to a slow alpha level while memorizing. Paradoxically, as you read earlier, the learners' brains were slowed to learn faster. To replicate this behavior in others, the Soviets tried sleep learning, hypnosis, and other techniques, but they had only minimal success transferring these results outside the lab.

Georgi Lozanov, studying for his doctorate at Kharkov University in the Ukraine, started to work with the suggestive power of music. He had studied music extensively and played the violin. As he continued his study of music at the Bulgarian Academy of Sciences and the Sofia Medical Institute, he discovered that what he called "mathematical" (60–80 bpm baroque) music could bring learners into a state of alert relaxation. He used this music as an integral part of his full learning program, called suggestopedia.

Originally called the "active and passive concert," suggestopedia is considered the beginning of accelerated learning by most practitioners, and many continue to practice Lozanov's techniques. The Bulgarian government restricted his work outside of the country until just recently, and many variants of his original work strayed from his research. His approach is described elsewhere in this chapter.

The active concert is used to introduce new material. Material is read dramatically to learners while music is played in the background, usually classical or romantic music with a tempo of about 80 bpm. Lozanov believed that the music helped create a limbic link for the words through aligned right and left hemispheres for better retention. Learners are conscious of the words and the learning. The active concert reenergizes the brain, rebalances the brain and body, and revitalizes the body system.

The passive concert is thought by some to teach the subconscious. Material that is the same as or similar to the active concert material is read more quietly to learners to slower music—60 bpm, usually baroque—following a relaxation exercise. The learners do not take notes; they simply sit and let the words flow over them. Combined, these two concerts create an accelerated way to replace standard lecture and are the basis of suggestopedia. Music researchers now believe that the learning effect comes from the capability of the music to decrease (fast) beta waves while increasing (slow) alpha waves in the brain. Although the brain isn't switched completely into alpha state, it moves toward it. The sounds of this type of music physically create energy in the brain and body. By aligning the whole brain with the body, the music allows the body to function more efficiently on less energy. Lozanov preferred a passive approach for review.

LEARNING POINT

Here is the original process used by Lozanov and still used by many AL practitioners today:

1. Preview: a quick introduction to the material with a chorus, parable, chant, or poem is performed over attention-getting, dramatic music for three to five minutes.
2. Active concert: detailed material using a dramatic reading is performed over classical or romantic selections for five to fifteen minutes.
3. Passive concert: detailed material, a review of the active concert material, is performed over baroque music for five to eight minutes at the end of a learning session.

If you are interested in trying this combination of steps, here is how to prepare:

1. Preview the material briefly and introduce the piece of music before you start. Set the stage.
2. Be well rehearsed with your music. Know the ebbs, flows, drama, and so on.
3. For the passive concert, prepare learners with reduced lighting and relaxation techniques.
4. Check the volume from the back of the room.
5. Let the music play for fifteen seconds or so before you start talking.
6. Finish with a spoken "big close" to music, at the end of the learning event.
7. Consider taping it so you can listen as well.
8. Preview and practice to ensure the proper feel.

Here are some additional tips for an active concert:

- Use classical and romantic music, such as Mozart, Beethoven, Haydn, or Brahms.
- Choose full-length concertos and symphonies. Be sure to honor copyright standards (more on this in a later discussion).
- Align the dramatic reading of stories and dialogue with the flow of the music.
- Read along and practice many times before presenting.

Here are some additional tips for a passive concert:

- Use baroque music deliberately written (by Handel, Vivaldi, Corelli, Telemann, or Bach) to lift the spirit and free the mind. Be sure to honor copyright standards (discussed later).
- Choose a major key, not a minor key. A minor key in music sounds sad or mysterious; a major key sounds more emotionally neutral or positive.
- Use slower movements, around 55–65 bpm (often called largo or andante). In baroque music, largo movements are usually short, so you may have to string some together.
- Choose pieces characterized by soothing strings with higher frequency. Violins, guitars, and harp are examples.
- Avoid music with brass or horns, which have lower frequencies and tend to sound too abrupt and noticeable for alpha music.
- Choose 4/4 time. You can tell what the time is of a piece by counting along with it. If you can count 1-2-3-4 repeatedly, then it is 4/4 time. In contrast, a waltz is in 3/4 time and would make you count 1-2-3.

- When combining pieces, sequence selections in ascending keys. In other words, start with the pieces with lower notes and move up to the pieces with higher notes.
- Play three minutes of faster, up-tempo baroque music at the end of the concert, to give a lift back to the present.

Many AL practitioners have adopted a less rigid approach to the use of music. In corporate training settings, learners may feel uncomfortable with relaxation exercises, dimmed lights, or closing their eyes. Here are some alternative methods for modified active and passive concerts:

- Have the learners read the active concert as a choral reading, each taking a different part after you have read it to them once. This participation adds the kinesthetic aspect to the concert (they do it), but it takes more time.
- Have the learners create an active concert from written material and perform it to each other. This approach takes even longer.
- Instead of reading to learners during the passive concert, ask them to relax and then, without speaking, slowly place review material on overheads for them to read silently. This is not quite as passive, but it may feel safer for corporate learning environments.
- Coordinate break music with your activities before and after the break. Do not make the musical transitions so abrupt that they are startling.

Another pioneer who heavily influenced the field of accelerated learning was Tomatis, whose influential work concerns how to manage your learners' ability to listen.

Alfred Tomatis and the Ear

Alfred Tomatis, a French ear specialist, continues to do extensive research on how sound frequencies affect people. Tomatis has found that fatigue and stress can eat away at the brain's electrical potential. In other words, the batteries start running out—a feeling that you are probably aware of. The interesting idea from Tomatis's research is that these little batteries are recharged not by the body's metabolism, as you might suspect, but by sound.

Tomatis researched higher frequency musical sound (produced by violins, for example) and found that these tones energize the brain while releasing muscle tension and balancing the body (Ostrander, Schroeder, and Ostrander, 1979). Different cultures hear differing ranges of frequencies. This healing benefit of high frequencies that Tomatis studied occurs only if the sound is heard. Depending on the culture (or existing hearing damage), the benefit may be lost on a specific listener. The American English listener has the narrowest listening spectrum, as a result of early learning geared toward the sounds of this language.

The other end of the frequency range triggered negative response in Tomatis's work. Low-frequency sounds, such as traffic, airports, and construction sites, burn energy, depleting the mind and body. Although Tomatis's initial research does not include rock music, this style frequently uses low, pounding, heavy bass sounds. For this reason, rock music is probably not appropriate in passive or active concerts.

Tomatis and Lozanov both reported that fluctuating sound between both ears seems to encourage processing effectiveness. Tomatis's father, Albert, had discovered, after working with the famous opera singer Enrico Caruso, that left-ear listening seemed best for matching tones. Caruso went deaf in his right ear after surgery but sang better than ever. By observing Caruso, Albert Tomatis and his colleagues learned how to help hearing-damaged professional singers hear a fuller spectrum of frequencies with their left ear. The left ear is the quickest path to the right brain, where musical tone matching resides. If the singers couldn't hear a tone, they couldn't sing it. Alfred Tomatis continued this research by inventing the electronic ear, which restores high-frequency hearing loss by exercising the middle ear with fluctuating high-frequency and low-frequency sounds.

In Chapter Five, you read about brain dominance and the roles the right and left brains play. The left ear has a longer, less efficient route to the language center of the brain. The right ear has a shorter route to the same language center. The right ear receives information more rapidly, so many people—especially people in auditory fields such as customer service or music itself—learn to depend heavily on their right ear to the exclusion of their left. In other cases, some people have never developed strength of listening in the left ear. Because learning first requires intake, some apparent learning problems may actually be listening or hearing problems.

 PRACTICE

Shifting between ears alternately stimulates each brain hemisphere and can be used to maximize memory (Ostrander, Schroeder, and Ostrander, 1979).

Place this familiar list in front of you:

apple, chair, newspaper, pen, cement, love, tree, dog, sign, bagel, desk, faith, queen, blue, book, pen, square, vine, orts, cup, down, coffee, peace, boot, smile

Listen to the piece "Falling Leaves" on the CD in this book, with headphones, if possible.
Close your eyes and take ten deep breaths, concentrating on your breathing.
When ready, open your eyes and take a "picture" of the list for seven or eight seconds.
Close your eyes and sink back into the music.
Repeat taking a picture and closing your eyes five times.
Now write the list on a fresh piece of paper.
Were you more successful this time than when you tried this exercise in Chapter Six? How stressful was this experience compared with your experience then?
Take a moment to reflect on the words that you still remembered from the first experience, and how that fact relates to memory theory. Now reflect on the words you remembered this time, and why you were able to retain them this time.

If the learners can't hear something, they can't learn it. Music fluctuating between the left and right ears can improve the listeners' ability to hear. By simply moving participants around every so often, a learning facilitator can ensure that both sides of the brain are being "spoken" to. Likewise, moving the music source to other corners of the room exercises both the left and right brains.

There is still much more research to do. People such as Anderson, Campbell, and Brewer continue to expand what is known about music and learning. Their research does not stop with what we typically define as music but extends to the research of rhythm and learning as well. You read more about body rhythms, for instance, in Chapter Eight.

The CD with This Book

As I thought about the challenge of modeling AL through a written book, I decided to include "music to read by." As you have read in the previous sections, music is an important part of accelerated learning. I asked my friend Marty Morrow to compose music to maximize the learning while reading. He has written two pieces, which you were introduced to in Chapter One: "Falling Leaves" and "The Stream." The titles clearly describe the restful, pastoral alpha state we were striving for in the music. If you are not interested in how music is composed, feel free to skip this section and go to "The Use of Music in the Classroom."

Now that you have read the theories associated with music and learning, here are some of the thoughts Marty incorporated into these two pieces of music when he composed them:

• The tempos of the pieces are both 65 bpm to stimulate as many alpha brain waves as possible.

• Both pieces are in the major key of D, consistent with the research on optimum frequencies of both Tomatis and Hans Cousto, a Swiss scientist who concluded that this key is best for calming, meditative, relaxing, and centering work (Ostrander, Schroeder, and Ostrander, 1979). While reading this book, I hope that you have found many opportunities to stop and reflect on what you have learned so that you can apply it to your corporate setting.

• The songs are intended to be "subtext" to other activities. They are not meant to be "active listening" pieces (which creates a problem for those who try to actively listen to this music—it can seem slow and boring!). Researchers have seen that learning effects seem to be more apparent when the music is barely audible, allowing it to get past the conscious mind. This means the readers should find that they "stop listening" to the music and are able to easily concentrate on what they're reading.

• The goal of the first piece is to synchronize both sides of the brain by providing a constant, repetitive beat. As Marty said, "I think I wore out my D on the keyboard!" Recurring patterns keep the listener from being distracted by the music. The lower-frequency sounds are minimized or eliminated—there are no drums and no lower frequencies. Everything resolves quickly so there is no phrase in the music that appears to be hanging waiting for resolution, as you find in many commercial new age songs.

• The first piece is designed to be long enough (eighteen minutes) to provide an uninterrupted environment for high concentration and comprehension. In my mind, I equated "reading" a book without practice to "lecture" in a classroom, so the idea was to minimize the lecture time to under twenty minutes to honor the attention span of adults, especially those who are highly kinesthetic or not strong in visual/linguistic aptitudes. My hope is that you work on application, perhaps through a Practice Box activity, after eighteen minutes.

• The goal of the second song, now that the alpha waves have been stimulated by the first piece, is to provide a higher level of energy in a manner that does not bring the music back to a conscious, active listening state. This second piece is the one you are encouraged to use for your practice work; it takes you to a relaxed beta state. You will notice more notes being played, but the tempo is still exactly the same as the first song with similar instrumentation. If you listen closely, you'll find something through-out the second song that is carried over from the first. This provides consistency from one piece to the next and will help you stay focused even though things become more upbeat.

• Higher piano tones were chosen, which is consistent with Tomatis's work (and because I like the piano).

I asked Marty to share with me how he creates original music. Consistent with the work of Gardner (Chapter Four) and Herrmann (Chapter Five), Marty says that he rehearses multiple pieces of compositions in his head over time until eventually only one theme is left. This theme is then manipulated through a synthesizer and built upon to create the final piece. Notice how effortless the creative work is—"the pieces pop into my head," he says—because of the strength of both his musical intelligence (songs in his head) and his bodily/kinesthetic intelligence (manipulating the key-board). To someone with less musical aptitude, this whole process might sound virtu-ally impossible. Marty has learned to maximize the strengths of his intelligence and is an example of accelerated learning in action.

A final personal note: this music has been played in the car and has worked great for putting children to sleep. It also made the driver pretty sleepy, so this is not good road music.

THE USE OF MUSIC IN LEARNING

It may come as a surprise to you, but according to the American Society of Com-posers, Authors, and Publishers (ASCAP), music purchased for personal use is licensed for personal use only. "If the performance is part of a face to face teaching activity at a nonprofit educational institution, permission is not required. Permission is required when music is used as part of training seminars, conventions, or other commercial pre-sentations" (ASCAP, 1999).

Using it in classrooms for large groups of people, especially while making a profit, is a violation of the copyright on most music. This requirement is very important to remember, even though it limits your flexibility in choosing pieces for classroom use. Just because you know someone who abuses this law doesn't make it any more legal. There are people who have written music specifically for classrooms, and you will read about them later in this section.

Beyond the legal issues involved in using music in a corporate workshop or other public setting, be aware that it is also very difficult to create on your own the consistency of sound that can be bought from people who produce music specifically for learning. Buying a CD with "Mozart's Greatest Hits" for one dollar is not going to work well. It will contain a mix of fast, slow, and vocal selections, and only a few of these will work. The slower sections of baroque music are usually fairly short—two to four minutes—so the right pieces of music will be few and far between on these CDs. Music from the music store is composed for listening, not learning.

Chris Brewer, president of LifeSounds, provides usable music for AL training through her company (see the Resources). She says: "I have contracts with specific artists or recording companies that indicate the music may be used for the methods we AL trainers use in training. This includes corporate settings but not profit-making entertainment, and certainly no reproduction of the music in any way. I send folks who buy this music for corporate training a contract about how they may use this music. I keep a copy on file."

Certainly, you can hire someone like Marty to compose music for you, but doing so may be a large and expensive undertaking. Luckily, there are people who produce and sell music specifically for public use with all rights included.

LEARNING POINT

Here are some composers and distributors used by accelerated learning practitioners (complete addresses are in the Resources).

Composers
Steven Halpern
Gary Lamb
Marty Morrow

Distributors
    Creative Training Techniques
    LIND Institute
    The Trainers Warehouse
    Zephyr Press

MAKING THE TRANSITION TO MUSIC IN THE CLASSROOM

Consider experimenting with music used in aerobics classes. There are many types to choose from, and any health club can tell you where to buy them in your area. These tapes are licensed for public use and often contain lively, fast instrumental music good for the times when people are coming in, taking breaks, or leaving. Likewise, dance and gymnastic studios also know where to get public-domain music. Finally, music studios have access to libraries of public-domain music if you are interested in constructing your own tapes.

To ease into using music in your classes, experiment. Use a workshop that you teach very often, so you are familiar with the pace, the amount of material normally covered in a day, and the flow of energy throughout the workshop. Use this knowledge as your baseline for comparing the effectiveness of pieces of music.

Start by playing alpha music during the team and individual exercises. If your learners are people you see in class often, they may react negatively to this change in the norm. Soothe their fears with minimal explanations of the research supporting music for increased learning, and move the music source away from any auditory learners who are distracted by it. Turn the music down if the learners complain, but resist removing it completely unless they are very unhappy. If you are able to continue the music, you will find that the learners forget all about it after a very short time.

By the end of the first day, you will probably notice the increase in energy level, retention, and enthusiasm compared with your other classes. After you are more comfortable with the benefit of music, start adding active pieces for coming-in music, break music, lunch music, and going-out music. Use slower and quieter music for review exercises (around 60 bpm) and faster and louder music for exercises (around 80 bpm).

Here are some additional suggestions for incorporating music into your learning events:

• Music used too much loses its effectiveness and the brain tunes it out. Jensen suggests using music no more than 30 percent of the time in the classroom, but I think that depends on the workshop, the learning objectives, and the learners. Limit the music to exercises and review, and leave it off during lecture and discussions.

• CD music is far superior to cassette music. The digital quality is much truer, so the listener hears more of the high frequencies. Best of all, selections can easily be repeated for as long as you need them to be. This allows more flexibility with the experiential activities. It is no longer necessary, as it was with cassette tapes, to find musical pieces that are long enough for each exercise. A small personal CD player with detachable speakers is only slightly more expensive than a cassette player, and it is easier to pack. If you are using a computer for your presentation, you may already have a CD player in the machine. The only downside of using CDS is that the truer sound causes the volume to move between greater extremes, requiring the facilitator to monitor it a little more closely than a cassette tape.

• Kinesthetic learners are influenced almost magically by music, which creates a focus and attention that are rare for these people. Focusing kinesthetic learners is a major benefit for the auditory learners, even if the music does bother them a little.

• Because auditory learners tend to sit in the front of the room and kinesthetic learners tend to sit in the back, move your music source from the front of the room to the back. This is not as convenient for the facilitator, but it is much better for the learners. As you move learners around to different seats, watch out for the ears of your auditory learners. It is really not as difficult as it seems, as there are rarely more than two or three auditory learners in a twenty-learner workshop.

• Avoid music that is very well known. Recognizable music can trigger memories and cause learners to temporarily tune out the learning. For example, Beethoven's "Für Elise" is wonderful for reflection, but so well known, and so often taught in piano classes, that it can be distracting. Purchasing music composed specifically for learning solves some of these problems.

• Walk around the room to test the volume of the music before the learning event, and whenever you switch to new music. All CDS and CD players have different default volumes.

• When you are turning music on or off, manage the transition. Slowly increase the volume when turning it on. When turning music off, initially raise the volume a little before slowly fading the volume off. This gives the learners time to make a transition out of the learning experience. Simply turning it off and on—"acoustical interruptus," as Brewer called it at the 1997 International Alliance for Learning (IAL) conference—is startling to the learners' ears. This takes a little practice to get used to the logistics, but the difference in the learners' ability to make the transition is noticeable.

• Music truly does seem to be a universal voice. In my own experience, it has worked as effectively in other cultures as it does here in my U.S. workshops.

• Place your music source so that it is closest to the left ear of your learners. This way the music does not interfere with the right ear. This only works if the learners are all facing the same way. Because this may rarely be true in an AL classroom, move the music around frequently.

• Put distracting noise sources that you can't get rid of (traffic, lights, air vents) on the left-ear side of learners if possible, keeping it away from the right ear. Listeners who have attention problems or who have to try hard to listen should be closer to your right side so that you can speak more directly into their right ears (right side to right side). Auditory learners tend to sit there automatically.

• Auditory learners are the ones who have the most difficulty learning to music. In fact, it may really jam their intake at first, although they will get used to it after a time. When learners complain about the music, make every attempt to make it better for them without losing the benefit to the rest of the class by moving the source away from them and turning the volume down a little. Turn the speakers to the wall so that the sound is buffered and not so intense.

• Move around the room as you speak so that eventually you speak to every learner's right ear. As you read earlier in the section on Tomatis and in Chapter Five, the right ear is best at retaining logical and linguistic information—it has the quickest path to the left brain. It is especially important to speak to the right ear when teaching technical or analytical learning objectives like computer skills, engineering, and accounting. For these topics, consider a seating pattern for the lecture activity that keeps the right ears toward you as you speak.

• Another technique for a highly left-mode, technical, or analytical topic is to play pieces by Johann Sebastian Bach during the exercises. His music is written with a theme played in multiple ways with multiple rhythms that are logical, linear, and complex, speaking to the linear left side of the learner's brain.

• You will get pressure from learners to play music that they like. Instrumental music is generally not what learners bring in. Do not give in. The music in class is not listening music. The type of music is critical to the success of the learning. In addition, as you read before, it is illegal in a commercial workshop to play music purchased for private use. If you have strong musical aptitude, choose a favorite musical phrase to hum (to yourself) when something in the learning event is making you feel a little reptilian. If you can catch yourself and do this, the little pause can help you regain your balance.

• To change the pace of an intense learning session, find out whose birthday is closest and lead everyone in singing "Happy Birthday," or see if more than one person has the same birthday and sing to them. You may have learned in your statistics class that it takes a group of only twenty or so people to have about a 50 percent chance that two people will share a birthday. Singing actually honors a music therapy principle called isoprinciple, which says that gradual changes in the speed of voice, music, or information presentation can change the mood. Moving from speaking to singing and then back to speaking creates a gradual change that may change the learning energy. If singing is too unsafe for your learners, suggest that they hum instead.

• Many well-known themes can be found in copyright-safe collections, especially on aerobics or dance collections. These themes can be used to empower learners and liven up the mood; they are best for breaks or leaving. These are not pieces that create learning. Their purpose is to energize the participant.

Here is a typical outline of use of music (recordings licensed for public use) in one of my corporate workshops:

1. As learners are coming in, play music that is uplifting, instrumental, and at a tempo of at least 80 bpm. I have found that very energetic music can be too much for people too early in the morning, so it's better to begin with music that is fast in tempo, but not so fast that it jars them.
2. For initial goal setting, play alpha music that is more "invisible" than the opening music. Baroque or classical pieces are useful as learners prioritize learning objectives.
3. During team or individual case study work, play alpha baroque music in the background.
4. The explanation of new material is done through lecture, but for no more than twenty minutes. The learners are encouraged to interact, discuss, comment, and question. There is no music playing.
5. This cycle is repeated for all learning objectives, alternating between team and individual work. For case-study work after lunch, the music is still instrumental, alpha, and at about the same tempo, but it is now new age.

6. For passive review (say, at the end of the day), play alpha music, dim the lights, and ask the learners to silently read and review the learning points projected on a screen.

7. As learners are leaving, play music that is as upbeat, fun, and energizing as it can be.

Instrumental music in major keys, whether energizing or reflective, works best in learning events. Keeping sung music out of the classroom ensures that no one is inadvertently offended by lyrics. It is also easier to find instrumental music for public use. The music played during my experiential learner activities is always instrumental (70–80 bpm), but it moves from baroque or classical pieces in the morning to more modern forms of music, such as new age, in the afternoon. This seems to help with boredom, oversensitization to the music, and basic biological rhythms (Chapter Eight).

CONCLUSION

Music is a magical force that researchers have only begun to understand. Even if it has never been a part of your life, begin to experiment with its power to grow learning. Get yourself a CD player and some learning music, like that found on the CD in this book, and play it while you work. Find the classical music station on your radio and switch to it the next time you are stuck in traffic. Try playing some passive music while your family is settling down in the evening. The results will astound you.

All brain researchers believe that there is more we can do with our brains. Music may hold one of the keys to maximizing our brains; it is one of the unique tools AL brings to the corporate classroom. Using music to learn is really not new; we have all been taught with music. For example, most people find it impossible to say the ABCs as fast as they can sing them.

Why do we stop using music as we "mature"? Ironically, it is the topic that most of my accelerated learning learners are least likely to choose as their learning objective, but the one that they tend to implement first. If you do nothing else, add a little music to your learning and learners.

PERSONAL ACTION PLAN

Please look back through this chapter, and jot down your thoughts below: insights, things you want to do, things you want to remember, games, and quotes. I've added a list of my own to supplement your list. It is better for your learning if you make your own list before you look at mine.

The learning objectives of this chapter were to

- Adopt specific improvements in how you communicate new learning to learners
- Identify how you learn best
- Identify and rethink those personal beliefs of yours that block learning
- Assess your preference for processing new learning to Gardner's multiple intelligences
- Use the multiple intelligences to design the logistical flow of a learning event
- Balance the use of both the left and right sides of the brain for learning
- Maximize memory in self and others for long-term retention
- Use music to create focused learning environments
- Create a personal action plan to increase personal learning and the effectiveness of your delivery of learning events

Your thoughts:

_____

_____

_____

_____

_____

_____

_____

_____

_____

_____

_____

Here are my thoughts:

- Music aligns both sides of the brain and taps into the limbic brain. Because the limbic brain is crucial to long-term retention, music can help increase such outcomes.
- Slower music has the effect of slowing down the pace so learners can focus.
- The best learning occurs through alpha brain waves, which enhance awareness, relaxation, calm, high suggestibility, and creativity in the learner.
- Baroque and classical are the types of music that researchers started looking at to learn how music and learning combine for wonderful effects. Some of these selections encourage the brain waves to change from beta to alpha.
- Lozanov uses music in active concerts to introduce new material and in passive concerts for review.
- Tomatis does extensive research on how sound frequencies affect people and the importance of fluctuating sounds between the right and left ears.
- Our left ears have a longer, less efficient route to the language center of the brain. The right ear has a shorter route to the same language center. Speak into right ears as much as possible.
- Auditory learners are the ones who have the most difficulty learning to music, while kinesthetic learners tend to receive the most benefit.
- Music purchased for personal use is licensed for that use only. Music used in corporate workshops should be purchased for that use from distributors or composers.

How Successful Learning Events Are Built

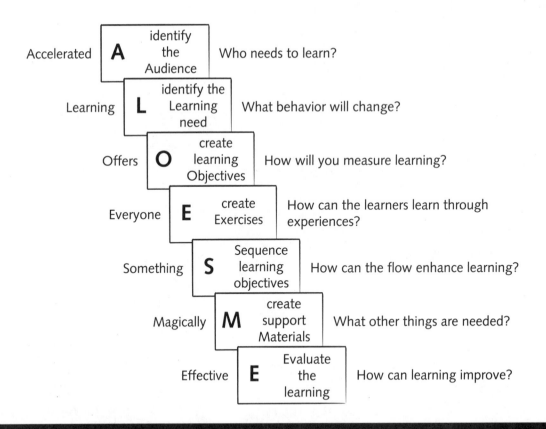

Accelerated	**A** identify the Audience	Who needs to learn?
Learning	**L** identify the Learning need	What behavior will change?
Offers	**O** create learning Objectives	How will you measure learning?
Everyone	**E** create Exercises	How can the learners learn through experiences?
Something	**S** Sequence learning objectives	How can the flow enhance learning?
Magically	**M** create support Materials	What other things are needed?
Effective	**E** Evaluate the learning	How can learning improve?

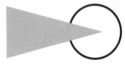

THE LEARNING OBJECTIVES OF CHAPTER 10

After reading this chapter, you will be able to

- Adopt specific improvements in how you communicate new learning to learners

- Construct and manage effective learning objectives for a learning event

- Adjust your intake styles to communicate more effectively with learners

- Use the multiple intelligences to design the logistical flow of a learning event

- Balance the use of both the left and right sides of the brain for learning

- Define the three primary functions (triune) of the brain in a learning event

- Maximize memory in self and others for long-term retention

- Develop classroom learning events to meet a specific learning need

- Measure the effectiveness of a learning event

- Create a personal action plan to increase personal learning and the effectiveness of your delivery of learning events

CHAPTER 10

Developing Learning Events

Because it is easy, you might be tempted to create and use inappropriate games. For example, you might try to use Jeopardy for teaching the Heimlich maneuver.

—S. Thiagarajan

Up to this point, you have learned many things about how people learn. But to truly accelerate learning, that's not enough. I have attended sessions by experienced trainers who are doing brilliant research in the field of learning but can't seem to design a learning event so that learning can occur. You have probably attended sessions where you were lectured to for an hour about alternatives to lecture. In this book or elsewhere, you have learned how to write behavioral and measurable learning objectives. Learning objectives help, but they are not enough either.

This chapter is dedicated to the nuts and bolts of creating and implementing learning events. In Part One, you read about the basics of how people learn: learning objectives, intake, processing, brain function, and memory. In Part Two, you read about how to successfully deliver learning through your own beliefs, the learning environment, and music. Part Three will focus on building successful learning events. In this chapter, you will learn a process to combine learning objectives, learner diversity, and environment for effective growth.

In this chapter especially, it is very important that you learn by doing. You will be coached to work on a real learning gap that you have in your business and create a dynamic AL event.

Think of a workshop that you need to design, a presentation that you need to make, or just part of a workshop you already teach that you have trouble with. The medium (live, video, computer, or Internet) doesn't matter; this approach will still work well. If you can't think of anything real to practice with while you read this chapter, here are some common business learning gaps for you to consider adopting for the purposes of this chapter:

- Help people become mindful of their own lack of customer service.
- Teach people how to construct a correct algebraic formula using Microsoft Excel.
- Teach people how to prioritize their time more effectively.

If you practice as instructed at each step, you will become a strong and valuable course developer. If you simply read each step, you may not.

The process that this chapter explores is called the *learner-first approach*. It is a process I have developed and tested as a synthesis of academic and corporate development processes. You will read about and practice each of the steps you see in the diagram on page 206 and then read how to ensure that your learning event is aligned to the needs of the business.

Memory is strengthened by review, as you learned in Chapter Six. Before going on, in order to honor your own learning style, say "accelerated learning offers everyone something magically exciting" a couple of times to yourself, or write it down on a piece of scrap paper. Go over it until you are comfortable that you have retained it. It's a mnemonic for the learner-first model of accelerated learning. Practice reciting the seven steps of the model after you read about each step.

IDENTIFY THE AUDIENCE

Accelerated Learning Offers Everyone Something Magically Exciting.

The first word of the mnemonic, *Accelerated,* begins with an A and is italicized to help you remember the **A** component of the learner-first approach: **A**udience. The first step of the learner-first approach is to identify the audience: figure out who has the learning gap that you have been asked by the business to help close.

There are four audiences to consider when you are creating a learning event: (1) the learner (the person who needs to learn), (2) the buyer (the person who writes the check), (3) the scheduler (the person who manages the logistics of the event), and (4) the supervisor or manager (the person the learner reports to).

One person may play multiple roles, or more than one person may play one of these roles. For example, there may be one learner while the supervisor, buyer, and scheduler are the same person. In another situation, you may have multiple learners, multiple buyers, multiple schedulers, and multiple supervisors. Depending on the situation, you may find that you are dealing with one person or more than four.

In many course-development models, the developer focuses primarily on the learning gap of the learner. In corporate training, this can be a fatal mistake. The buyer, the scheduler, and the supervisor have needs to be met that are as important to the learning as the needs of the learner are. For example, it is possible for learners to feel that they have had their learning needs met in a workshop even while several disconnects occur:

- The supplies arrive at the wrong location, causing the scheduler a lot of extra work.
- The buyer is billed for a higher price than originally agreed to.
- The supervisor does not get the skills or knowledge desired for the team.

If any of these problems occur, whether with an external training company or an internal training organization, the learning may fade because of negative reinforcement back in the trenches. In addition, you will not get return business.

 PRACTICE

First, write a brief statement of the situation, the learning gap, you chose at the beginning of the chapter:

_____

Next, answer these questions:

1. Who are your customers (learner, buyer, scheduler, supervisor)?

_____

_____

2. What does each of them want to achieve? What will satisfy each one?

_____

_____

_____

3. What are the issues that you must be aware of as you proceed?

_____

_____

Clarity as to the customers of a learning event is critical to successful learning and to successful business performance improvement. Taking a little time at the beginning of learning-event development ensures that you are connected to the needs of the business.

IDENTIFY THE LEARNING NEED

Accelerated *Learning* Offers Everyone Something Magically Exciting.

In the second step of the learner-first development approach, we turn to the **L** component: the **Learning** need. The course developer determines what the business problem is that the company is trying to solve with the learning event. Business problems can be broken down into three major categories:

1. Increase **Revenue**
2. **Avoid Cost**
3. Improve **Service**

(To remember these categories, use the mnemonic *IRACIS,* the name of the ancient Greek goddess of business reasons!)

In other words, some gap in skills, knowledge, or attitude is preventing the company from increasing revenue, avoiding cost, or improving service (a quicker way to think of these is MMM: **Make More Money**). As for not-for-profit organizations, they must **Make Enough Money** (MEM) to wisely spend their funds. In addition, companies often have to implement strategies to deal with a changed government regulation or as a reaction to competition.

Here are some examples of how learning events might help:

Increase revenue. When new products are released, the sales staff has trouble adjusting quickly. If the sales staff could learn about the products faster, the company could increase its sales revenue.

Avoid cost. The average project in a company is delivered with an 80 percent overrun on time and cost. If the project teams could learn to manage the projects more effectively, this cost overrun could be lessened.

Improve service. Customers of a call center are getting so annoyed with the service representatives' treatment of them that they are switching to competitors. If the service reps could learn to communicate more effectively with the customers on the phone, the business would improve service and keep its customers.

Government regulation. The government has issued a ruling that all manufacturing staff must attend one hour of safety training per quarter. If the company can hold one workshop quarterly for all one hundred members of the manufacturing staff, it can efficiently meet the regulation and avoid costly fines.

Competition. The competition has just announced that it will now provide customers with a special computer and modem to link them into a system that will take their orders automatically. Your company believes it can do them one better if it can deliver an Internet Website, which will allow customers to place orders without any special computer or software. Right now, no one on staff has the skills to develop such a site.

PRACTICE

For the situation you chose at the beginning of the chapter, determine what the business reasons (the learning needs) are for this learning event. Consider that there is probably more than one.

Increase revenue:

_____

_____

Avoid cost:

_____

_____

Improve service:

_____

_____

Government regulation:

_____

_____

Competition:

_____

_____

Business reasons must drive learning objectives in corporate training. Not only does this approach make the learning events easier to sell but it also ensures that the money being invested in the learning event produces a good return for the company. Focusing on business reasons helps guarantee that the learners will learn what is need-to-know, not nice-to-know.

By clearly documenting the business reasons, the course developer will also have the criteria required to go back after the learning event and assess the return on investment. These business criteria also help the course developer clearly explain what other changes must take place in the business for the training to be effective. Chapter Twelve discusses how these business reasons driving learning objectives are used to evaluate the success of learning events.

The first two steps of the learner-first method, "identify the **A**udience" and "identify the **L**earning need," are what people mean when they say they are doing a needs analysis. The scope of a needs analysis can be very broad (determine the needs or gaps present in the entire company), or very specific (determine the needs for a particular audience group). Nailing down the scope of a needs analysis is pretty tough to do because it is difficult to predict how long it will take and to know when you are done. Many rookie course developers have been lost to the dreadful disease of analysis paralysis. In the next couple of paragraphs, you will read about how to control creeping scope.

The issue is how to do "good enough" needs analysis. When a supervisor is looking for help with a performance problem, there is not a lot of tolerance for analysis time. Course developers must be able to move quickly through the needs analysis without compromising much of the learning, though focus on speed means some quality will be lost. Difficult times demand difficult choices. Here are some time-saving tips:

• Trust your instincts and your experiences. As a course developer, you will often see things that you have seen before. Know when to jump to a solution, but also know how to ask the right questions to make sure you've jumped to the right solution.

• Don't be afraid to look at other people's outlines for content. I browse many of the public course offerings that come through my in basket to see what other developers think should be the content of topics, such as working in teams, negotiating, conflict resolution, and so on. This is market research and is not the same thing as plagiarizing other people's course materials, which is illegal and unethical.

- Interview a top performer and a less stellar performer (but don't let them know why you picked them). You are shooting for 70–80 percent competency in a workshop. Use these two people and their performances to quickly identify the learning needs.
- As long as it meets the needs, use as much of your existing course material as possible. If you keep your existing material in small reusable chunks, the pieces can be easily reassembled as needed. Using learning objectives to organize the chunks helps make the small pieces cohesive and easier to pull and plug together.
- Keep asking yourself, *Is this learning objective need-to-know or nice-to-know?* There is no time for nice-to-know learning in business today.
- Consider buying games and simulations, or mixing purchased materials with homegrown. Again, be sure that you have not compromised a learning objective. Be careful buying games and simulations, though. It is always tempting to let a really fun exercise sway you from the real learning objective.
- Even within need-to-know, there are various levels, and shrinking the duration of a learning event may mean that some need-to-know must be cut out as well. Consider prioritizing your learning needs as you create them: rate them A = must have, B = should have, and C = could delay and do later or not at all. If you are under the gun to deliver, focus your efforts on top priority needs exclusively.

After you have done a good-enough needs analysis, you can roughly estimate how long the project will take. Table 10.1 gives guidelines—and estimates of my own—for planning how long a learning-event development project will take.

Bear in mind that 40–60 percent of your total time will be spent in identifying the audience, identifying the learning need, and creating learning objectives.

In addition, certain other factors can add time:

- Multiple organizational areas with multiple subject-matter experts, especially if they are feuding.
- Meetings with more than one person.
- Multiple geographic locations for customers.
- Technology of any kind. Video, Internet, and computer-based training take substantially more development time (perhaps as much as one hundred hours for each hour of instruction). These media should be used only for learning that won't need to be changed often.

TABLE 10.1. Estimating Development Time Per Hour of Instruction.

For each hour of classroom time

If . . .	and . . .	and . . .	then plan on . . .
You are starting from scratch	the material is very new to you	you have no subject-matter expert to ask	35 hours of development time
You are starting from scratch	the material is very new to you	you do have a subject-matter expert to ask	25 hours of development time
You are starting from scratch	you know something about the material	you do have a subject-matter expert to ask	15 hours of development time
You are starting from scratch	you are an expert on the material	you do have a subject-matter expert to ask	10 hours of development time
30–70 percent of the material exists			10 hours of development time
70 percent or more of the material exists			5 hours of development time

PRACTICE

For the learning-gap situation you chose at the beginning of the chapter, determine the following.

How much expertise do you have in the topic?

_____

_____

How much existing course material can be used?

_____

_____

Will there be other people involved?

How much of their time will you need?

Will you have any trouble getting that time from them?

Are there any other constraints that might slow the project down?

How long do you estimate it will take from start to finish to implement the learning event?

You now have all the information you need to create a contract with your learners. In the next section of this chapter, you will read about the most critical part of course development: writing appropriate, concrete, and measurable learning objectives. You have seen how to use them in class, and now you will read about how to construct them.

CREATE LEARNING OBJECTIVES

Accelerated Learning *Offers* Everyone Something Magically Exciting.

Once the business reason is clear and the needs are understood, the learning **O**bjectives can be created by clearly stating the audience and the behavior you will be able to observe during the learning event. The objectives provide direction for the course developer, the facilitator, and the learner. They are the core, around which the entire learning experience is built.

Creating learning objectives can also be time consuming. In order to simplify the process, here is a pared-down version of more academic approaches to creating objectives. In this section, you will learn how to create good learning objectives by specifying the ABCD: audience, behavior, condition, and degree.

A = audience   Who will be learning? Who is this objective geared toward? (See first step of the learner-first approach.)

B = behavior   What will the learner be able to do differently, and how? How will the facilitator know?

C = condition   What will the environment be where the learning is needed?

D = degree   What amount (degree) of performance is required by the business?

The Audience

In the first step, you analyzed your learning-event audience and customers. As you have read, the more specifically you understand your learners, the more effective the learning experience will be.

As an example of a problem with not defining the audience completely, consider developing a software testing workshop. From a marketing standpoint, it's great if this class can be sold not just to computer programmers but also to their software clients. Unfortunately, from a learning standpoint, these two groups have very different learning needs for this topic. Programmers need very detailed testing techniques and plans, while software clients need an overview of the testing that should be done and of the impact on their schedules. If you try to develop one class to meet these divergent needs, each group will like and dislike different parts. The workshop will be more successful written as two separate workshops for the two audiences. A single learning event really can't serve that many masters.

The earlier section in this chapter on "Identify the Audience" provided you with specific questions to consider in defining the audience. It is also a good idea to look at the types of learning styles that are prevalent for a particular audience; for example, graphic designers tend to be more visual than the average person. In Chapters Three, Four, and Five you learned how to do this.

Here's another example of why material focused on a specific audience matters so much. Suppose you have a need to learn project-management skills. You are given the choice of attending either a five-day public workshop with one hundred other learners or a one-on-one session for a day with the informal guru of project management at your company. Personality issues aside, most learners would pick the guru if they felt they had a true need to learn. Why? There is no time in business today to sort through a lot of information that is not relevant to your situation. Learners want *their* questions answered, not someone else's. Trying to create a workshop for everyone, like a generic project-management class, risks degrading the learning for everyone.

The Behavior

What good facilitators really want is that the learners learn. But learning can take many forms and happen in degrees, and with varying progressions. For example, not everyone at your company needs to be an expert at depreciating fixed assets. Your business likely requires that the accountants be experts in depreciation, but the managers only need to be aware of it as they manage their budgets, and some line workers don't need to know about it at all. The learning event created for a specific audience must facilitate learning at the degree required for the staff member.

How do developers of learning events begin to define the behavior completely? You have already started the process by identifying the learning need. Many educators have researched the acquisition and levels of knowledge over the years. For example, in 1956 Benjamin Bloom saw learning as a hierarchy from basic to complex, which came to be known as Bloom's taxonomy. In 1974, Robert Gagne grouped learning into five parallel types. The big difference between the two was that Bloom believed you learned and taught from basic to complex, but Gagne believed the sequence of learning could start anywhere and depended on the learning style of the learner. Bloom went on with others in 1964 to research what motivates people to learn. Recognition of the importance of learning physical skills prompted Elizabeth Simpson in 1966 to prepare a list of characteristics of the "psychomotor domain" (Heinich, Molenda, and Russell, 1989).

So what? The learning objectives specify the behavior the learner will be able to demonstrate after the learning has occurred. For example, will it be sufficient to spout back the steps of saving a file in Microsoft Word, or will learners be able to figure out Save by using the Help function, or will they have to be able to do it without any help? The learning objectives need to define what the behavior is and how proficient it needs to be.

Focus the learning objective on the three types of learning that can occur:

1. Will the learner have a new *skill*? Will the learner be able to do something new?
2. Will the learner have new *knowledge*? What level of expertise will the learner have?
3. Will the learner have a new *attitude*? Will the learner have a new belief?

Most learning in business requires all three, but attitude is the most prevalent need—and the most difficult learning to facilitate. Let's say your business has a group of managers who are having problems managing their projects. Their bosses would like the managers to be taught how to get projects done on time, with high quality and within the budget.

The next list contains the behavior changes the bosses would like to see after training. As you read through the list, notice that the most important outcomes, the ones that most closely map to the needs of the business, are the ones involving attitudinal learning. In fact, if the managers don't believe in project management, they will never open up enough to learn the knowledge and skills specified in the first three.

- The managers will be able to use Microsoft Project to document and track their projects. (Knowledge, skill)
- The managers will have the ability to create a correct critical-path diagram. (Knowledge, skill)
- The managers will have the ability to estimate hours for project resources. (Knowledge, skill)
- The managers will choose to take the time to create the above project-management deliverables. (Attitude)
- The managers will believe in the value of project management. (Attitude)

As you ask your customers to describe how the behaviors will change after a learning event, many will list skills and knowledge, forgetting about attitude. As you gather the needs, ask questions to ensure that the customers have considered all the learning needs.

 LEARNING POINT

Most business learning needs are usually involved with attitude. Although course developers in corporate training focus on teaching lots of skills and knowledge, they are usually really trying to teach attitude under the guise of skills and knowledge. In terms of classroom learning time, the type of learning determines the amount of time required:

- *Skill* requires the least time to learn.
- *Knowledge* demands a little more time to learn.
- *Attitude* requires even more time to learn.

The learning objectives describe the behavior change desired from the learner after the learning event. Statement of an objective includes an action verb. It is something the learner, not the facilitator or someone else, will do. It is something that the learner can demonstrate and the facilitator can observe. It is something that is needed by the business for the learner to be more valuable.

Learning objectives are written with observable behavior. What will the behavior look like after learning? Here are some examples of good action verbs for observing behavior change:

apply	categorize	compare
complete	conduct	construct
defend	define	demonstrate
describe	design	evaluate
identify	install	modify
outline	predict	prepare
revise	select	specify
state	time	verify

Here are some verbs that don't work well for learning objectives because the behavior can't be observed:

appreciate	believe
know	understand

Here's a good example of a learning objective that measures behavior change:

> After completing the workshop, the supervisor will be able to apply the five coaching questions to a job feedback session.

Writing learning objectives for attitude learning still requires verbs that can be observed. Here's a list:

appraise	contrast	criticize
demonstrate	detect	discriminate
justify	practice	

Notice how the action expressed by these verbs can be practiced and tested. A good example of a learning objective for attitude learning is

> After completing the workshop, the supervisor will be able to contrast the benefits of 180- and 360-degree feedback.

Condition

The condition specifies what the environment will be when the learner demonstrates the behavior. To put it more in real-world terms, the condition describes what will be in the work environment as the behavior is performed:

- What tools will be used during the application of the newly learned behavior?
- What timing or sequencing is required?
- What job aids will be available to help?
- What equipment will be used?
- What things can the learner not depend on?

Building on our last example, the learning objective might be

> After completing the workshop, the supervisor will be able to apply the five coaching questions to a job feedback session by consulting the reference card.

Here is an example of specifying what the learner cannot depend on:

> After completing the workshop, the supervisor will be able to apply the five coaching questions to a job feedback session *from memory.*

In the learning event, the supervisors will practice and demonstrate applying the five coaching questions to a simulated job feedback session strictly from memory. They cannot depend on the reference card or any other job aid.

Sometimes conditions make a lot of sense, but they aren't always needed. Putting arbitrary conditions in a learning objective is as detrimental to the learning as having no learning objective at all. Adding this condition to the end of this example doesn't help at all:

> After completing the workshop, the supervisor will be able to apply the five coaching questions to a job feedback session while sitting at a desk.

You may also have to specify how proficient the learners need to be in the new behavior. Often there is a business requirement to be able to perform some act in a specific amount of time or to a specific level of quality. An example might be

> The customer service representative will enter completely correct orders into the accounts receivable system 75 percent of the time.

Put another way, 25 percent of the time a bill entered into the business system will be inaccurate. The practice and reinforcement that goes on in a workshop that is shooting for 75 percent accuracy is different from the learning for 100 percent, or even 20 percent, accuracy.

There is a wonderful saying: we value what we measure. Many ridiculous stories attest to how the wrong metrics and measurements can accidentally create behavior in individuals and teams that is counterproductive to the needs of the company. Specifying a meaningless degree in a learning objective has the same effect. If the learning objectives are wrong, so is the learning.

Training managers can easily track the long-term value of training if a degree is specified. Learning objectives can be mapped to dollars in added productivity from hours saved. For example, if a customer service representative raises her productivity from 50 to 75 percent, there is a real return in dollars.

However, it is often very difficult to specify degree. How do you measure the accuracy of a person's time-management or leadership ability? In some cases it may be possible to use a comparison to quantify the learning objectives that are hard to measure. For example:

> The supervisor will be able to list his or her top three leadership strengths when compared to a list of Abraham Lincoln's leadership characteristics.

There has been a tendency with some overly ambitious course developers to embed meaningless degrees (numbers) in their objectives. Often this is a marketing ploy, not a learning enabler. For example:

> The trainer will learn forty-seven ways to open a workshop.

Stipulating forty-seven has no relevance to a real-world learning gap. Why not twenty-three? Fourteen? Three? Learners resent learning objectives that sound irrelevant, disconnected, and marketing-oriented.

In summary, here is an example of good and bad learning objectives, using audience, behavior, condition, and degree (ABCD):

(Bad) After completing this course, the learner (A) will be able to understand why stress management is important (B).

(Good) After completing this course, the supervisor (A) will be able to list at least three ways (D) stress has a negative impact on performance (B) on the job (C).

Let's look at the bad example. Notice that although the first objective weakly specifies an audience and a behavior, it does not specify a condition or degree. The vagueness may create varying expectations in the learners and their managers, and will make it very difficult to observe whether the learning has occurred. Some of the unanswered questions: "Will this workshop be relevant to the stress in all aspects of my life, including my personal life? Will it help me save my marriage? Will it make my children behave? Will it help me get over the stress I have because of the idiot manager I work for?"

The audience is vague and undefined, which suggests that the workshop is going to try to be all things to all people. The behavior that is stated as "understand" is impossible to measure. You can ask people if they understand something, but you (and they) may not really know. Objectives need to focus on outcomes that can be observed during the training event and encourage learning that is needed on the job.

The good example fixes these problems. The audience has been tightened up: this learning event is specifically geared toward people with supervisory roles. Adding the degree to the behavior makes it easy to create an exercise in the learning event. Framing the condition in terms of the job helps avoid developing a therapeutic workshop that deals with stress at home in families—and also avoids inadvertently misleading learners.

 PRACTICE

Now you try it! Pretend that you are going to teach someone how to manage his time more effectively. Come up with three learning objectives for this learning event:

1. _____

2. _____

3. _____

Use these criteria to judge the quality of your objectives:

Did I specify the audience? The behavior? Condition? Degree?

_____

_____

Is my objective easily measurable? Easily observable?

_____

_____

Is my objective possible within the constraints of the learning? (For example, have you indicated what media will be addressed? Do you need e-mail, voice mail, or any other technology as part of the condition?)

_____

_____

Here's an answer for comparison (yours may be much better):

After completing this class, the employee (A) will be able to create (B) a to-do list (C) with three categories: highest-priority, high-priority, and low-priority (D).

A final edit should be made to ensure that you have not followed the rules to the detriment of the needs of the business. The effort it takes to write good learning objectives can sometimes distract from the true needs of the business. It is possible to create very tight behavior and conditions for very specific audiences and yet completely miss the reason the workshop is needed.

Bob Mager is _the_ expert at creating good objectives. Mager was a research scientist at Fort Bliss, Texas, focusing on how to improve an existing U.S. Army course. He used the objectives as a contract with the authorities before rolling out a new workshop for comparison with an old one. Later he published a classic book, _Preparing Instructional Objectives_ (1997). When faced with arguments about the value of objectives, Mager wrote, "How do YOU know? Have you ever tried seriously to specify exact objectives for an academic course? Or are you upset simply because what is being suggested sounds like work?" (Mager, 1976, p. 4).

 PRACTICE

Creating learning objectives is probably the most critical step of course development. If this is a trivial exercise for you, you have done it wrong. Spending time here creates accelerated learning; skipping or neglecting creates, at best, accelerated entertainment.

For the situation you chose at the beginning of the chapter, what are the learning objectives?

_____

_____

It is critical to create explicit learning objectives. That said, I recommend that you balance writing the perfect objective with the need to deliver learning in a timely manner. I have seen enthusiastic course developers spend so much time on objectives that they never deliver a learning event. At the other extreme, I have seen enthusiastic course developers do course development without creating learning objectives and forget what learning they were supposed to deliver. Learning objectives will pave the way for more learning when created correctly.

CREATE EXERCISES

Accelerated Learning Offers *Everyone* Something Magically Exciting.

As the italicized word *Everyone* helps you remember, the fourth component of the learner-first approach is the **E**xercise.

People learn best when they try it themselves. I'm sure you are already convinced, but here's an example. Suppose you ask your friend to give you directions. Chances are she will visually describe streets and turns, talking at you about what you will see.

Assume the directions are either completely auditory or auditory with some visual. This does not honor all three intake styles (Chapter Three) or the multiple intelligences (Chapter Four). Depending on your preferences, you may ask her to repeat, you may rush to write everything down, or you may go ask someone else to draw you a map.

Many traditional course-development methodologies encourage course developers to create lecture notes as soon as learning objectives are finished, and then create the exercises. As in all projects, the things that are left for last are done least well. Accelerated learning practitioners believe that learners learn best from experience, so the exercises are the most critical part of the event. In the learner-first approach that you are reading about now, the exercises come before all the other support material, including lecture notes, to ensure that the exercises are well planned and implemented. This way, if the developer runs out of time, she short-changes the lecture instead of the practice.

This is the step in course development that requires the most creativity and that most differentiates AL from traditional classes. The goal is for the learners to be actively involved in the learning 80 percent of the time. No more than 20 percent of the time will be lecture. That said, learners will get exhausted if they are doing exercises for 80 percent of the workshop. In corporate training, learners may feel that the learning facilitator is not adding much value to the learning experience. "Actively involved in learning" includes

- Review sessions (see Chapter Six and the Appendix for examples of reviews)
- Silent reading
- Answering questions from the facilitator
- Trying, on their own, something the facilitator has just demonstrated
- Filling in the blanks on a worksheet
- Discussing pros and cons with the people at their table

Not every experience has to be a huge, complicated exercise. You can simply avoid lecturing for more than twenty minutes at a time without getting the learners actively involved. This section of the chapter will focus on

- Choosing the right exercise
- Creating a learning game or simulation
- Debriefing the exercises

Choosing the Right Exercise

The medium that will be used for the learning event strongly influences which exercises make the most learning sense. For example, playing a game of Clue to discover quality standards will be designed according to whether it will be played alone through Web-based training, through computer-based training, or in a team during a workshop. Each medium carries its own limitations and strengths. In a perfect world, the learning objectives and the optimum exercise to experience the learning should drive the choice of media. In the real world, the available media for the training are often constraints.

It is not uncommon for companies to decide to do all their training with one medium, for cost reasons. When this is the case, it is important to consider the limitations of the media while designing the exercises. Regardless of the medium, the learning event should always honor the learning objectives (earlier in this chapter) and the learners' diversity (Chapters Two through Five).

Matching learning objectives to learner diversity drives your exercise choices. The Appendix can get you started in thinking of creative exercises that honor the multiple intelligences.

 PRACTICE

For the situation you chose at the beginning of the chapter, pick one of your learning objectives (or more than one if they seem to go together):

_____

_____

Using the Appendix, and your own creativity, describe an exercise for your learning objective(s). You may find it necessary to combine several suggestions into one idea of your own.

_____

_____

_____

_____

_____

Creating a Learning Game or Simulation

The difference between a game and a simulation is that the simulation looks more like the real world. This is the best way to learn, because the closer the experience is to the real world, the easier it is to transfer the learning. However, the more similar the experience is to the real world, the more painful the learning may be initially and the greater the chance that learners will not be safe. This can be a challenge to a learning facilitator, because the real-world stress can create a reptilian response during a simulation that's too close to home.

Here are the steps to use when creating a learning game:

- Gather a couple of creative thinkers (they don't have to be training people).
- Review the learning objectives. Spend some time pulling out two or three main things that you would like the learners to learn from the game.
- Brainstorm games that you have played before (Clue, Jeopardy, Pictionary, Trivial Pursuit, The Game of Life, Risk, and so on). Find one that seems to have the type of processing that your learning objectives require, or make up a new one.
- Go back to the learning objectives. Work on the details of the rules until you have the objectives covered.
- Create the debriefing questions, ensuring they are also aligned with the learning objectives (described in the next section of this chapter).
- Play the entire game; then troubleshoot the stumbling points.
- Write up all the rules and directions, watch while novices play the game, and then make necessary changes.

Here's an example. You have been asked to teach a group of professionals the quality standards of the organization. The quality process is lengthy and full of jargon. It specifies multiple techniques and roles that must be honored for a number of situations. The material, a large standards manual, is dry at best. To identify the learning objectives you hope to build the game around, declare that after completing the workshop the professionals will be able to

- Select the correct tasks to implement a quality initiative.
- Identify the roles played in the quality process.
- Match the correct quality technique to the appropriate situation.

You gather your team of brainstormers and start. First, you talk about games that you have played. You settle on the game of Clue. (For those of you who have never played this board game, you move your player through rooms around a board trying to uncover clues to a murder. To win, you have to be able to identify the murderer, the room the murder occurred in, and the weapon used.)

Your team decides that to win the game of "Quality," the winner must be able to identify the correct tasks in the quality process, the correct role(s), and the correct technique(s), given clues to the business situation. Teams of three will play together, and each team will be assigned a name from the board game (such as Colonel Mustard), with a small sign in the corresponding color. Each team will be given a different clue at each round. They will be given the quality standards manual to use as a reference while they try to figure out the clues.

Here is how this game maps to the multiple intelligences:

Intelligence	Aspect of the Game
Interpersonal	The learners work with their team and the class.
Logical/mathematical	There is a defined process and rules.
Spatial/visual	The team colors and the charts with the roles, techniques, and main phases of the quality process are visual.
Musical	Music plays while the teams strategize.
Linguistic/verbal	The written and spoken word are used.
Intrapersonal	The learners read and think by themselves.
Bodily/kinesthetic	The learners move their pieces on a large board.
Emotional	It is fun to play a game from childhood.
Naturalist	Weak; consider plants and flowers in the room, or full windows.
Existential	Weak.

Notice that the bodily/kinesthetic could be weak, but it is easily shored up with a tactile addition such as moving game pieces around on a large board. The only intelligence that is not honored well, other than naturalist, is existential. It would be possible for an individual to play this game and still not change her attitude about the quality process. Therefore, it would be necessary to follow this game with a more intrapersonal, reflective exercise to encourage learners to buy in to the quality process or build an additional simulation that shows the importance of quality.

This is an example of how to design a game. When this game is tried out with real students, you learn more about the logistics—which are much more complex in a game than in a traditional exercise. For example, playing as individuals is much faster than playing as a team, and practice might not show you this problem in advance. In this situation, you might modify the approach so that individuals play within small groups, with several games of "Quality" going on at the same time; you could debrief the entire group at the end.

I encourage you to check out www.thiagi.com because Sivasailam Thiagarajan (who goes by the easier name of Thiagi) is a master of creating wonderful games and simulations. He has written many resources to help you either adapt his games or create your own.

Debriefing Exercises

The learning occurs when people reflect on an experience. While they are in the learning experiences, they don't have time to notice that they are learning. The debriefing is the most important part of the exercise, but it is often the part facilitators and developers devote the least time to. Truth be known, in execution most facilitators wing the debriefing with very little planning.

The purpose of the debriefing is to move the learners to a new state of mind. They entered the learning event with unconscious incompetence—they didn't even know what they didn't know. Slowly, through the learning experience, they become conscious of how little they know. Finally, as the debriefing begins, the learners become conscious of growing more competent. Only with practice in the real world can a learner continue to learn and grow into unconscious competence.

 LEARNING POINT

Thiagi once told me that the debriefing should last at least as long as the exercise. This is where the learning occurs. It is the ethical duty of the facilitator to allow learners to discuss and work through all the emotions associated with the learning before they leave, especially in a competitive setting where teams win and lose.

Debriefing should cover the following:

- What did you do that was successful during the experience? What would you do the same way the next time?
- What did you do that was unsuccessful? What would you change or do differently next time?

This is the starting place for creating debriefing questions. The goal is to stimulate open discussion and learning, so it is important to take it to the next step and make the questions as specific to the learning event as possible. In his game books, Thiagi lists debriefing questions specifically tied to the learning objectives. It is better to have more debriefing questions than you need, because the flow of discussion will change with the group of learners.

For example, consider this learning objective:

> After completing this learning, the project team member will be able to choose between collaboration and competition in a project situation.

Using the two generic questions as a starting point, you might create these questions for the debriefing:

- What did you like about the collaboration of your team during this exercise?
- What did you learn about collaboration that you could use during your work with teams?
- What was the cost of the collaboration to your team? To other teams?
- How could you minimize the cost without losing the benefit during your work with teams?
- What did you like about the competition in your team during this exercise?
- What did you learn about competition that you could use during your work with teams?
- What was the cost of the competition to your team and others?
- How could you minimize the cost of competition without losing the benefit during your work with teams?

As you are creating your initial list, you might think of other questions that would be interesting, such as:

- Do you think it's possible for a team to both compete and collaborate? Why or why not?
- Which (collaboration or competition) has more long-term benefit to a team? Short-term benefit? Why do you think this?
- Did time influence your team's ability either to collaborate or to compete? How?

Sometimes you ask a debriefing question and realize that the learner is resisting the learning for whatever reason. Let's suppose you observed the teams actively competing, and now they claim that they were collaborating. You can't let that go if learning is to occur. You must continue to rephrase your questions, pointing out in a safe way the discrepancies in their observations. Think of yourself as a mirror when you are debriefing—you are reflecting back to the learners things they already know but may not have accepted consciously. It is important to be ready with follow-up questions to lead them to that learning.

Here's a sample dialogue.

FACILITATOR: How'd that last exercise go? Were you successful at collaboration? How do you know?

LEARNERS: Yes, we were very successful at collaborating because we all communicated our needs effectively.

FACILITATOR: I noticed that each of the teams had a very different score at the end. How did you resolve this discrepancy with collaboration? [Notice that the feedback is safe, factual, and nonjudgmental.]

LEARNERS: Maybe we stopped collaborating because of time constraints, and turned competitive at the end. The teams did stop communicating at that time.

FACILITATOR: I also noticed that the teams isolated themselves about five minutes into the simulation. How do these communication patterns influence collaboration?

LEARNERS: That's when we started to get more competitive. We felt that if other people weren't going to share, we weren't going to either. Some trust was lost in that behavior.

Even with thorough debriefing, some people refuse to accept the learning, at least publicly, especially if it's very personal or attitudinal. It is not the role of the facilitator to make learners admit that they have learned, but good debriefing questions can up the odds that they, at least internally, do think differently.

Success or failure in an exercise just drives which direction the debriefing questions come from. In that sense, no simulation or game can fail. For example, suppose you open a project-management workshop with this team exercise. Teams are each assigned one piece of data (for example, name, occupation, learning goal, and the like) to get from everyone else in the room within a very challenging time frame (say, three minutes). Team one might get everyone's name, team two everyone's occupation, and so forth.

Normally, competition erupts right away and the teams jump up and start running around trying to gather their data, no matter what the other teams are trying to do. Once in awhile, someone will stand up and convince everyone to collaborate so the teams can easily accumulate the data they need, but this is rare. When collaboration occurs, the usual debriefing questions don't work, because there is no competition. Instead, you must be prepared to debrief about what went well and how this is different than what happens to them at their real jobs.

In summary, here is a checklist for success in creating debriefing questions:

- Plan to spend a significant amount of time creating debriefing questions. You should have twice as many questions as you think you will need.
- Start with the generic debriefing questions as a starting point; discuss the good and the bad of the exercise.
- Include questions that map the learning to real-life settings: How would this transfer?
- Don't ask yes or no questions, unless it's for a show of hands to get started.
- Consider using words that generate more thinking: *what, how, why.*
- Be prepared to use different debriefing questions in each class. The learners, learning, and context will be new, so the debriefing will be as well. Do not stick to a script.
- When you are debriefing, never avoid emotions. Air out all that is negative and draw out all that is positive. Negative emotions stifled will hinder the learning (perhaps forever) on that particular topic.
- Don't challenge an answer directly, even if you truly believe the learner is wrong. For example, never say, "That's not what I saw happen." Instead, ask more questions to get them to discover the learning themselves or allow other learners to chime in.
- Catch people in their beliefs, and reflect the beliefs back gently with active listening. For example, "Let me see if I understand. I think I hear you saying that your company's culture prevents you from collaborating. Is that what you believe?" Contrast this to the confrontational question "You think your company prevents you from collaborating?" Use *I* instead of *you* whenever possible.
- Don't give up. Be prepared to ask the same question from multiple directions when your class clams up. For example, the question "What did you like about collaboration?" could also be asked as:

"Let's brainstorm all the pros and cons of collaboration on the flipchart."
"Collaboration has some unique benefits—what did you experience?"
"Where do you see a lot of collaboration around you at work?"
"How did the other teams that you interacted with collaborate?"

• If the answers are not what you expected

Play hotter-and-colder: "That's not what I'm looking for. . . . yes, that's getting
   hotter. . . ."
Ask the learner to say more to clarify.
Ask others to comment after a period of silence to think through the point made.
Walk learners through their logic, and point them toward a better answer.
Rephrase the question.
Give credit for a nice try, and then quickly move on.
Give partial credit or a prize for trying.

• Let the learners come up with the debriefing questions to use to facilitate a discussion by

Asking the learners to generate the open-ended questions to be asked.
Asking learners to link ideas to other subjects (for example: How is project man-
   agement like a surprise birthday party? Both have a beginning and an end).
Having teams of learners brainstorm as many questions as they can in five minutes.
Having a contest for the "ultimate" question.

• Let the learners debrief each other. Have each team share a lesson learned after
the debriefing. Some ways to do this are

Having learners ask each other open-ended questions.
Having teams of learners create written questions for other teams.

PRACTICE

For the learning game that you've just created or the exercise you designed earlier, design at least five debriefing questions.

1. _____

2. _____

3. _____

4. _____

5. _____

Validate your list against the checklist above. Adjust as needed.

In summary, the best learning occurs when the learner discovers it himself or herself through an experience and then has time to reflect about what has happened. Learning is not limited to a classroom—it can happen through online discussion, a simulation, a book group, or an informal brown-bag lunch discussion. Open your mind to the many creative ways of accelerating learning (see the Appendix for ideas).

SEQUENCE LEARNING OBJECTIVES

Accelerated Learning Offers Everyone *Something* Magically Exciting.

The fifth (S-) step of the learner-first approach is to figure out the **S**equence—that is, in what order to cover the learning objectives. There is a sense or intuition about sequencing that comes from experience in the classroom. That said, there are a couple of helpful hints that will help you learn from others' experience if you have not had much classroom experience up to this point.

Backward chaining is a concept that flips traditional sequencing. Many educators have found that starting with the outcome will accelerate the learning in the classroom. If learners understand *why* they are learning something, it is easier for them to digest the steps along the way.

For example, suppose you are creating an introduction to word processing for your executives. Most course developers would probably start by demonstrating to the learners what all the keys on the keyboard do and what all the drop-down menus mean. These little pieces of information, out of context, are very difficult for a learner to retain.

Backward chaining suggests, instead, that you teach from the end. Here's an example of how this approach works. When the executives get to their computers, there is a piece of paper there telling them to "Push the ENTER key." When they do so, a personalized letter comes out of the printer next to them, welcoming them to class. The learning facilitator then shows the executives the steps and drop-down menus to get the letter to print again. The next thing the learning facilitator shows them is how to change the name on the letter and print it again. Finally, the last thing the facilitator does is show them how to create a new letter. Margins, spell check, formatting, and other topics are introduced in context as needed or as requested by the learners.

 LEARNING POINT

When creating learning flow or working out the glitches of an existing learning event, think about answering this question first: "*Why* does the learner need to know this?" Start by letting learners experience the end result. Then, working backward, show them how to get there themselves. Or, thinking in metaphorical terms, sketch the outlines of the picture before painting in the detail.

The quite natural thought that you should define terminology first turns out to work more poorly than introducing terminology in context. In technical modeling classes, it is typical to spend the first half-day on symbols and terms. Instead, using AL with backward chaining, the facilitator covers a complete model with the learners, first showing the usefulness of the model and introducing symbols and terms at the same time. This approach makes complex material much less intimidating, takes far less time, and gives learners help linking the new knowledge to existing knowledge in their memory (see Chapter Six).

PRACTICE

For the situation you chose at the beginning of the chapter, consider a learning objective with multiple steps, or work on the flow of all the objectives. Sequence the learning using backward chaining. A worksheet has been provided for you here. Start by defining the end result. Work backward for as many steps as it takes until you can define the first step. You may not need all the steps that have been provided, and that's OK. If you need more, you may have too large a learning objective to cover as one topic.

End result:

_____

_____

Steps, chaining backward:

10. _____

9. _____

8. _____

7. _____

6. _____

5. _____

4. _____

3. _____

2. _____

First step:

_____

_____

CREATE SUPPORT MATERIALS

Accelerated Learning Offers Everyone Something *Magically* Exciting.

The next-to-last step of the learner-first approach is to figure out what **M**aterials you will need to supplement the exercise, so that the learning objectives are achieved by the learners. Today, you have myriad choices of support materials. In this section, you will read about creating

- User guides, reference manuals, learner guides, and prerequisite work
- Presentation media
- Facilitator notes
- Learning-event supplies

User Guides, Reference Manuals, Learner Guides, and Prerequisite Work

Learner documentation and prerequisite work can require a lot of preparation time. It is important to be clear about the benefits of each and plan your time accordingly. There are three types of printed learner material: user guides, reference manuals, and learner guides. Confusion occurs when course developers try to make one document meet the needs of all three.

User Guides

A user's guide is created to answer the learner's questions about the topic she is trying to learn. It is designed to be used on the job by a novice learner who might not even know the right way to ask the question she needs answered. An example would be the user manual that comes with your VCR. Mini–user guides may also take the form of a job aid—an abbreviated "help" document. Software packages often come with a user's guide. It is designed to be used alone, without a learning facilitator.

Reference Manuals

A reference manual is created to answer learners' questions about a topic they already have some experience with. It assumes that the learner will be able to format the correct question and will know what to call it so as to look up the term. For example,

Microsoft Word Online Help is a form of online reference manual. If you want to know how to put the contents of a table in alphabetical order by last name, it will be difficult to find the answer unless you know you should use the term Sort. Like a user's guide, a reference manual is designed to be used alone.

Learner Guides

A learner guide, often called a student workbook, is created to supplement the facilitator's presentation of the topic, the discussion, and the experiences in the learning event. It assumes the learner will use it primarily in class and is designed to be a supplement to, not a replacement for, the learning event. In corporate training, it is pretty much standard to provide a copy of the visuals, exercises, and resources and a place to take notes, all together as the learner guide. The learner guide is not the class. The guide, learners, facilitator, and context make up the class, so just reading the learner guide does not meet the learning objectives.

When you try to create all three—user guides, reference manuals, and learner guides—in one document, you will find that you are trying to meet too many goals at once. You may have experienced the frustration of trying to listen to an instructor while scanning a full page of book-size text. It splits your focus. Supplementary learner documentation should be designed differently if its goal is to be used alone rather than during a learning event. Instead, when needed, provide user guides and reference manuals for the learners to use during exercises; that way, you are helping to acclimate learners to materials they can use to continue learning on their own after the learning event ends.

Certainly, learners (visual learners, anyway) would like an easy way to find specific material and notes once they get back to their jobs. We have experimented with providing indexes in the back of our learner guides, but feedback has told us that people really don't use them much. Visual people seem to be able to remember and find what they are looking for after the fact, and auditory and kinesthetic people rarely take the book out again.

It is valuable, though, to put a resource list in a learner guide; include book, article, and Web references for continuing learning. Glossaries are also very useful, especially in technical workshops. Ask your learners to flip back and add to the glossary any terms that they ask about. Doing so helps stimulate their multiple intelligences to maximize retention of the new term.

When laying out learner guides, remember Chapter Six on memory. Every page should have the following:

- Visuals to link to the learner's memory.
- For text, minimum of 18 point type for overheads (Times Roman is easiest to read in lowercase).
- For titles, minimum of 24 point type (Arial is good for titles).
- No more than three fonts (for example, Times Roman, Arial, Helvetica; bold and italics count as an additional font).
- Honor the design quadrant (see Exhibit 10.1).
- Include copyright information if needed.
- Include logo and company information if needed.
- Follow a standard format (title always in same place, margins the same, and so on).

During review sessions in class, it is amazing to see how the visual learners rebuild memory from the visual that was on the page. The visual learners stare up toward the ceiling and say things like "OK, I can see the little man on the left of the page, and the bullet point says. . . ." The visual does not have to be fancy; it just has to be meaningful to the content of the message. In fact, if the graphic is too fancy it may distract from the content.

If your learner guide is modular and reusable, it will be easier for you to create new, customized learning events when needed. Store each unit, roughly tied to one or two learning objectives, in its own separate file on a computer disk.

The learner guide should follow a standard template, similar to this one:

- Preliminary unit: title, table of contents, learning objectives
- For each unit:
  Page 1: table of contents for the unit
  Learning material (headings match unit table of contents)
  Summary page
- Last unit: overall summary, bibliography, glossary
- Appendix unit (if needed)
- Exercise unit

Prerequisite Work

Prerequisite work can take many forms:

- Prereading assignments
- Preworkshop worksheets (especially useful for assessments, evaluations, and so on)
- Prerequisite workshops
- Background information

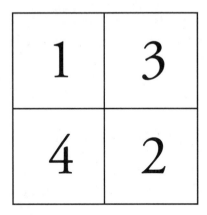

Without color or graphics, the U.S. learner's eye will travel in this order (from 1 to 2 to 3, and maybe 4 if boredom hasn't set in) on a page. The most important information should be in the top left (such as headings), and the least important in the lower left (maybe nothing). If you are putting important information elsewhere on the page, use graphics or color consciously to move the eye where you want it to focus, to direct attention to what's important:

- Use pictures to get more attention. Make important information stand out by showing it as a picture.
- Repeat the same cues (arrows, frames, instructions) to direct attention.
- Use a bit of bright color to attract attention, but remember that too much is distracting.
- The eye is drawn to change and movement. Emphasize what is important by making it colored, larger, underlined, or moving, depending on the medium.

EXHIBIT 10.1. Sample Learner Guide Layout.

Prereading assignments are wonderful to level the playing field in the learning event, but few people take the time to get them done. In fact, most try to read them quickly while waiting for class to begin. If it is necessary for you to use prereading assignments, you run into the problem that some in the class will read them and some won't. You may have to have a creative way for people to catch up, such as a team scavenger hunt (see the Appendix for more information about this). The challenge is finding a technique so that the people who did the work won't feel used by the people who didn't. It may be more useful to pass out reading material after class or between days of classes.

Preworkshop worksheets can be useful to minimize the time that must be spent together. For example, a leadership workshop might ask each learner to create a personal time line before the class begins. Again, any work expected before class can make a person who didn't get to it, didn't notice it, or basically didn't do it feel unsafe, which hinders learning for everyone. Unless there is a manager who actively makes everyone get it done, prerequisite work is rarely completely done before a corporate workshop.

Prerequisite workshops sound like a good idea, but they are challenging to implement. When you create a curriculum with this type of dependency, the facilitators are usually left to deal with the wrong people showing up. Instead, design your workshops to be as stand-alone as possible; use unique material and minimize the need for prerequisite workshops.

Presentation Media

Here are some pointers about common presentation media. Currently, the informal business standard for creating course materials is Microsoft PowerPoint. This powerful software tool allows you to create overheads, slides, or personal computer (PC) projection presentations. (There are some relevant additional guidelines on use of color in Chapter Eight.) Consider the audience and the environment where you will be offering the learning event. Which delivery mode works best for your specific need? (See Table 10.2.)

Facilitator Notes

If you purchase training material from a supplier, you can expect to get very, very detailed facilitator notes. I have seen facilitator notes that were so detailed they included the questions the instructor should ask and the answers the learners would give. They were also so long that few facilitators ever took the time to read them. The key is to have notes that are useful, and they can't be useful unless facilitators read them.

I admit my bias against facilitator notes written in the belief that anybody can teach

TABLE 10.2. **Presentation Media Compared.**

Media	Audience Size	Printing Cost (Each)	Production	Advantages	Disadvantages
Overheads	10 to 100	B/W = 50¢ Color = $1	Can print on your own printer	• Room lighting OK • Can write on, interactive • Students can create in class by hand • Projectors readily available	• Color may require dimming lights • Bulbs blow • Changes require reprinting overheads
Slides	<500	$2–4	5–7 days externally	• Very formal, fancy • Vivid color • Looks expensive	• Room must be dark • Trays are cumbersome • Projectors hard to come by • Bulbs blow • Changes require reprinting slides
PC projection	<500	None	1–2 days to enter	• Status quo today • Allows animation and music • Runs on standard PC • Easy to change	• Room must be dark • More technology means more chance of technology failure • Can't write on • Bulbs blow • Special adapters may be needed • Medium so high-tech it can interfere with the message

the class with them. In fact, because learning happens through interactions, not through lecture, the facilitator notes should never be a substitute for facilitator experience. They should fill in the gaps and serve as a good review, but no facilitator should trust them to predict every detail in a learning event.

It is very important for the facilitator to be knowledgeable and experienced in the topic. She may need to review some specific facts supplied by the facilitator notes, but her own stories, experiences, and interaction with the learners will supply the learning. Try to have a new facilitator observe an experienced facilitator teaching a class before the novice himself teaches it. He can then create his own facilitator notes through observation, questions, and research, adding to the notes provided with the course materials.

The age-old question is, Can you teach something you have never done? Gardner has shown through his research that intelligence is best developed through mentors having strength in that intelligence (Gardner, 1993). There is evidence that masters should teach, for optimum learning to occur. In business, it is not always possible to have a master in the classroom. Facilitators can become "masterful enough," though, through experience and practice. Classroom experiences with the topics also serve to develop expertise, as long as it builds on some existing expertise. Learning occurs most successfully when the learning facilitator has real-life experiences to share.

PowerPoint lets you record notes with each page of the presentation. This capability can be handy, but when you remove or add pages you have to be very careful about notes that might be lost or need to be added. The challenge with AL is that there are two types of facilitator notes: content notes and logistical notes. The content notes include the background material the facilitator needs; they are used before (not during) the class to prepare. These notes are pretty easily associated with a guide page. Logistical notes contain such things as debriefing questions, metaphors and analogies, good posters for peripheral learning, good quotes for peripheral learning, preparation information, and research details. They aren't really associated with a specific overhead and may, depending on the workshop, need to be moved to another part of the session. For this reason, you may decide to keep these notes in a separate document.

Each facilitator should create her own logistics notes. They are a plan of the flow of the class—how the open will be done, where the breaks will be, what the review exercises will be, and other sequencing details. This is a useful guideline to help the facilitator manage the time constraint. The plan is changed by the priorities of the learners; logistics never go exactly as the notes plan.

Learning-Event Supplies

Along with increased emphasis on experiential learning comes a pretty extensive, though not necessarily expensive, supply list. Each workshop needs two supply lists: the standard AL list (see Chapter Eight) that creates the learning environment that each workshop needs, and the specials that only this workshop requires either for a specific audience need or for a specific exercise.

EVALUATE THE LEARNING

Accelerated Learning Offers Everyone Something Magically *Exciting*.

The last step of the learner-first approach is **E**valuation—continuously monitor the success or weaknesses of the learning event over its lifetime. This topic is covered in more detail in Chapter Twelve; here I simply offer an overview section. Once the learning event is finished, it is tempting to think you're done, but much work still remains. A tremendous amount of attention has to be paid to keeping everything synchronized as you make changes. Think of your workshops as never finished and constantly evolving. This continuous change must be managed to maintain the quality of the learning.

Consider the ripple effect of a change on one page of a presentation. It could also affect

- The overhead or slide
- The learner guide
- The facilitator notes
- The prework
- The exercises, games, and simulations
- The marketing material (in numerous places)
- The supply list
- The room setup

At this point in the learning-event development, establish a plan for ongoing evaluation of the workshop (see Chapter Twelve) and how the maintenance of all the pieces will be handled. The rollout of the learning event is the first part of this plan. Here is the best sequence of events for the rollout:

1. Alpha class: facilitate the class with a group of experts, then update the workshop
2. Beta class: facilitate the class with a hand-picked group representing the target audience, then update the workshop
3. Production: roll the class out to the masses

This sounds wonderful, but in business you almost never get the time to do this type of rollout. You may be in a work environment that demands that your learning events hit the ground running. If this is the case, substitute less time-intensive improvement:

- Walk through the material, flow, and exercises with other course developers and trainers.
- Try out as many of the exercises as possible with friends.
- Walk through the material, flow, and exercises with a group of subject-matter experts.
- Be prepared to change a lot after the first couple of workshops.
- Be prepared to improve during the workshop.

 PRACTICE

For the situation you chose at the beginning of the chapter, consider whether you would need to develop the following, and create a plan for the development.

- Prerequisite work
- Learner guide
- Job aid (user guide, reference manual, or other)
- Presentation media (overheads, slides, or other)
- Facilitator notes
- Marketing information
- Supply list
- Room setup
- Change or maintenance plan
- Evaluation strategy

Development Plan:

_____

_____

_____

_____

BUSINESS ALIGNMENT

An important business question in developing learning events is "How much learner time will the training take?" In an ideal world, the course developer would answer the question after analyzing all the needs. In the real world of business, which is very time constrained, the time is usually a given that the course developer must work around.

As of the late 1990s, workshops in the business world rarely last more than two days, which is down from four or five days as recently as the beginning of the decade. This is why *accelerated* learning is so pertinent to today's business environment: there is less time to learn. This limitation may not be desirable to a course developer, but it is a priority for the business. Alignment to the business requires that the course developer work creatively within the time constraints.

Here are some tips for shortening workshops without losing much of the learning:

• Assign reading assignments, computer-based training, or worksheets prior to the learning event. Coach the requesting manager that this work is to be done instead of additional days of training, and ask for help in ensuring that it is. Be prepared to deal with the fact that people may not have time to complete the prework.

• Spread the learning event over more time but in smaller pieces. Many organizations will tolerate two days every other month for a year but would never tolerate twelve consecutive days.

• Hold all or part of the learning event in the evening or on a weekend day.

• Sandwich self-paced material in between facilitator-led work—for example, a Microsoft Project workshop might have a one-day facilitator-led overview, followed by a practicum assignment, followed by a one-day facilitator-coached review of the practicum.

• Let technology help you. There are tremendous computer, video, and Internet-based materials that can supplement learning events outside of a facilitator-led classroom event.

 PRACTICE

For the situation that you chose at the beginning of the chapter, determine the following.

Are there any time constraints?

_____

_____

What are they, and who are they from?

_____

_____

Based on the tips you have just read, how can you work within the constraints and still promote learning?

_____

_____

CONCLUSION

Like all project work, course development is really a never-ending story. The learner-first process is meant to get you started developing learner-focused learning events, but it does not guarantee that you will be successful. The best thing you can do to improve at development is practice. Here are some final tips to help you get started with your own learning about course development:

- Create fewer exercises, but make them more complex and detailed.
- Use guest experts, but beware of "talking heads." If you have an expert with good content but too much lecture, consider using Thiagi's lecture bingo game.
- Let learners self-discover through reading articles, writings, checklists, and Web (or computer-based or video-based) information before, during, or after class.

Whether you are creating a one-hour miniworkshop or a four-month certification program, practice the steps you have read about in this chapter to ensure that you keep your focus where it belongs: on the learning objectives and the learners. The business and the learners will benefit, and so will you.

 ## PERSONAL ACTION PLAN

Please look back through this chapter, and jot down your thoughts below: insights, things you want to do, things you want to remember, games, and quotes. I've added a list of my own to supplement your list. It is better for your learning if you make your own list before you look at mine.

The learning objectives of this chapter were to

- Adopt specific improvements in how you communicate new learning to learners
- Construct and manage effective learning objectives for a learning event
- Adjust your intake styles to communicate more effectively with learners
- Use the multiple intelligences to design the logistical flow of a learning event
- Balance the use of both the left and right sides of the brain for learning
- Define the three primary functions (triune) of the brain in a learning event
- Maximize memory in self and others for long-term retention
- Develop classroom learning events to meet a specific learning need
- Measure the effectiveness of a learning event
- Create a personal action plan to increase personal learning and the effectiveness of your delivery of learning events

Your thoughts:

_____

_____

_____

_____

_____

_____

_____

_____

_____

_____

Here are my thoughts on the learner-first approach:

Identify the audience	*Who* needs to learn?
Identify the learning need	*What* behavior will change?
Create learning objectives	*How* will you measure learning?
Create exercises	*How* can the learners learn through experiences?
Sequence learning objectives and exercises	*How* can the flow enhance the learning?
Create support materials	*What* other things are needed?
Evaluate the learning event	*How* can the learning improve?

This can be remembered by using the mnemonic:

ALOESME
Accelerated Learning Offers Everyone Something Magically Exciting

- There are multiple customers of learning: the learner, the scheduler, the supervisor, and the buyer (and perhaps others).

- All business-oriented learning events must be tied to a business objective that
  Increases revenue
  Avoids cost
  Improves service (*IRACIS*)
  Or is a reaction to government regulation or competition
- The debriefing, which is when learning occurs, should be as long as the exercise. Learners need to know that they know.
- The sequencing of learning is most effective when you demonstrate the outcome or the *why* to the learners first.
- Support materials are critical to the learner's learning but challenging to keep synchronized as changes occur.
- Evaluation ensures that you stay focused on the learning objectives and that the learning always increases over time.

**Business
Success**

CHAPTER 1
Starting the
Learning Journey

CHAPTER 12
Your Learning
Journey
Continues

PART ONE
How People Learn

CHAPTER 2
A Contract for Learning

CHAPTER 3
Learning to Take More In

CHAPTER 4
Learning Through All
Your Intelligences

CHAPTER 5
Learning with
Your Whole Brain

CHAPTER 6
Remembering What
You Learned

PART TWO
**How Successful
Learning Is Delivered**

CHAPTER 7
You Are the Deliverer

CHAPTER 8
The Environment
Delivers Learning

CHAPTER 9
Music to Deliver
Learning

PART THREE
**How Successful
Learning Events
Are Built**

CHAPTER 10
Developing Learning
Events

► **CHAPTER 11
Selling the Dream**

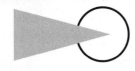

**THE LEARNING
OBJECTIVES OF
CHAPTER 11**

After reading this chapter, you will be able to

- Adopt specific improvements in how you communicate new learning to learners

- Identify and rethink those personal beliefs of yours that block learning

- Develop classroom learning events to meet a specific learning need

- Create a personal action plan to increase personal learning and the effectiveness of your delivery of learning events

CHAPTER 11

Selling the Dream

In learning organizations, leaders are not heroes, but rather designers, teachers, and stewards. These roles require different skills: to build shared vision, to bring out and challenge prevailing mental models, and to foster more systemic patterns of thinking.

—Robert J. Graham and Randall L. Englund,
Creating an Environment for Successful Projects

There are people at some of the largest companies in the United States who are passionately committed to growing the learning in their organizations. They will work unlimited hours writing new workshops, and they will devote massive energy to thinking up new ways of facilitating the most learning in the least amount of time.

Some of these very same, passionate facilitators of learning will quickly turn and run when anything having to do with "sales" is mentioned. There seems to be a belief that if the learning event is good enough and needed enough, it will sell itself. With a little reflection, corporate training people will admit that there really isn't a strong link between what the organization really needs to learn and what its employees choose to learn. The most-needed learning events often need the most selling.

What makes corporate training people so afraid of sales? Perhaps it's the negative emotions associated with the word—somehow you might become the negative stereotype. Perhaps professionals in training perceive themselves to be lacking in sales expertise. In fact, sales and marketing have a great deal in common with learning: getting to the right learners, at the right time, with the right learning for the business. The process of marketing and selling learning events requires

- Identifying the correct audience (the first step in the learner-first approach)
- Correctly identifying their needs (the second step in the learner-first approach)

- Implementing a solution to these learning needs (the complete implementation of the learner-first approach)
- Communicating to learners what has been done

This chapter will focus on communicating. If you are a professional responsible for internal training, you may be struggling with the need to market. Many corporate training managers fail because they do not feel it is their job to "sell." Instead, training managers often do a careful, thorough needs analysis, place training events on a schedule, and wait for people to sign up—and then, often, people don't do so. In today's chaotic business environment, even when the learners do sign up, they don't show up. Eventually, the corporate training manager's job will fade away when the business perceives that no business value has been added from the oft-canceled training.

If you are an external vendor, you already know how critical marketing is. In this chapter, you will learn to create a strategy to focus your marketing dollars on.

As you read through this chapter, you will notice that the learning theories in Part One of this book, how people learn, are as applicable to communicating in sales and marketing efforts as they are in a learning event. Selling the dream requires the same techniques, the same beliefs, and the same audience (if not a larger one). Customer service consists of two things: the *what* and the *how.* The previous chapters have taught you the *what* and the *how* of classroom delivery, and this chapter will focus on the *how* that occurs before a learning event can begin. The first step is that you must truly believe that the learning event is the right solution to the business problem. If you don't, this chapter won't help you at all.

In this chapter, you will read about how to continue your partnership with your learners, both in and outside the classroom. This is a core part of creating a learning organization—sharing the business vision through the development of personal mastery. It really isn't enough to "tell them." You will learn how to communicate not only the learning objectives but also why they are important to the learner and the business. You must sell managers on the entire context of the learning to earn their commitment. This approach is a variation of relationship selling: as you foster a trusting relationship with your customer-learners, it gets easier for you to sell them and, soon, easier for them to ask you before you have to.

This chapter is divided into five main sections:

1. Defining your learning promise
2. Creating a learning mission and vision
3. Creating a marketing strategy

4. Budgeting maintenance
5. Marketing and learning theory

DEFINING YOUR LEARNING PROMISE

Brand management (which includes creating a brand promise) is an important concept in the field of corporate marketing. To sell your learning events, it is critical that you understand what your learning promise is to your customers and your business. What makes your product or service unique? What are the reasons your customers should get these products and services from you? Who are the customers you seek to serve?

First, ask yourself what you are great at. What are the things that your training area does better than any other? If you adopt AL techniques, you will be much better than most at the delivery of learning. Thinking about what benefits you provide forces you to face up to things you aren't very good at. For example, maybe your facilitators do not have the depth of technical knowledge required to lead quality personal computer workshops.

Next, turn your focus to your learners. What do they need? What are the benefits that they ask from you? For example, most business clients want a quick response and a customized business solution. Do your clients want speed, cost, quality, or something else? For an interesting take on this, check out the wonderful book *The Discipline of Market Leaders* by Michael Treacy and Frank Wiersema (1997). What emotions or feelings would your clients like you to trigger in them? Do they want you to reduce their stress, reduce their time pressures, make them look good, or something else? See where you can match your features with what will benefit your customers. A clear understanding of the match will ensure that you are focusing your limited resources on the right products and services for the benefit of the business.

 PRACTICE

Use the following questions to create a learning promise:

What are the *features* you excel at?

_____

_____

What are the *benefits* your customers want?

_____

_____

What are the customers' *emotions* that your features trigger?

_____

_____

Fill in the blanks to create your learning promise:

Our learning events will provide _____ [features] that will make our customers feel _____ [emotions] about their _____ [benefits].

As a corporate training company, we have found it challenging to market one of our strong features: use of accelerated learning in all our services. On the one hand, AL can be perceived as a fun way to learn, a way that maximizes retention. On the other hand, people who have not experienced its power may perceive it as a silly way to teach that wastes time. Accelerated learning carries a lot of baggage; very few people who have heard of it define it in the same way. We find ourselves in the position of selling accelerated learning in addition to our service, which just adds to the complexity of the sales call.

Instead, we sell the benefit to the customer rather than the feature that we provide. The benefit to the customer is that our workshops let the learners learn by doing, which creates increased long-term retention while reducing the time needed in the classroom. The feature is that we achieve this benefit through applying AL principles. Notice the difference: talking about the feature (from our perspective) versus the benefit (from our customers' perspective).

PRACTICE

Now that you have a clearer picture of your position in your marketplace, fill in the chart below. Assess each of your products and services in terms of your learning promise; can you deliver your promise through them? It is usually better to deliver fewer products and services with higher quality than to deliver many lower-quality options.

Product or Service	Customer	Value Compared to Competition
1.		
2.		
3.		
4.		
5.		

Prioritize your products and services according to how they fit your learning promise. Which ones (pick three to five) seem to fit best with the direction you have defined? How can you better focus your limited resources on these priorities?

CREATING A LEARNING MISSION AND VISION

The piece that many corporate training organizations are missing is a real mission. A mission contributes to creating a shared vision, one of the five disciplines of a learning organization, according to Senge. After thinking about your products, services, customers, and the need you best meet in your marketplace, it is a good time to step back and figure out your mission, which is the *why.*

Creating an organizational mission statement clearly captures the reason the business is funding your team. A well-written mission statement can align your entire organization and maximize your resources. A poorly written mission statement, posted on the wall on a pretty plaque but with no real buy-in, can have the opposite effect.

The book *The Path,* by Laurie Beth Jones (1998), has a clear process for creating a personal mission statement. I have modified this process so that you can use it to create a mission statement for a training organization, either internal or external. To begin, think of a noun that best defines all of your products and services. Here are a few suggestions:

Creativity	Customer knowledge	Customer service
Effectiveness	Efficiency	Growth
Knowledge	Learning	Performance
Productivity	Product knowledge	Quality

Now, think of two or three verbs that capture how you deliver the noun you picked. For example, if you picked *learning* as your noun, you might think "create, model, and promote learning." Play around with different combinations of verbs until you come up with one that you think summarizes the promise you outlined above.

 PRACTICE

In big, bold letters, write your organizational mission here:

The other part of creating a shared vision is to create a step-by-step plan for getting from where your organization is right now to where you need to be to fulfill your learning promise. This plan is often called a vision. Using the practice area below, quantify what you'd like your organization to be like in the next year.

PRACTICE

Answer the following questions as specifically as you can. Add your own thoughts until you have a clear, measurable picture of your future. This vision will be your plan for moving your learning organization to where it must be to meet the needs of the business.

1. How many learning events will you hold per month? How many participants will be in each? What will the format be?

   _____

   _____

2. How many vendors (or client organizations, if you are a vendor) will you work with? Who will they be?

   _____

   _____

3. What are the new products and services you will develop? By when?

   _____

   _____

4. How many learning facilitators will you need to deliver the learning events detailed above?

   _____

   _____

5. Where will the money come from? Who will pay for the learning events?

   _____

   _____

6. How will you determine the ongoing needs of the business?

   _____

   _____

7. How will you market the learning events? (You may add to this after you've read this entire chapter.)

_____

_____

8. How will you continue to grow the strengths of your staff? How will you model learning?

_____

_____

9. What partnerships and alliances can be created to help you meet the needs of your business?

_____

_____

10. How will you measure the success of learning?

_____

_____

Now that you know what you want to accomplish and why your customers need your product or service, it's time to let them know how you are going to help the business.

CREATING A MARKETING STRATEGY

The vision drives the marketing strategy. If you are in a typical corporate training organization, there is no limit to what learning objectives you can cover. Over the years, your list of learning events may have become too much for your customers to remember. Creating a marketing strategy means focusing your message by marketing specific topic areas at different points in the year. Although you will sell many topics as the business requests them, your marketing strategy is a plan for gauging the needs of the business and communicating specific products that fit with it.

A corporate learning professional must be in touch with the priorities of the business and must learn to read signs both internally and externally that will help predict the learning gaps hindering the productivity of the staff. Here are some ways you can anticipate needs:

• Track all topic requests, no matter how informal. Even topics that are outside your scope will be a clue to the growing needs of your audience. For example, if you have had two or three customers talk to you about their struggling teams, you could guess that something in the business is putting pressures on teams to perform more effectively. This observation will tell you what people need, but they may not perceive yet that they need it. That's why marketing is important.

• Track completions and no-shows. When people sign up but don't attend a learning event, it says a lot about the changing priorities of the business. Investigate why people are really not showing up. Time pressure is usually the stated culprit, but why is there so much time pressure? Is there some opportunity for learning that is creating the time pressure, such as poor task prioritization, project management, or communication?

• Ask on your evaluations what other topics the customers have a need for.

• Watch the flyers from conferences, especially nontraining conferences. Watch the mailings you get from outside training companies. Observe which topics they think have the biggest draw. This tells you what people want (though not necessarily what they need).

• Monitor listservs on the Web, especially training lists. What are people asking for? What are the trends?

• Interview some of your internal managers to see what business problems (not training problems) they see in the next six months or a year. Note that this is a different question from "What workshops will your people need?" Very few managers know how to answer that, so they make up an answer that does not represent what their people will actually attend; the results can be very misleading.

Spend a morning with the other people in your training area, and compare notes. Come to a consensus about the topics that the business needs for the next four quarters. If you are a vendor, this may be your guess; internally, you may have to do some form of a needs analysis. This topic list should be revisited at least every six months. For example, suppose that your team has come up with something like the following:

Time Period	*Priority Topic*
First quarter	Project management
Second quarter	Leadership
Third quarter	Communication
Fourth quarter	Sales

Now, define no more than three learning solutions for each topic. Depending on the breadth of your services, these may be instructor-led workshops, and they may also include self-paced learning, coaching, or focus groups. You may have many more than three solutions, but the marketing effort should be concise and focused, so pick up your strongest three. Once the customers are interested, you can then unveil the depth of your services for that topic. Use a catchy title to honor the memory principles you read about in Chapter Six and the importance of meeting your audience's needs, as in Chapter Ten. Contrast "Introduction to Project Management" with "Minimal Project Management for Professionals." Notice the use of emotion in these titles—the first has none, but the second plays on the emotions of an overworked, undervalued learner.

Here is an example of a prioritized list of learning events for each topic of the four business needs in the example above:

Priority Topic	*Learning Events*
Project management	Self-paced: "Minimal Project Management for Professionals"
	Workshop: "Project Management Simulation"
	Coaching: "Project Team Kick-off and Mentoring"
Leadership	Self-paced: "Principle-Based Leadership"
	Workshop: "The Inner Works of a Leader"
	Study group: "Becoming an Effective Leader"
Communication	Workshop: "Assessing and Improving Communication Patterns"
	Study group: "Becoming an Effective Communicator"
	Coaching: "Executive Mentor"
Sales	Self-paced: "Relationship Selling," "Selling the Dream"
	Workshop: "Growing Sales through the Sales Automation System"

This list can and should contain diverse services, to maximize the appeal to your customers. For example, one customer might prefer to learn in a self-paced environment, while another might like an ongoing study group format. Obviously, the topic must guide the type of service offered; for example, communication is not learned well completely alone.

The next step is to brainstorm the most effective way to communicate these three services within the time period specified. The tools you use must be consistent with the learning promise, mission, and vision. In addition, they have to be geared to the customer, and they should address benefits, not features. Finally, the learning theories you read about in Chapters Three through Six, especially multiple intelligences, should be used to maximize communication. You'll read about ten options.

- Topic flyers
- Springboard pages
- Course pages
- Postcards
- Company newsletter ads
- Newsletters
- Web information
- Online intranet or e-mail notices
- Speaking
- Booths

Topic Flyers

These one-sided flyers are used to group your associated services into a concrete whole. Use the memory principle of information chunking that you learned about in Chapter Six; your customers will find it easier to understand your services if you help them picture how the pieces fit together. These flyers work well for new customers to introduce them to your products and to remind them of your products.

Here's how a topic flyer can map to the multiple intelligences:

Interpersonal	Learning points speak to needs of a project team
Logical/mathematical	Sequence is implied by the list of services
Spatial/visual	Graphic draws the eye, color on the page is also useful
Musical	None

Linguistic/verbal	Written word
Intrapersonal	Written for processing alone
Bodily/kinesthetic	Graphic shows movement, and learning points are written actively
Emotional	Graphic implies a feeling of losing control
Naturalist	None
Existential	Learning points speak to the personal need to excel

Flyers can be distributed innovatively. You can put flyers about new classes on the back of the bathroom stall doors or on the mirrors in the bathrooms—nobody misses those. Or try creating little table tents to advertise your products and services in the cafeteria and break rooms.

Springboard Pages

Every time you provide a service to a customer, there is an opportunity to continue to market. For example, after learners complete a workshop, they often ask the facilitators what they should take next to continue learning. Consider creating a one-sided flyer to distribute in each event, detailing the products or services that make sense for the learners as next steps. These springboard pages map to the multiple intelligences as flyers do.

Course Pages

Course pages are two-sided detailed descriptions of products and service. The front side contains a description, designed to speak to the emotions that the customer is currently experiencing combined with the benefits the customer seeks. The learning objectives are also on the front. The back contains the detailed outline or flow of the event. These can be mailed, faxed, and kept on the Website so they are available whenever and however the customer wants them. Both existing and new customers benefit from these detailed marketing pieces; they also map to the multiple intelligences in the same way the flyers do.

Postcards

Postcards are very popular. Put an intriguing graphic or cartoon on one side of the card and your message on the back. A good postcard will end up hanging in people's cubicles communicating your message. You can also use your postcards to send out registration information. Put training department information on the front as well as the back so the source is obvious when the postcard is hanging up. Find a creative and talented graphic artist to give your postcards a consistent look and tone, but be careful to keep the message clear as well as fun. Postcards work equally well for new and existing customers.

Here's how this piece maps to the multiple intelligences:

Interpersonal	Learning points speak to the need for better team communication
Logical/mathematical	Text is bulleted to make information easy to find
Spatial/visual	Graphic draws the eye
Musical	None
Linguistic/verbal	Written word
Intrapersonal	Written for processing alone
Bodily/kinesthetic	Graphic shows movement, and services are written actively
Emotional	Picture is a humorous take-off of a well-known story
Naturalist	Lighting sets an outdoor feel
Existential	Graphic points out the personal importance of communication

Company Newsletter Ads

If you are part of an internal training department, consider advertising in your own company paper. Stress the benefits, make it flashy, provoke a response, and repeat it often. It is a little more challenging to map all the multiple intelligences to a small ad, but it can be done in the same fashion as the postcard.

Newsletters

Newsletters take a lot of time and coordination, so carefully plan how often you do them. The best dates for delivery are right after winter break (around the first of January), right before summer begins (June), and right after Labor Day (September). These seem to be the times when people are looking forward and planning their activities for the future.

The lead article should address your marketing strategy topic for the time period. (Note that marketing strategy is quarterly, but by the timetable just suggested the newsletter is three times a year so that it can span quarters.) Inside, have smaller articles that are written by your facilitators and suppliers, including the topics that are coming up in later periods. This arrangement helps you test level of interest by checking the number of comments you hear. Include a schedule of learning events coming up, some marketing blurbs about your top three services, and a contest to get a feel for how many people actually look inside your newsletter. To generate interest, include a pertinent tip or technique, such as a meeting tip, plus a humorous sidebar and a book review. Promise (and deliver) prizes for anyone who responds to a contest. Keep articles to no more than a page in length, and limit the newsletter to three and a half pages of content, leaving half a page for mailing address information.

If the newsletter is mailed out, it gives you the opportunity to clean up your mailing list. If mailing outside your business, first-class mail is more costly but guarantees that either the newsletter gets to the person or it's returned so you can update your list.

Electronic newsletters through the Web or e-mail are enticing because they are virtually postage-free. However, there are some logistical problems that lower the likelihood that your newsletter will be read. For example, if the newsletter is sent as an attachment to an e-mail, the receiver may not take the time to look at it or save it. In addition, because of the array of technology, the look of your newsletter (including the fonts, spacing, graphics, and color) may vary greatly depending on who has received it and what software is used. When using e-mail, the articles must be limited to one or two pages to keep the size of the message congenial.

The most important thing to remember about newsletters is that they need to add value for the people receiving them. They are more a learning event than they are a marketing piece, although marketing is a subtheme. Newsletters tend to communicate better with existing customers than they do with new customers, because the tone often implies an existing relationship.

Here's how newsletters can map to the multiple intelligences:

Interpersonal	The tone of the newsletter can mimic a conversation between the reader and the writer
Logical/mathematical	Table of contents, headings, page numbers all add structure for navigation
Spatial/visual	Graphics, color, and charts communicate to visual learners
Musical	None
Linguistic/verbal	Written word
Intrapersonal	Debriefing-style questions and reflection points are built into the articles
Bodily/kinesthetic	A contest invites participation
Emotional	Humorous stories and pictures keep the tone light and inviting
Naturalist	Only through articles or graphics
Existential	The articles must speak to the personal mission of the reader

Web Information

Welcome to the twenty-first century. Training organizations must have a Website to be considered serious, even as an internal organization. Your Web page can act as a catalog with all the current descriptions of products and services. When customers ask for information, they can be referred to the Web, where they can access information immediately. This works extremely well in the time-constrained business world. More and more, your customers expect immediate answers.

Linking from your internal Website to other sites is also an added value to your customers. Many vendors, including Amazon at www.amazon.com, will let you link a bibliography to their site for ordering and will pay you a small commission for the reference. More costly options for your site include animation, video, a listserv, a discussion group, and the ability to e-mail from your site.

A Website requires a Web master to administer it. For example, our Web master spends about eight hours a month on enhancements, and this time obligation is growing. Web pages need to change often for people to return to them. Consider which parts of your Website will change often and which parts will be more stable. Always pay special attention to your topic of the quarter. Even with the overhead cost, the Website is less expensive than fax or mail alternatives. In fact, the site is available to anyone—new and old customers—regardless of whether you are aware of them or not.

Here's how you can map your Website to the multiple intelligences:

Interpersonal	Design the Website to simulate a conversation with your customer
Logical/mathematical	Design frames that are easy to navigate, consistent, and quickly loaded
Spatial/visual	Color and graphics are powerful, but balance with speed of access
Musical	Music can be offered
Linguistic/verbal	Written word
Intrapersonal	Websites, by their nature, are accessed by a person working alone
Bodily/kinesthetic	Animation and interaction are features of Websites
Emotional	Humor and other positive emotions can be triggered by good Web choices
Naturalist	Only through graphics or stories
Existential	The Website should speak to the priorities of the customer

Online Intranet or E-Mail Notices

E-mail can be used to let clients know about services, but use it sparingly. People are getting very good at ignoring e-mail now that they are buried in it. Be sure to include a provocative title so they will open it, and keep it brief, enticing, and to the point.

Speaking

Some of the best prospecting comes from speaking. Businesspeople are buying a service from you, and a service depends on the people who provide it. Demonstrating the expertise of your facilitators through speaking and the like creates customer trust. Plan your speaking topics and align them to your marketing strategy as much as possible. Look for opportunities to have your vendors or facilitators give presentations to your target audiences—or you could do it yourself. Treat the speech as a sneak preview of your workshops, and honor the diversity of the learners by creating a lot of interaction. The multiple intelligences map the same way they would in a learning event.

Whenever you speak, maximize the opportunity it presents. Be prepared to have a table with your latest marketing materials, including your newsletters and postcards. Tie the marketing material to the speech topic to fulfill your marketing strategy.

A word of caution: people don't like to be marketed to, so make sure your speech adds value and is not just a sales pitch. Don't hand them marketing material; put it in an easily seen place where the participants can choose whether to pick it up or not. An interesting technique is to place your marketing material on the floor by the door, surrounded by candy and prizes to draw the eye. People always seem to notice items on the floor.

That said, you still need something to help them remember you if they are interested. You need a hook. The hook should be something that will motivate a new prospect or an existing customer to contact you for more information. For example, at a speech, offer to mail something to your participants that is of value to them. Make marketing fun for you and your customers.

Booths

Many large corporations have enough training departments to conduct their own conferences each year. In this case, you will want to have a booth to share your message. Consider a booth at your local professional training organization show as well. If you are competing against external training vendors for your internal customers' needs, it makes sense to be where the vendors are.

A booth can be a big investment, and it works only if you are clear and concise about the message you are communicating. The message should be driven by your marketing strategy. Think of how you can stand out from all the others, making use of the memory research indicating that people recall things that are unusual (Chapter Six).

Here's an example of how a booth can map to the multiple intelligences:

Interpersonal	Welcome each visitor in a friendly but nonaggressive way
Logical/mathematical	Visually and concisely list your services in the booth
Spatial/visual	Color and graphics are powerful, but balance with simplicity
Musical	Music can be played
Linguistic/verbal	Written word on literature, spoken word in conversations
Intrapersonal	Allow people enough space to look at things on their own
Bodily/kinesthetic	Provide take-aways that are clever and tactile, such as yo-yos
Emotional	Humor and other positive emotions can be triggered
Naturalist	Put plants or fresh flowers in the booth
Existential	Let the customer speak more than you do

Booths, like speeches, require a defined, repeatable process and a hook for follow-up. Consider how you will stay in the minds of your customers after they return to their desks.

BUDGETING MAINTENANCE

The more diverse and frequent the marketing pieces, the more likely the message successfully gets to the right people at the right time. However, the more diverse and frequent your marketing pieces are, the more work it takes to roll them out and keep the process going. Prioritize your marketing time and dollars carefully around a marketing strategy, and be prepared to fund not just the rollout but the entire life of the strategy. Many efforts fail because people think marketing means telling them once.

Marketing is not work that any one individual can do well. Good marketing takes right-brain processors to invent and left-brain processors to implement. When all is said and done, the success of your marketing comes down to a documented, repeatable process designed by the right brains and implemented by the left brains of your staff. What appears seamless to your customers will keep your staff, or just you, very busy.

 PRACTICE

Look back at the marketing strategy you created in the last practice. Using the list of ideas in this chapter as a starting point, create an implementation list for yourself:

Time Period	Topic	Marketing Tool	Who and How
First quarter			
Second quarter			
Third quarter			
Fourth quarter			

MARKETING AND LEARNING THEORY

Marketing your products and services and then selling them to the right people is a part of facilitating learning. You are transferring learning about why an employee needs to improve for the good of the business, and about how the employee can acquire the new skills and knowledge necessary.

All the knowledge you have gained in the previous chapters of this book on how people learn and remember is critical to good marketing and sales. Keep in mind the multiple intelligences; tapping both the right and left brains; seeking out the visual, kinesthetic, and auditory learner; and calming the reptilian brain by creating a limbic sense of hope—a direct line to the neocortex and marketing success. Use what you know about memory to help your customers learn about your services. Stay close to learning objectives. Whether in a speech, sales presentation, workshop, or consulting session, the learning objectives should always be clearly communicated.

CONCLUSION

This chapter has given you many examples and details of how to market. You have some ideas of your own and will soon learn to watch and learn from others. Your competition, especially external vendors, knows the importance of an effective marketing strategy to ensure sales. The world is screaming at your customers. How are you going to stand out so that they can see how you can help them meet the needs of the business?

 ## PERSONAL ACTION PLAN

Please look back through this chapter, and jot down your thoughts below: insights, things you want to do, things you want to remember, games, and quotes. I've added a list of my own to supplement your list. It is better for your learning if you make your own list before you look at mine.

The learning objectives of this chapter were to

- Adopt specific improvements in how you communicate new learning to learners
- Identify and rethink those personal beliefs of yours that block learning
- Develop classroom learning events to meet a specific learning need
- Create a personal action plan to increase personal learning and the effectiveness of your delivery of learning events

Your thoughts:

_____

_____

_____

_____

_____

_____

_____

_____

_____

Here are my thoughts:

- Learning and retention are maximized when the learners are clear about what they need to learn and why.
- Creating a learning promise, a mission, and a vision is the cornerstone to managing an ongoing marketing strategy for a corporate training organization.
- Marketing should emphasize what benefits are provided to the learner, not the features that the learning event possesses.
- Manage, prioritize, and focus your marketing efforts through a marketing strategy.
- A hook helps you track leads, especially for speeches, booths, and even newsletters.
- Fund not just the rollout but the entire life of the marketing strategy.
- Apply all you know about AL to your marketing pieces for maximum knowledge transfer and retention.

CHAPTER 1
Starting the
Learning Journey

**Business
Success**

CHAPTER 12
**Your Learning
Journey
Continues**

PART ONE
How People Learn

CHAPTER 2
A Contract for Learning

CHAPTER 3
Learning to Take More In

CHAPTER 4
Learning Through All
Your Intelligences

CHAPTER 5
Learning with
Your Whole Brain

CHAPTER 6
Remembering What
You Learned

PART TWO
**How Successful
Learning Is Delivered**

CHAPTER 7
You Are the Deliverer

CHAPTER 8
The Environment
Delivers Learning

CHAPTER 9
Music to Deliver
Learning

PART THREE
**How Successful
Learning Events
Are Built**

CHAPTER 10
Developing Learning
Events

CHAPTER 11
Selling the Dream

THE LEARNING OBJECTIVES FOR THIS BOOK

After reading this book, you will be able to

- Identify times in a learning event when you play the roles of facilitator of learning, trainer, and learner
- Adopt specific improvements in how you communicate new learning to learners
- Identify how you learn best
- Identify and rethink those personal beliefs of yours that block learning
- Construct and manage effective learning objectives for a learning event
- Identify your learners' preferences for receiving new learning (intake styles)
- Adjust your intake styles to communicate more effectively with learners
- Assess your preference for processing new learning in terms of Gardner's multiple intelligences
- Use the multiple intelligences to design the logistical flow of a learning event
- Balance the use of both the left and right sides of the brain for learning
- Define the three primary functions (triune) of the brain in a learning event
- Maximize memory in self and others for long-term retention
- Use music to create focused learning environments
- Develop classroom learning events to meet a specific learning need
- Measure the effectiveness of a learning event
- Create a personal action plan to increase personal learning and learning event delivery effectiveness

CHAPTER 12

Your Learning Journey Continues

When my students and I discover uncharted territory to explore, when the pathway out of a thicket opens up before us, when our experience is illuminated by the lightning—life of the mind—teaching is the finest work I know.

—Parker J. Palmer, *The Courage to Teach*

I n reaching this chapter, you are well into your journey to improve learning for yourself and for others. Take a moment to congratulate yourself on a job well begun.

You alone decide how to proceed. Only you know what your audience is like, what the business objectives of your organization are, and what the learning objectives need to be. This chapter is created as a worksheet for you, to help you begin the transition.

PRACTICE

Delivery is the personal aspect of adapting an accelerated learning approach. This practice exercise will help you jell your thoughts about your own delivery techniques. Think of the teacher from whom you learned the most. List the characteristics of that person in the first column of the table below. Reflect on why you learned as much as you did.

Now, think about the learning events that you facilitate. How would you rate yourself? In the second column, rate yourself for each characteristic that you listed in column one for your favorite teacher. At any time, feel free to add additional important characteristics as you think of them.

What would you like to improve? It is not necessary, or helpful, to rate a 10 at everything; if you are honest, you'll admit your favorite teacher did not. As Robert Greenleaf wrote in *Servant Leadership* (1977) "Strengthen the hands of the strong." How can you maximize your strengths? Figure out how much growth is important to you for each characteristic, if any. Is there a characteristic you'd like to temper? For example, you might think you tell too many personal stories. Put that rating in the third column.

Finally, create action items in the fourth column to move you from your current to your future rating.

Characteristics	Current Rating (1 low, 10 high)	Future Rating (1 low, 10 high)	Action
1.			
2.			
3.			
4.			
5.			
6.			

In the words of Thiagi's mission statement, "We specialize in improving human performance efficiently, enjoyably, and ethically."

We have all been greatly influenced by the teachers in our lives. As a learning facilitator, you also have the power to influence people in your learning events. You can create miracles for them and for yourself. In addition to the delivery techniques you bring to the learning events that you facilitate, you have the power to make influential changes in course development, facilitator development, classroom design, course marketing, and course evaluation. By improving these factors, you also help your company or your clients become a learning organization by growing personal mastery, team learning, systems thinking, truth about mental models, and shared vision. By constantly improving the learning process, you lay the building blocks for initiatives such as knowledge management, thus enabling companies to create, exchange, and transform personal and organizational knowledge.

PRACTICE

You are now going to create a personal action plan based in part on the reflection you did during the previous exercise. In addition, take a moment now and review your notes from this book. Reread the summary boxes at the ends of the chapters that were important to you, especially your own take-aways.

In column 2, brainstorm the things you would like to do differently, whether it's honoring the diversity of the learner, creating great learning events, designing a learning environment, implementing a marketing strategy, or building an evaluation strategy. Don't worry about quantity—list as many as you like. List actions from the previous exercise as well.

After you have listed the actions, go through the list and think about which ones are high priority, which ones are low priority, and which ones are medium priority. Restrict yourself to ten or fewer high-priority actions. Enter the ratings in column 1 for each action in column 2.

For each of the high priorities, consider what activities the action depends on, and enter them in column 4. You may find that there is more than one activity that must take place before you can implement your action item. For example, if your action item was to "increase the training budget," then "prove the return on investment to the business from the training department" might need to be done before that.

Think about anything that might hinder your progress, and what you will do about it. Put that thought in column 5. Add a note about any action you could take to address that hindrance. The more realistic you are about the troubles you will encounter, the more likely you will be prepared to deal with them effectively.

Create a reminder note on your calendar to revisit your plan two weeks before you are scheduled to have your high-priority actions completed. At that time, you can add new action items to the list, and reprioritize on the basis of business requirements at that time. You may find that medium- and low-priority actions have moved to high priority.

A blank table is included here, but you may need more room. If you have a spreadsheet like Microsoft Excel, it can be a helpful tool for building this action plan. In addition, it is useful to keep your plan handy, so you may find it helpful to carry a printout of it in your organizer.

	Priority	Action Items	Due Date	Depends on . . .	Hindrance and Action
1.					
2.					
3.					

	Priority	Action Items	Due Date	Depends on . . .	Hindrance and Action
4.					
5.					
6.					
7.					
8.					
9.					
10.					
11.					
12.					

Finally, assign yourself a realistic due date for the high-priority actions (in column 2).

I have shared my passion for learning with you. I'm guessing that you have a strong passion for learning too. Through the next exercise, you will translate your passion into a plan of action.

PRACTICE

Create a time line for the high-priority actions you will take. Consider any subactivities that you haven't thought of yet that will need to be done to achieve your final goal. Add these to the plan. Create a picture that clearly shows the dates and the deliverables. Read your final plan out loud. As you accomplish actions, mark them out with a big red X. Notice how this process will reinforce visual, auditory, and kinesthetic learning. Here is a sample time line:

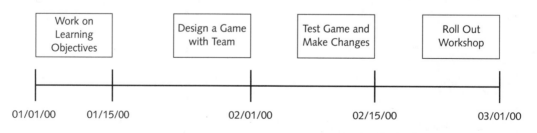

CONCLUSION

"We teachers have been invested with great authority," a learning expert named Lynn Dhority writes:

> Our voices, our eyes, our facial expressions, our body language, our enthusiasm or boredom, our capacity to foster an engaging atmosphere (or its opposite), our encouraging attitude or our withering critical mien, our joy or our mechanical routine. The messages contained in such unconscious forces can literally create success or failure in our classroom. To become aware of the tremendous power we individually possess and to take proper responsibility for it challenges us deeply, yet provides a wonderful opportunity. Recognizing, strengthening and further developing ourselves as the prime carriers of the essential stimuli for success becomes a major area of continuing development for the teacher [1991, p. 1].

I would love to hear about your experiences, good and bad. Feel free to contact me with questions, triumphs, failures, and dreams (see the Resources). Occasionally you will get tired and frustrated, but even then you will be learning. Honor that learning in yourself and in others.

I leave you with the lyrics of a song from a wonderful video, *It's in Every One of Us* (Krutein and Pomeranz, 1987):

> It's in every one of us to be wise.
> Find your heart, open up both your eyes.
> We can all know everything without ever knowing why.
> It's in every one of us by and by.
>
> It's in every one of us—I just remembered.
> It's like I've been sleeping for years,
> I'm not awake as I can be, but my seeing's better—
> I can see through the tears.
>
> I've been realizing, I bought this ticket,
> And watching only half of the show.
> But there's scenery and lights and a cast of thousands
> Who all know what I know—and it's good that it's so.

It's in every one of us to be wise.
Find your heart, open up both your eyes.
We can all know everything without ever knowing why.
It's in every one of us by and by.

In this part of the book, you will read about tips and techniques for facilitating accelerated learning. Some of them you can use exactly as written, but most will have to be modified to fit the specifics of your learning situation. There are many other sources of ideas for tips and techniques, which are cited in the Resources. These ideas are some of my personal favorites.

The tips have been put into these categories:

- Opens
- Interpersonal exercises
- Intrapersonal exercises
- Review exercises
- Other classroom delivery techniques

OPENS

Opens set the stage for learning and initiate a positive learning environment. Here are some examples you might like to try.

Famous People

Use: this is an interesting, reflective open for a class about leadership or management. This can also be used during class.

1. Ask learners to pick a famous person they admire.
2. Ask each of the learners to share: why do you admire this person? How would you like to be like him or her? Different?
3. Use the criteria discussed to start a list of good leadership or management characteristics on a flipchart or board.

You can use the list to ask learners to create an assessment and action plan for an intrapersonal second exercise, in which the focus is to choose actions they will take to get them close to their individual goals.

Four Facts

Use: for lengthy classroom experiences where it will be necessary to build a large amount of trust so as not to arouse the reptilian brain. This exercise is also good for showing participants that the other learners are more special than they may have thought and is useful if team building is one of the learning objectives.

Ask each person to write down four interesting facts about himself or herself, but one should be a lie. The facilitator should begin by listing her four facts and reading the list. The rest of the group votes on which they think is the lie. Each person takes a turn reading his or her list to the class (or to the people at the same table, depending on the size of the class).

Quirky Facts

Use: for lengthy classroom experiences where it will be necessary to build a large amount of trust. This is useful if the learners will be in a long workshop (more than one week) and will have to work well together.

1. Ask each learner to write down a fun fact on a piece of paper.
2. Collect them and read one at a time.
3. Ask the class to guess, either aloud or on paper, who goes with each fact.

Word Association

Use: for lengthy classroom experiences where it is a learning objective that the learners work together better.

Ask each learner to introduce himself with a word association. A word association is another word that describes the learner that begins with the same letter or rhymes with his name, for example, Brilliant Brian. Challenge the learners to use words that relate to the workshop content. Have the class repeat each new one in order as the names are announced until at the end they are reciting the entire list. To add more bodily/kinesthetic stimulus, add physical movement, like clapping hands, while reciting people's word associations.

INTERPERSONAL EXERCISES

Interpersonal exercises, in which participants work with each other, honor the interpersonal intelligence principle.

Breaking into Teams

Use: as you have read in many places in this book, it is important that learners work with a variety of teams during a learning event to build a complex context for retention. Here are some safe ways to move people into new teams:

- Use stickers on learner guides, for example, four types of stickers to create four teams.
- Use hard candy, for example, divided up by color.
- Use comic strips cut into frames for teams of three or four. Pass the frames out and ask the learners to find the other people needed to complete their comic strip.
- Write the names of common songs (for example, "Row, Row, Row Your Boat") on slips of paper. Learners must hum their song while walking around the room to find the others on their new team.
- Put the names of famous people on the board. Ask each learner to sign up under his or her favorite, but limit the number per famous person.
- Print the titles of popular movies on small pieces of paper. On other pieces, print clues that refer to the movie. For example, on the title paper write *Sound of Music* and on a clue paper write "Julie Andrews." Have everyone circulate until all movies are matched to clues.

Team Process Guidelines

From early school experiences, we've all learned to love field trips. Learning is accelerated when there is a new context.

Field Trips

Use: everyone likes to play a little hooky, and there are some days that just seem to call people outside. Letting your learners do an exercise outside will instill some fun in the learning, increase learning energy, honor the naturalist intelligence principle, and create stronger links to long-term memory through diverse context.

Teams of learners love the adventure of working somewhere other than the classroom. Because some exercises can be done as easily outside as they can at a table in a classroom, you can release the learners to go either to a specific location (for example, the tables around a pool in a hotel) or to a place of their own choosing. Follow these suggestions:

- The facilitator needs to know where the teams are so she can check on them occasionally.
- The learners need to respect the come-back time.
- The learners need to be mindful of not disturbing other individuals in the business, conference center, or hotel.

Group Discussion Guidelines

Use: this is a structured approach to discussion that ensures that each learner gets an equal chance to participate and use interpersonal intelligence. If you are facilitating a group with one or two learners who monopolize the discussion, consider a technique like this. This process can be applied either to the whole group or to smaller teams working in parallel.

1. Identify the issue for the group to discuss.
2. Give each learner three blue poker chips and three red poker chips.
3. As the discussion begins
   If a learner makes a point, he plays a blue chip.
   If he disagrees with another, he plays a red chip.
   No one may talk without playing a chip.
   The discussion cannot end until all the chips are played.

Team Conflict Resolution Guidelines

Use: these guidelines should be established before the learning event begins and used as a process for working through emotions that may arise from disagreements, which honors the emotional intelligence. This approach is especially needed if the learning topic is emotional, such as sexual harassment or managing diversity. It is also a useful process to learn for managing any conflict effectively.

1. Identify and define (out loud) the conflict, including facts and feelings.
2. Brainstorm possible solutions to the conflict.
3. Discuss the pros and cons of each solution.
4. Select the best solution as a team.
5. Develop a plan to implement the solution, specifying owners, outcomes, and time frames.
6. After the session, select time in advance to review and adjust the solution.

Guidelines for Role Plays

Role plays are a good way to have learners practice new skills in the safety of the learning environment. Good planning is critical to their success.

Guardian Angels

Use: many learners fear role-play activities, but such practice as role play is necessary for some learning objectives. Role plays are best for topics that relate to communication, including managing conflict, negotiating, coaching, customer service, and project management. This addition to traditional role plays ensures that all learners are safe.

1. Establish the number of roles for the role-play scenario.
2. Break the class into teams, with one team for each role.
3. Give each team the resources needed and time to brainstorm how the role should be played.
4. Ask the team to select a volunteer to play the role in front of the class.
5. The volunteers begin the role play in front of the class, but they can freeze the action and ask for help from their team (the guardian angels) at any time. Other members of the team can substitute for the player. In addition, the guardian angels may freeze action to coach their player at any time.
6. Debrief about the learning associated with the role play.

Debates

Use: this structured technique ensures that learners carefully consider both sides of an issue. It allows learners to represent positions without owning them, so they can safely explore the issue, and it is useful for problem solving. The debate is a variation of the guardian angel role-play technique.

Assign teams to take positions on an issue, and give each team time to prepare its message. Then conduct the debate, using one member from each team. The team selects which member will do the debate. At any time, the person debating can freeze the action and go back to the team for help. These guidelines keep the debate safe on two counts: no one plays the role unless she wants to, and the player is never alone.

Brainstorming Techniques

Brainstorming, often used in learning events, taps into the wisdom and energy of the group of learners.

Mind maps, or another variation, are great for brainstorming, but they aren't as effective for communicating to others or for review later. Encourage the learners to convert mind maps to notes to save for future use or share with others.

Group Sharing

Use: this technique is good for brainstorming because it engages the bodily/kinesthetic aptitude, and it also keeps the participation balanced. By limiting the initial brainstorming and grouping to nonverbal activity, the team is able to share as equals.

1. Give everyone Post-its and a pencil.
2. Ask each individual to brainstorm as many ideas as he can (one idea per Post-it).
3. Ask teams of two to four to silently place all Post-its on a wall together.
4. Ask the teams to silently group the Post-its for about two minutes.
5. Ask teams to verbally continue to group and label each grouping.
6. Share the results of each group brainstorming effort.

Relationships and Connections

Use: this technique is good for starting a difficult discussion about a topic. It is also useful for allowing learners to vent about a topic without feeling unsafe.

Use analogies to get learners thinking about a topic. Here's an example: How are learner-focused learning events like a seagull? (My answer: they allow a learner to soar!)

Scenario Planning

Use: good for providing a structure for learners to think about multiple futures. This approach can be especially useful for strategic planning, budgeting, and project management and is a technique recommended by Senge in *The Fifth Discipline.*

The learners begin by considering events that could happen in the future and placing them in the first column of this table. The event is rated, either by teams or by individuals, for the likelihood that it will happen, and for the impact if it does. Both likelihood and impact are rated high, medium, or low. A high-level action plan is created for each event. If time is limited, consider building an action plan for only the high-impact, high-likelihood events.

Scenario	*Likelihood*	*Impact*	*Action*
1.			
2.			
3.			
4.			

Systems Thinking Wheel

Use: good for problem solving and analyzing the entire issue. Also good for learning systems thinking, a discipline from Senge's *The Fifth Discipline,* prior to learning more complex causal loop diagrams.

1. Draw a circle in the middle of a sheet of paper and write the issue in the circle.
2. Brainstorm the other things that will be affected by the issue, and draw these as circles hooked to the middle.
3. Draw a third level of circles hooked to those in the second level to reflect potential consequences of the next level.
4. Debrief the impact of the issues.

This exercise can also be done from the outside in, by starting with an outer circle, analyzing what issues affect the outer issue, and then moving inward.

Team-Building and Communication Exercises

Even more than in other types of interpersonal exercises, those involving team building and communication offer multiple opportunities for learning.

Compliment Circles

Use: good for team building, increasing self-esteem, and stretching interpersonal intelligences. Useful for teams that will work together for long periods of time.

The circles can be done either in person or even on cassette tape in advance.

1. Each learner takes a turn sitting in the middle of the team.
2. Each member of the team takes a turn saying a compliment to the person in the middle.
3. The compliments must be honest and sincere, and no one can pass.
4. The receiver can only smile and say thank you.
5. A scribe records each compliment, and the list is given as a gift to the receiver.

Construction

Use: construction exercises are great for team building, team communication, project management, conflict resolution, and planning learning objectives. The debriefing is the key component that ensures that learning occurs, and that the learners are aware of it. The first example is useful for topics relating to communication. The variation can be used in reengineering, project-management, and analysis workshops as well.

1. Break into teams of three to four. Have one team build an item out of Tinker Toys (or a similar construction set) in secret.
2. Give the other teams the same construction materials.
3. Have the original builders describe to the other teams how to replicate the design. Continue until each team has been successful. The design team cannot touch any blocks or show its creation at any time to the coached team members.
4. Debrief on what enhances and what detracts from good communication.

Variation:

1. Ask for one volunteer in class to play the role of the customer. Give the customer a picture of a constructed design, or use a picture of a design.
2. Break the rest of the class into teams of three or four. Tell them that they are going to build what the customer asks for, but they will not be able to ask any questions. If the teams would like something repeated, any member can raise a hand and the facilitator will ask the customer to repeat what was just said.
3. The customer, with back turned to the teams, describes the picture. It is impor-

tant that the customer not be able to see what is being built. Ask the customer to repeat if hands go up.

4. When the customer is done, give the teams a few minutes to finish. Pass out pictures or show the model to the teams so that they can compare their creations with what the customer asked for.

5. Debrief about why it is difficult to meet the needs of the customer.

6. For reengineering and process-improvement groups, add another level of complexity: ask each team to design a better creation for the customer than the one in the picture. Each team will be required to sell its design in a three-minute sales presentation once the design is finished. The customer will select the winner.

7. Debrief about how the designs are different and why.

The Penny Game

Use: this quick exercise is good for highlighting the limited effectiveness of most people's powers of observation, or for emphasizing the challenges inherent in planning and estimating. It also works with bodily/kinesthetic and spatial/visual intelligences.

Ask each participant to write down the number of pennies she's handled in her life. Record the figures on flipchart or overhead from some or all of the participants (depending on group size).

Next, ask each participant to draw two large circles on a blank piece of paper. Ask them to draw the front and back of a penny in one minute, without actually looking at a penny.

Debriefing: tell them they can now look at a penny. Share that the U.S. Treasury Department estimates the average person handles one thousand pennies per year. Refer back to their estimates. Many will be over one hundred thousand, and some may be over a million. Point out how we can be overly familiar with an object or situation or event and not really see it.

For team-building use: ask the learners to each share one thing they have on their drawing of a penny with their team. As each gives a feature, the others add the feature to their own drawings, so that each one's picture becomes more and more complete through shared knowledge. Debrief about the value of the team.

Rigatoni "Necklace"

Use: this is a variation of a construction exercise, good for creativity and outside-the-box thinking. It requires interpersonal and bodily/kinesthetic aptitudes.

1. Break the class into two or three teams. This exercise works best if the teams are larger than usual, with five or more participants.
2. Give each team a box of large rigatoni and a roll of string. Tell the learners that there will be a contest to see who can "put the most rigatoni on the string in five minutes."
3. Give the teams five minutes to strategize, and then begin.
4. Debrief on communication, competition, team dynamics, "cheating," leadership, diversity, and creativity.

Note: some teams tie the string around the box instead of trying to string each piece of rigatoni. This approach demonstrates creativity!

Structures

Use: this construction project is good for creative thinking, project management, valuing diverse skills and knowledge, and communication topics. Again, this is strongly interpersonal and bodily/kinesthetic.

Pass out straight plastic straws (not the kind that have accordion flexible ends) and paper clips (small enough to fit snugly in the ends of the straws). Challenge the learners, in teams, to build the tallest structure they can in ten minutes. Debrief about why teams work or don't work, the value of having diverse abilities on a team, and other topics related to the learning.

INTRAPERSONAL EXERCISES

In intrapersonal exercises, individual learners have the opportunity to work alone and tap into their personal resources. They honor the intrapersonal intelligence principle.

Drawing

Use: asking learners to draw is a very powerful way to get them to reveal their personal beliefs. It also honors the spatial/visual aptitude.

The most important thing about drawing (for adults especially) is to keep it very safe. No one should have to share her drawing with anyone. Sharing isn't necessary for the learning to occur.

For example, you might ask learners to draw themselves as a leader, and then have them refer back to the drawings as you work through learning objectives. The picture may help them clearly see their behavior and values.

Collage

Use: also a favorite of K–12 teachers, collages reinforce both bodily/kinesthetic and spatial/visual aptitudes. They can be used as reviews or as way of revealing the inner beliefs of a learner.

Provide individuals or teams with magazines and let them create a collage around a topic. For example, in a leadership class, teams could create a collage about misconceptions on leadership using headlines and ads from current business and technical journals.

Journals

Use: journaling is an important learning activity for highly spatial/visual and linguistic/verbal aptitudes. Learners can be encouraged to journal in class or outside of it. The journal serves as a review, reinforces learning, and strengthens the existential intelligence.

Provide learners with a notebook to log their learning, thoughts, to-do action items, and even questions. Alternatively, provide blank pages at the end of each unit in the learner guide for more frequent reflection.

Observation

Use: this quick exercise is wonderful to point out to learners that things are not always as they seem. It stimulates spatial/visual intelligence.

Put the following on a board or poster (or give each learner a copy):

> The Earl of Fomme,
> father of Frederick,
> fell off his horse on
> the fifth of February.

Ask learners to count the *f*'s and write down the answer. Most readers skip the *f*'s in the three words "of," because it sounds like *v* and because people tend to skim over small words when they read.

Pie of Life

Use: this intrapersonal exercise is good for learning about time management, personal values, and prioritization.

Each learner draws a circle on a piece of paper, representing the Pie of Life. The learners reflect on how they are currently spending their time and mark slices on the pie to represent the proportion of time spent on each of their activities. Debriefing occurs with reflection about whether this is the way the learner wants her pie and time divided up.

Reflection

Use: reflection is critical to learning, as you have read throughout the book. The more the learning objectives have to do with attitude, the more reflection is needed. Reflection stimulates the existential and intrapersonal aptitudes.

Here are some ways to facilitate reflection:

- Lower the lights and provide quiet music to create an environment for reflection.
- Provide ways for bodily/kinesthetic learners to move while reflecting without disturbing others who do not have that need. Note taking, drawing, and reading are examples.
- Before a team exercise is to begin, allow learners two minutes to decide what they want to do.

Sculpture

Use: similar to drawing, this tactile exercise can reveal inner values and beliefs that a learner may not be conscious of, as with learners in a customer-service class drawing pictures of themselves interacting with their customers.

The tactile nature of clay brings out the whole brain. For example, facilitators can have individuals or teams construct a sculpture representing their evaluation of the leadership in the organization. Again, debriefing is critical to learning.

Visualization, Imagery

Use: visualization and imagery are used to relax and focus the learners. Some corporate learners are uncomfortable with visualization, so be sensitive. As you read in Chapter Nine, use music and visualization to introduce and review learning. Here is a basic process for visualization led by a facilitator:

1. Ask the learners to think about an issue or challenge they are now facing pertaining to the learning. Ask each of them to list several questions on a piece of paper, which they'd like help answering.
2. Ask everyone to sit in a comfortable position so they can completely relax. Have them focus their attention on their breathing. As they breathe in, coach them to feel themselves relaxing. Invite them to close their eyes if they wish.
3. Continue by speaking these directions to the learners with a slow and peaceful voice:

"Picture yourself at a gate. Behind the gate is a pathway through a beautiful wooded area. Picture yourself opening the gate, and walking down the path. Imagine what you hear, feel, see, smell."
(pause)
"As you walk along, you hear running water. The path leads you to a beautiful, clear stream running over rocks. Imagine what it is like to be here next to the stream."
(pause)
"You notice a friendly-looking person sitting in the grass downstream. The person waves to you, and you instinctively understand that this is someone you would like to get to know. You walk to the person and sit down."
(pause)
"You spend a few minutes talking with the friendly person. You have many, many things in common and you enjoy the conversation. Think about what you are talking about."
(pause)

"Ask this person one of the questions you wrote down earlier. Wait for an answer. Notice everything this person tells you, including gestures, emotions, feelings, and words."

(pause)

"You thank your new friend and say good-bye, promising to visit again. Make your way back to the path and leave through the gate."

(pause)

"Slowly return to the present. Feel free to stretch as you open your eyes."

(pause)

"Write down everything you remember about the answer to your question."

If you are a novice facilitator, you may find it easier to tape your voice before class and play it back, rather than reading the exercise live. This method also allows you to experience the visualization with the learners. Quiet, instrumental music is essential to this type of exercise, and it is helpful to dim the lights, if it can be done in the classroom, after step 1.

REVIEW EXERCISES

Because of the recency effect (see Chapter Six), review is a critical element in effective learning.

Baseball Review

Use: this creative alternative for a review exercise honors the bodily/kinesthetic and mathematical/logical aptitudes. If you are facilitating a multiday workshop, use this activity in the morning for review of the material from the day before.

Lay out a baseball diamond on the floor using tape and construction paper. Break into two teams. Toss a coin to decide which team is first. Give the first batter a question—the team can yell hints. If the answer is correct, a large die is tossed:

1 = first base
2 = second base
3 = third base
4 = home run

5 = foul (another question)

6 = out (pop fly)

Outs come from wrong answers or from rolling a six. There are three outs to a team, and the facilitator can determine how many innings to play.

Envelope Sort

Use: this is used when you are teaching teams to reinforce a series of steps where order is important—for example, the steps to develop a new product. This stimulates mathematical/logical intelligences.

1. Create an envelope for each team containing the steps of the process, written on individual strips of paper.
2. When the facilitator says "Go," the teams race to put the strips in the right order. A team is finished when the facilitator has approved its ordering.
3. Ask teams to discuss how to better their time.
4. Race again (same envelope, same flowchart).
5. Debrief about whether they improve or not, and why.

Jeopardy Review

Use: this is a very effective technique to use at the beginning of the day in a multiday workshop to review the material from the day before. Review is a critical component of memory retention, as you read in Chapter Six.

Before class, the facilitator creates a list of questions about the material covered. Start with a couple of true-false questions to warm up the group, and then continue with harder "essay" questions.

Break the class into teams to compete with the following rules:

• The game is closed-book, open-team (and open to job aids, wall posters, and the like).
• In turn, each team will get a question to answer. A right answer wins each member of the team a point; players are part of different teams over the course of the learning event, and the individuals with the most points at the end of class win prizes.
• Each team has one minute to come up with its consensus answer. Individual answers blurted out are not accepted as the team answer.

- If a team can't answer or answers incorrectly, the question is passed to the next team (true-false are not passed).
- Intrateam whining is OK, but whining to the facilitator or other teams is not.
- If a question is passed through each team without a correct answer, the facilitator loses and the material will be covered again.
- It is the quality of answers that matters, not the quantity.

Koosh Ball Review

Use: Koosh ball reviews can be very unsafe if implemented without care. When well defined, however, this type of review can effectively strengthen learning through bodily/kinesthetic stimulus.

Ask the learners to read through the notes and material that have been covered. Review the rules while demonstrating them:

1. Ask the entire group to stand.
2. Share something that you have learned.
3. Say another person's name clearly (or ask for it if you don't know it).
4. Make eye contact.
5. Gently toss the ball underhand to the person.
6. Sit down, unless you want to go again.
7. The person who receives the ball stands, shares, and tosses.

Share something that you've learned in class to model the behavior you expect from them or to finish the review round when you get the ball back at the end.

Mind Mapping or Mindscaping

Use: mind mapping or mindscaping is great for brainstorming and review and builds spatial/visual intelligence. The technique allows individuals or teams to collect their thoughts without being limited by the hierarchical flow of a traditional outline. Many elementary teachers use a similar technique, called "story spiders," to aid in reading comprehension.

Tony Buzan introduced mindscaping. Mind mapping is the variation developed by Nancy Margulies. There are visual differences in the pictures created by each, but the process is similar. Either one is a powerful tool when used for brainstorming or review. Here are some guidelines.

Be careful not to put too much structure around mind mapping or mindscaping. The idea is to leave the brain unencumbered and to open creative thinking. Give minimal directions by modeling these steps:

1. Put the topic in the center of the page.
2. Work outward on branches as your mind thinks of things.
3. Feel free to add to branches or start new branches whenever it makes sense to you.
4. Use abbreviations, pictures, keywords, and arrows to create quick visual notes.
5. Put the words on the lines, not at the end.
6. Move fast, and don't think long about anything you add.
7. Let yourself play, and make it fun. It's wonderful to laugh as you do this.

Initially, some learners may feel very uncomfortable doing mind mapping. After modeling the technique for the class, assign the first use to teams rather than an individual.

Music Performance

Use: this technique does require a higher level of trust than others, but it is highly effective and fun. It honors the musical aptitude. Music performance can be used for reviewing an entire day or more of material; in this way, it requires the learners to prioritize and pull out the key points of the learning.

Learners can review material by adapting raps, songs, or even opera to the course material that has been covered. Set the stage by explaining to teams that they will be asked to perform (through raps, songs, skits, or whatever they choose) to show what they've learned about a specific point. For example, a pharmaceutical company used this technique after a one-day workshop for highly technical learners on data-gathering techniques to review facilitation guidelines. The quality of the review and the creativity of the performances, especially the raps, were inspiring.

Pair Interviews

Use: this technique is a good alternative to entire group reviews. Although interpersonal, this review lessens the amount of auditory input from all the groups taking turns sharing. To ensure that the entire class learns from all, another step may have to be added for the "question people" to share key points. For example, this technique could be used to review a change-management process.

One person in each pair prepares questions while the other reviews notes so as to be prepared to answer. Then the pair conducts a mock interview, with the question person pretending to be writing a newspaper article on the topic. To make it consistent and more challenging, the facilitator provides the question person with a couple of samples to get answers for—such as finding a significant quote, a catchy title, business value, or other pertinent information bits.

Snowball Fight

Use: this review exercise incorporates intrapersonal, interpersonal, and bodily/kinesthetic aptitudes.

Ask learners to think about one thing they've learned and write it on paper without their names. When everyone has written one thought, have the learners crumple up the paper into balls and throw them gently at each other on the count of one, two, three. Have each learner read another's paper aloud before throwing it in the trash.

Terminology Review

Use: this is a bodily/kinesthetic approach to reviewing the meaning of terminology.

Give learners each a term to be reviewed by writing it and sticking the paper to their backs with tape. Each learner must ask the others yes-no questions while the other learners are asking them as well. The first learner to discover what the term is and define it wins a prize.

OTHER CLASSROOM DELIVERY TECHNIQUES

Obviously, the AL classroom has virtually endless possibilities. Here are a few more suggestions. You'll soon be creating plenty of your own.

"Fabulous Merchandise" (Prizes) Guidelines

Use: good for all facilitated learning events to reward and entertain learners. This encourages fun, which is a strong emotional link to memory retention.

It really doesn't matter what you pass out as prizes; it only matters that you do so with great tongue-in-cheek flourish. Here are the basic tips to increase learning with prizes:

- Never reveal what you have (don't let the learners pick from a bag, for example). The surprise and anticipation are the motivators, not the item itself.
- Always act tongue-in-cheek. Many facilitators refer to the prizes as "fabulous merchandise," while clearly knowing that it is merchandise, but hardly fabulous. In other words, have fun while you reward the learners: "Oh! You win a shiny rock!!"
- Reward the behavior you want to encourage, but don't be predictable. Keep the learners guessing about what it will take to get a prize. When learners ask you, "Don't I get a prize for that?" say, "No, but thanks a lot for asking!" Again, the surprise is the motivator.
- Consider rewarding teams especially if team building and communication are learning objectives. Pass out playing cards as individual rewards. The teams can turn in pairs for prizes at the break. Using cards can encourage networking, sharing, and maybe fighting, so watch out for behavior that could make learners feel unsafe.
- Strive to reward all participants at least once.

Facilitator as Model

Use: in all facilitated learning events, this builds a safe learning environment.

Learners respond much more enthusiastically if the facilitator models the behavior first. If you want them to draw a picture, draw one (not too perfectly) first. If you want them to list their leadership strengths, provide them with your list as an example. This makes it safer for them to step forward and risk because you yourself have risked and survived.

End on a Peak

Use: this is good for all facilitated learning events for both interpersonal and intrapersonal activities.

Don't wait for all the learners to complete an exercise before going on. Shoot for 80 percent complete. If you wait until everyone is done, it will eventually drag down the pace of the class. Eventually, the people who are finished will leave the room out of boredom. The learners should always feel they are being pushed a little bit, which will keep them energized and the pace upbeat. At the start of the exercise, give the learners an ambitious time estimate ("We'll take about three minutes to do this"), play quiet music, and then watch until 80 percent of the learners are done. Strike a balance between a lethargic pace and a frenetic one.

Lecture as a Last Resort

For a variety of reasons, there may be times when a lecture is the only feasible approach. The challenge is to use AL principles even during lecture.

Layered Learning

Use: this is an interesting alternative to a traditional lecture. Because the topics in the lecture jump around a little, the learner needs to work a little harder to stay connected and engaged in the process.

Instead of lecturing from beginning to end (linear), introduce a little detail about a topic, move on, come back to it with more detail, move on, and so on, up to four or five times. Here's an example that teaches two concepts in parallel, jumping between them:

1. Explain the topic of work breakdown structure (WBS). A WBS is a chart showing the breakdown of activities necessary to complete a project.
2. Convert a WBS to a schedule, and show learners a sample using the critical path method (CPM). A CPM is a model of the dependencies between activities needed to complete a project.
3. Return to the original WBS and add people to the chart.
4. Show the ramifications on the CPM by adding the people detail.
5. Return to the WBS and show how resources can be overscheduled.
6. Show how the CPM would not allow this.

Peer Teaching

Use: as an alternative to lecture, let the learners teach each other to "earn what they learn" through discovery.

Assign topics and resources to teams, and give them a fixed amount of time to present the material back to the class. Encourage the teams to teach innovatively, such as through a poem, song, poster, skit, or commercial.

Model Making

Use: this technique is useful when learners need to be able to know, in detail, the pieces and interactions of machinery or processes. It especially honors the mathematical/logical and bodily/kinesthetic aptitudes.

David Meier has worked with teams who create wonderful examples of model making for learning. In his speeches on AL, he tells of a team of people who had to learn to troubleshoot a type of nuclear plant equipment. The team members taught themselves by modeling the machine on the floor with string, tape, construction paper, blueprints, and their imagination.

Performance

Use: this lecture alternative is useful for introducing lengthy and complex terminology and process steps. There is still a strong emphasis on linguistic/verbal, but additional aptitudes such as bodily/kinesthetic and emotional are also engaged.

Some lecture material can be written in a choral reading format. You will find an example of a choral reading about multiple intelligences at the end of Chapter Five. Learners either read parts aloud or read along silently and fill in the blanks.

Some material lends itself to skits. When teaching the dull and academic steps of data normalization, we have learners act out what happens to each field in each record. They simulate the computer pointers by pointing their fingers at each other. Learning through movement and play acting is long lasting.

Storytelling

Use: when introducing a concept in a lecture, consider a metaphor or story. An important memory technique, this approach is especially useful for learning about multistep procedures or standards, such as the sequence in a problem-solving process.

Many of the classic myths are wonderful metaphors for business. A utility company acts out the Sophocles play *Antigone* to help learners experience and discuss how different values and visions can drive behavior, instead of lecturing on these topics.

Here are two additional examples, using different types of stories. To introduce a systems-development methodology, a pharmaceutical company used the segment "The Sorcerer's Apprentice" from the Disney film *Fantasia*. In the video, when Mickey Mouse has the sorcerer's hat on (which equates to following the methodology), he can do magical things. Sometimes things get out of control, for many reasons, which experts (who equate to the Sorcerer) can fix because of their experience (sometimes without the methodology).

A university program included a fairy tale with characters representing different commands used in the FOCUS programming language. These characters portrayed the behavior of the commands, but in a story format.

Variation: use "sound alikes" to teach new terms. For example, "green megs and RAM" can be used to humorously remember the relationship between megabytes and random access memory in a computer class.

Stump the Expert

Use: this exercise can be used as an alternative to lecture. The learners will learn more effectively when they discover the learning through their own questions.

1. Present a short overview of the major topic and identify three or four subtopics.
2. Distribute index cards to the participants and ask them to write at least one question on each subtopic.
3. Collect the question cards and divide the participants into as many teams as there are subtopics.
4. Give each team the set of questions dealing with a specific subtopic, many of which will not be their own.
5. Ask the team members to organize the questions in a logical order, eliminating any duplicates.
6. After a suitable pause, play the role of an expert and invite one of the teams to grill you for ten minutes.
7. At the end of the ten minutes, ask members of each team to review their notes and identify what they consider to be the two most important pieces of information given in your answers.
8. Repeat this activity with the other teams.

Window Pane Agenda

Use: this is a technique that I learned when I attended the Bob Pike Creative Training Techniques seminar; it can be used to visually display the flow of the learning event.

Draw a square for each unit and, from left to right, put a simple line drawing in each one that represents each unit in order. In their learner guides, participants will have a table of contents with words. Ask them to follow along with this list as you explain the pictures. Place a Post-it note with a large, red arrow on it on the first square, and then say "Anyone who catches me forgetting to move this arrow will win fabulous merchandise!" This is a wonderful challenge for left-brain learners and keeps them engaged. Here is an example:

Unit	Picture
Changing the way we train	Picture of change
Who is the audience?	Picture of an owl saying "who?"
What is the learning goal?	Picture of a football goal post
Building support material	Picture of sequencing, "support hose," evaluation report, or report card
Growing learning	Picture of learner with flowers growing out of his head
Fine tuning the class	Picture of a violin

Word Scramble

Use: this is a technique to engage a learner's bodily/kinesthetic aptitude while listening to a lecture with technical terms.

Give each learner a sheet with a list of scrambled terms on it (for example, "visual" is shown as L U A S V I). As learners listen to the lecture, they try to unscramble the terms on the worksheet. Every time someone solves a term, he is rewarded if he can define it.

Here's another for you to try:

H N S T T I I E E K C

The solution: kinesthetic. The definition: preference for learning by touching or doing.

RESOURCES

This list of resources (as well as references cited in the text) is alphabetized within four sections: books and articles; individuals and organizations; music; and Websites.

After most entries in the first section are letters in parentheses. (L) denotes Learning, that is, readings on how people learn; (D) denotes Delivery, for readings on delivery techniques.

Books and Articles

Anderson, O., Marsh, M., and Harvey, A. *Learn with the Classics.* San Francisco: LIND Institute, 1999. (D, L)

Arch, D. *Tricks for Trainers.* Minneapolis: Resources for Organizations, 1993. (D)

Arch, D., and Pike, B. *First Impressions.* Minneapolis: Resources for Organizations, 1993. (D)

Arch, D., and Pike, B. *Lasting Impressions.* Minneapolis: Resources for Organizations, 1993. (D)

Armstrong, T. *Seven Kinds of Smart: Identifying and Developing Your Many Intelligences.* New York: Penguin Books, 1993. (L)

Birren, F. *Color Psychology and Color Therapy.* Secaucus, N.J.: Citadel Press, 1961. (D)

Buzan, T. *Use Both Sides of Your Brain.* New York: Dutton, 1983. (L)

Campbell, D. G. *100 Ways to Improve Teaching Using Your Voice and Music.* Tucson, Ariz.: Zephyr Press, 1992. (D)

Campbell, D., and Brewer, C. *Rhythms of Learning.* Tucson, Ariz.: Zephyr Press, 1991. (D, L)

Campbell, L., Campbell, B., and Dickinson, D. *Teaching and Learning Through Multiple Intelligences.* Seattle: New Horizons for Learning, 1992. (D, L)

Chapman, C. *If the Shoe Fits . . . How to Develop Multiple Intelligences in the Classroom.* Palatine, Ill.: IRI/Skylight, 1993. (D)

Cowley, G., Underwood, A., Springen, K., and Gegax, T. "Tested Your Memory Lately?" *Newsweek,* June 15, 1998, pp. 50–51. (L)

Dhority, L. *The ACT Approach.* Bremen, Germany: PLS Publishing, 1991. (D, L)

Dickinson, D. *Creating the Future.* Aylesbury Bucks, U.K.: ALS, 1991. (D, L)

Durie, R. "An Interview with Howard Gardner." *Mindshift Connection,* Apr. 1997, p. 1. (L)

Edwards, B. *Drawing on the Right Side of the Brain.* New York: St. Martin's Press, 1988. (L)

Forbess-Greene, S. *The Encyclopedia of Icebreakers.* San Francisco: Jossey-Bass/Pfeiffer, 1983. (D)

Frender, G. *Learning to Learn.* Nashville, Tenn.: Incentive Publications, 1990. (L)

Frick, D. M., and Spears, L. C. (eds.). *On Becoming a Servant Leader: The Private Writings of Robert K. Greenleaf.* San Francisco: Jossey-Bass, 1996. (L)

Gardner, H. *Frames of the Mind.* New York: Basic Books, 1985. (L)

Gardner, H. *Multiple Intelligences.* New York: HarperCollins, 1993. (L)

Gardner, H. *Are There Additional Intelligences? The Case for Naturalist, Spiritual, and Existential Intelligences.* (White paper.). 1996. (L)

Goleman, D. *Emotional Intelligence.* New York: Bantam Press, 1997. (L)

Graham, R. J., and Englund, R. L. *Creating an Environment for Successful Projects.* San Francisco: Jossey-Bass, 1997. (D)

Greenleaf, Robert K. *Essay: Servant as Leader.* Indianapolis: The Greenleaf Center for Servant-Leadership, 1977.

Greenleaf, Robert K. *Servant Leadership: A Journey into the Nature of Legitimate Power and Greatness.* Mahwah, N.J.: Paulist Press, 1977.

Greenleaf, Robert K. *On Becoming a Servant-Leader.* San Francisco: Jossey-Bass, 1996.

Grinder, M., and Grinder J. *The Educational Conveyor Belt.* Portland, Oreg.: Metamorphous Press, 1991. (L)

Hale, J. *The Performance Consultant's Fieldbook.* San Francisco: Jossey-Bass/Pfeiffer, 1998. (D)

Healy, J. *Endangered Minds.* New York: Simon & Schuster, 1990. (L)

Heinich, R., Molenda, M., and Russell, J. D. *Instructional Media.* New York: Macmillan, 1989. (D)

Herrmann, N. *The Creative Brain.* Lake Lure, N.C.: Ned Herrmann Group, 1995. (D, L)

Herrmann, N. *The Whole Brain Business Book.* New York: McGraw-Hill, 1996. (L)

Hersey, W. D. *Blueprints for Memory.* New York: AMACOM, 1990. (L)

Jensen, E. *Superteaching.* Del Mar, Calif.: Turning Point for Teachers, 1988. (D, L)

Jensen, E. *Brain Based Learning and Teaching.* Del Mar, Calif.: Turning Point, 1995. (D, L)

Jones, L. B. *The Path.* New York: Hyperion Press, 1998. (L)

Karten, N. "Influence: Science and Practice." *Perceptions and Realities,* 1995, *1*(3), 8. (D, L)

Kawasaki, G. *Selling the Dream: How to Promote Your Product, Company, or Ideas—and Make a Difference—Using Everyday Evangelism.* New York: HarperBusiness, 1992. (D)

Kearns, D. T., and Doyle, D. P. *Winning the Brain Race.* San Francisco: ICS Press, 1989. (L)

Kline, P. *The Everyday Genius.* Arlington, Va.: Great Ocean, 1988. (L)

Kolb, D. A. *Experiential Learning.* Upper Saddle River, N.J.: Prentice-Hall, 1984. (L)

Larson, K. *The Trainer's Handbook.* San Francisco: Jossey-Bass/Pfeiffer, 1998. (D)

Lawler, M., and Handley, P. *The Creative Trainer.* Berkshire, U.K.: McGraw-Hill, 1996. (D)

Lazear, D. *Seven Ways of Knowing.* Palatine, Ill.: IRI/Skylight, 1991. (D, L)

Lazear, D. *Seven Pathways of Learning.* Tucson, Ariz.: Zephyr Press, 1994. (D, L)

Lozanov, G. *Suggestology and Outlines of Suggestopedia.* Newark, N.J.: Gordon and Breach Science Publishers, 1978. (D, L)

Mager, R. F. *Measuring Instructional Intent.* Belmont, Calif.: Fearon Pitman, 1973. (L)

Mager, R. F. "Why I Wrote. . . ." *NSPI Journal,* Oct. 1976. (D, L)

Mager, R. *Preparing Instructional Objectives.* Atlanta: Center for Effective Performance, 1997. (D)

Margulies, N. *Mapping Inner Space.* Tucson, Ariz.: Zephyr Press, 1991. (D, L)

Margulies, N. *Yes, You Can . . . Draw!* Aylesbury Bucks, U.K.: ALS, 1991. (L)

Margulies, N. *Inside Brian's Brain.* Tucson, Ariz.: Zephyr Press, 1997. (L)

McPhee, D. *Limitless Learning.* Tucson, Ariz.: Zephyr Press, 1996. (D, L)

Melymuka, K. "Crazy Correlations." *Computerworld,* 1988, *32*(29). (L)

Nawa, P. "Letter to the Editor." *Indianapolis Star,* Jan. 16, 1998. (D, L)

Newstrom, J. W., and Scannell, E. *Games Trainers Play.* New York: McGraw-Hill, 1980. (D)

Nonaka, I., Takeuchi, H., and Takeuchi, H. *The Knowledge-Creating Company: How Japanese Companies Create the Dynamics of Innovation.* New York: Oxford University Press, 1995. (L)

Ostrander, S., Schroeder, L., and Ostrander, N. *Super-Learning.* New York: Dell, 1979. (D, L)

Palmer, P. J. *The Courage to Teach.* San Francisco: Jossey-Bass, 1998. (L)

Pfeiffer, J. W. *The Encyclopedia of Group Activities.* San Diego: University Associates, 1989. (D)

Richards, R. G. *L-E-A-R-N.* Tucson, Ariz.: Zephyr Press, 1993. (D, L)

Rose, C. *Accelerated Learning in the 21st Century.* New York: Delacorte Press, 1997. (D, L)

Scannell, E. E., and Newstrom, J. W. *More Games Trainers Play.* New York: McGraw-Hill, 1983. (D)

Scannell, E. E., and Newstrom, J. W. *Still More Games Trainers Play.* New York: McGraw-Hill, 1991. (D)

Senge, P. M. *The Fifth Discipline.* New York: Doubleday, 1990. (D, L)

Senge, P., and others. *The Fifth Discipline Fieldbook: Strategies and Tools for Building a Learning Organization.* New York: Currency/Doubleday, 1994. (D, L)

Sylwester, R. *A Celebration of Neurons.* Alexandria, Va.: Association for Supervision and Curriculum Development, 1995. (L)

Thiagarajan, S. *Framegames by Thiagi.* Bloomington, Ind.: Workshops by Thiagi, 1992. (D)

Thiagarajan, S. *Games by Thiagi.* (Series.). Bloomington, Ind.: Workshops by Thiagi, 1994, 1995. (D)

Treacy, M., and Wiersema, F. *The Discipline of Market Leaders.* Reading, Mass.: Perseus Press, 1997. (L)

Toll, C. "Creating Environments for Successful Learning." In *Mindshift Connection: Learning Environments.* Tucson, Ariz.: Zephyr Press, 1998.

Vaill, P. B. *Learning as a Way of Being.* San Francisco: Jossey-Bass, 1996. (L)

Von Oech, R. *A Kick in the Seat of the Pants.* New York: HarperCollins, 1986. (D)

Von Oech, R. *Creative Whack Pack.* Stamford, Conn.: U.S. Game Systems, 1990. (D)

Von Oech, R. *A Whack on the Side of the Head.* New York: Time Warner Books, 1990. (D)

Other Items

ASCAP. "Frequently Asked Questions About Licensing." [http://www.ascap.com]. 1999.

Chant. (Music CD.). Madrid: Angel Records, 1994.

Krutein, W., and Pomeranz, D. "It's in Every One of Us." (Video.). New Era Video, 1987.

Thiagarajan, S. International Society for Performance Improvement (ISPI) conference presentation. Session 37: "Interactive Experiential Training: Eight Breakthrough Strategies." 1997.

Individuals and Organizations (General)

Brain Store
11080 Roselle St., Suite F
San Diego, CA 92121
800/325-4769
Use: delivery, resources, fun

Chris Brewer
LifeSounds
160 Seashore Dr.
Jupiter, FL 33477
888/687-4251
fax: 561/575-0929
e-mail: music@flite.net
Use: music research, workshops

Don G. Campbell
P.O. Box 4179
Boulder, CO 80306
303/440-8046
fax: 303/440-3353
Use: music research

Center for the Neurobiology of Learning and Memory
University of California
Irvine, CA 92717
949/824-5193

Creative Training Techniques
Robert Pike
7251 Flying Cloud Dr.
Eden Prairie, MN 55344
800/383-9210
www.cttbobpike.com/catalog
Use: music, *Creative Training Techniques* (newsletter), supplies, workshops

Steven Halpern
Steven Halpern's Inner Peace Music
524 San Anselmo Ave, Suite 700
San Anselmo, CA 94960-2614
800/909-0707
fax: 415/485-1312
e-mail: innerpeacemusic@innerpeacemusic.com
Use: music research

Herrmann International
Ned Herrmann Group
794 Buffalo Creek Road
Lake Lure, NC 28746
800/432-HBDI
www.hbdi.com
Use: brain dominance assessment, resources

Kipp Bros.
P.O. Box 157
Indianapolis, IN 46206
800/428-1153
Use: inexpensive prizes

LIND Institute
Ole Anderson
P.O. Box 14487
San Francisco, CA 94114
415/864-3396
Use: resources, music

Georgi Lozanov
International Association for Desuggestology and Suggestopedagogy
P.O. Box 132
1101 Vienna, Austria
tel/fax: +43 1 651 50 69
Use: delivery, resources

Masie [Institute] Center
10 Railroad Place, Suite 401
P.O. Box 397
Saratoga Springs, NY 12866
800/986-2743
www.masie.com
Use: learning and presentation resources

David Meier
Center for Accelerated Learning
1103 Wisconsin Street
Lake Geneva, WI 53147
414/248-7070
fax: 414/248-1912
e-mail: alcenter@execpc.com
Use: workshops

Oriental Trading Company
P.O. Box 3407
Omaha, NE 68103-0407
www.oriental.com
Use: inexpensive prizes

Pegasus Communications, Inc.
One Moody Street
Waltham, MA 02453-5339
www.pegasuscom.com
Use: learning organization resources

Russell Martin and Associates
6326 Rucker Road, Suite E
Indianapolis, IN 46220
317/475-9311
www.russellmartin.com
Use: consulting workshops, coaching

Tomatis Listening Centre
Timothy Gilmore, Director
600 Markam Street
Toronto, Ontario M6G 2L8 Canada
Use: listening research

Trainers Warehouse
89 Washington Ave.
Natick, MA 01760
800/299-3770
www.trainerswarehouse.com
Use: music resources, magic tricks

Turning Point for Teachers
Eric Jensen
P.O. Box 2551
Del Mar, CA 92014
Use: brain research, workshops

University of Houston
Division of Distance and Continuing Education
Houston, TX 77204-3901
713/743-0983
Use: AL workshops

U.S. Toy Co.
1227 E. 119th Street
Grandview, MO 64030
816/761-5900
Use: inexpensive prizes

Whole Person Associates
210 West Michigan
Duluth, MN 55802-1908
800/247-6789
www.wholeperson.com
Use: videotapes

Workshops by Thiagi
4423 East Trailridge Road
Bloomington, IN 47408
812/332-1478
www.thiagi.com
Use: simulations, workshops, books, *Thiagi GameLetter* (newsletter)

Zephyr Press
P.O. Box 66006
Tucson, AZ 85728-6006
520/322-5090
www.zephyrpress.com
Use: books, newsletter, conferences, workshops, resources

Individuals and Organizations (Music)

Creative Training Techniques
Robert Pike
7251 Flying Cloud Dr.
Eden Prairie, MN 55344
800/383-9210
www.cttbobpike.com/catalog

Steven Halpern
524 San Anselmo Ave., Suite 700
San Anselmo, CA 94960-2614
800/909-0707
fax: 415/485-1312
e-mail: innerpeacemusic@innerpeacemusic.com

Gary Lamb Recordings
Golden Gate Records
333-B Castle Dr.
Santa Cruz, CA 95065
800/772-7701
www.garylamb.com

LifeSounds
Chris Brewer
160 Seashore Dr.
Jupiter, FL 33477
888/687-4251
fax: 561/575-0929
e-mail: music@flite.net

Marty Morrow
e-mail: morrow@iquest.net

Relax with the Classics
LIND Institute
Box 14487
San Francisco, CA 94114

Trainers Warehouse
89 Washington Ave.
Natick, MA 01760
800/299-3770
www.trainerswarehouse.com

Zephyr Press
P.O. Box 66006
Tucson, AZ 85728-6006
520/322-5090
www.zephyrpress.com

Brain and Learning Websites

www.sciencenews.org
A weekly newsmagazine covering all areas of science. You can read it online every week. To find the brain articles, do a search by keyword "brain." Each issue usually has some new data on the brain.

www.brain.com
A colorful, fun site with a free five-minute IQ test.

www.dana.org/dana/publications
Download any issue of *Brain Work,* "the neuroscience newsletter."

www.hbp.scripps.edu
The Human Brain Project, launched in 1993. A wealth of brain information that connects to about a dozen related Websites such as the International Consortium on Brain Mapping.

www.ialearn.org
Headquarters of the Internal Alliance for Learning.

Eric@ericir.syr.edu
Education source for hundreds of AL resources.

www.ascd.org
Association for Supervision and Curriculum Development.

Mbb.harvard.edu.HPZpages/Whatsnew.html
Information from the Mind/Brain/Behavior interfaculty initiative at Harvard University.

www.indiana.edu/~eric_rec/ieo/bib/multiple/html
The ERIC link to other MI sites.

www.neuroguide.com
Guide to the neurosciences online.

www.heartmathe.org
Articles on the relationship between mental and emotional balance.

www.pbs.org
Search for information from public television (the Public Broadcasting System).

www.newshorizons.org/ofc_21cli.html
Twenty-First Century Learning Initiatives synthesis.

www.fidalgo.net/~indigo
Alison Miller, certified trainer for Lozanov methods.

www.cttbobpike.com
Bob Pike's Creative Training Techniques.

www.thiagi.com
Free games and tips.

www.alcenter.com
David Meier's Institute for Accelerated Learning.

www.mindtools.com
Thinking skills.

www.superlearning.com
Source for superlearning and music information.

www.liszt.com
More than ninety thousand mailing lists, with 112 education lists.

www.teachnet.org
Teachers Network, with classroom activities.

www.ritaderbas.com
Articles and a listing of brain-related Websites.

INDEX

A

Accelerated learning: benefit of, to business, 8–9; benefits of, 11; definition of, 4–8; and learning organization disciplines, 10; traditional learning *versus,* 6

Active concert, 187–189

AL. *See* Accelerated Learning

Alert relaxation, 186

Alertness levels, 163

Amazon, 267

American Society of Composers, Authors, and Publishers (ASCAP), 193

American Telephone and Telegraph (AT&T), 123

Andersen, O., 161

Anderson, O., 181, 191

Apple Computer, 102

Armstrong, T., 56

ASCAP. *See* American Society of Composers, Authors, and Publishers

AT&T. *See* American Telephone and Telegraph

Attitude objectives, 124, 219

Audience: and diverse intake styles, 48–49

Ayers, M., 3

B

Bach, J. S., 185, 197

Baroque music, 185

Beanie Babies, 68

Beethoven, L., 185, 188

Benedictine Monks of Santo Domingo de Silos, 184

Binet, A., 55, 59

Bird, L., 65

Bloom, B., 217

Bodily/kinesthetic intelligence, 65–66. *See also* Multiple intelligence

Bolanos, P., 4

Brahms, J., 188

Brain Based Learning and Teaching (Jensen), 45, 151

Brain dominance: impact of, on learning, 93–94; theories of, 88–92

Brain dominance theories: and corpus callosum, 90; and left brain, 89; and Ned Herrmann's brain quadrants, 91–92; and Ned Herrmann's whole-brain model, 92; and right brain, 89–90; and two sides of brain, 88–89

Brain function, four-quadrant model of, 91–92

Brain quadrants. *See* Brain function, four-quadrant model of; Ned Herrmann's brain quadrants

Brain stem, 95

Brainstorming techniques: and group sharing, 288; and relationships and connections, 288; and scenario planning, 289; and systems thinking wheel, 289

Brewer, C., 37, 161–163, 191, 194, 197

Bulgaria, 186–187

Bulgarian Academy of Sciences, 186

Business learning, holistic approach to, 79

C

Campbell, B., 63

Campbell, D. G., 37, 93, 161–164, 174, 191

Campbell, L., 63

Caruso, E., 190

CAT scan, 88, 94

Celebration of Neurons, A (Sylvester), 21

Center for the Neurobiology of Learning and Memory (University of California at Irvine), 181

Challenger space shuttle, 126

Chant (Benedictine Monks of Santo Domingo de Silos), 184

Chopin, F., 185

Cialdini, R. B., 172

Classroom delivery techniques: and ending on a peak, 300–301; and fabulous merchandise (prizes) guidelines, 300–301; and facilitator as model, 301; and layered lecturing, 302; and model making, 303; and peer teaching, 302–303; and performance, 303; and storytelling, 303–304; and stump the expert, 304; and window pane agenda, 305; and word scramble, 305

Columbia University, 111

Computerworld, 63

Conseco (insurance company), 56

Cooper, L., 182

Copeland, A., 185

Corelli, A., 188

Corpus callosum, 90. *See also* Brain dominance theories

Courage To Teach, The (Palmer), 137, 277

Cousto, H., 192

Cowley, G., 111, 115

Creating an Environment for Successful Projects (Graham and Englund), 9, 253

"Creating Environments for Successful Learning" (Toll), 149

Creative Brain, The (Herrmann), 87, 92

Creative discomfort, 23

Creative Training Techniques, 195

D

Debriefing exercises, 229–234

Debussy, C., 185

ABOUT THE AUTHOR

MG Photography (317) 773-8598

Lou Russell is president of Russell Martin and Associates, a training, workshop, and learning company that works with clients in areas such as project management, information systems infrastructure, accelerated learning, performance consulting, and course development and delivery. Russell has published articles in journals such as *Data Training, Computerworld,* and *Auerbach Journals,* among others. She holds a master's degree in instructional technology from Indiana University. Russell has worked with Ameritech and McDonnell Douglass, among others. She lives in Indianapolis, Indiana. Website: http://www.russellmartin.com